A CENTURY
OF HOPE
1866-1966

by

WYNAND WICHERS

President Emeritus

Hope College

WILLIAM B. EERDMANS PUBLISHING COMPANY
GRAND RAPIDS, MICHIGAN

2|8290   5-154

FOREWORD

HOPE COLLEGE: Not just another educational institution, but the crowning effort of a group of immigrants to maintain their ethnic identity, and even more to preserve and promulgate their religious faith. It is fortunate that this history can be written by a man as competent and informed as Dr. Wynand Wichers. For he was born and spent his boyhood in the little city of Zeeland, Michigan, where the tradition of the Netherlands and the memory of the Dutch pioneers were retained long after most of the communities in which the Dutch had settled were pretty well Americanized.

He is a graduate of Hope College. For a dozen years he was Professor of History at his Alma Mater, and for fourteen years he served as its President. After his retirement, he remained on the Board of Trustees until 1963. He knows of its struggles and problems — problems of finance, problems of administration, problems of curriculum and discipline. This background of ancient lore and knowledge, coupled with his powers of incisive thinking and clear expression, have enabled him to write a story interesting not only to thousands of Hope's alumni, but to all students of the culture and the ethical progress of the United States.

For us who live in the latter half of the twentieth century, when men have, as Arnold Toynbee suggests, put their trust in the discoveries of their minds and the ephemeral institutions of their own making — national sovereignties and their armies; science and technology rather than in eternal verities — it is difficult to understand the religious zeal of these immigrants from the Netherlands. The dominant motif of this emigration to America was religious. They sought freedom to worship according to the dictates of their conscience. The memories of the Inquisition, of the Huguenot massacres, were interwoven into the history of their country. In the first half of the nineteenth century, while physical torture was not practiced, the Netherlands government, which was so tolerant under William the Silent, had taken a stand against the dissenters. Meetings of more than nineteen people were forbidden. When the dissenters practiced civil disobedience and held meetings of larger groups, contrary to law, they were broken up by the King's officers, and the sponsors and preachers were fined heavily. The Constitution of the United States of America guaranteed freedom of worship.

The economic motive was also present but it was secondary. For the religious faith of these dissenters was "otherworldly." To the fact that life on this earth held little promise for them, save toil and trouble, they could reconcile themselves; but they firmly believed that in the hereafter they would be fully recompensed if they kept the faith. The old Hervormde Kerk, they felt, had strayed away from the true doctrine. It had also been infected, as had all society, by the wave of materialism and modernism that had swept over Europe after the Napoleonic wars. From this they revolted to return to the true doctrine, based on Scripture as interpreted by the Synod of Dort. Tolerance of the faith of others they had not achieved, save to the extent that they would live in peace with people of other faiths and would cooperate with them in civil matters.

It is significant that, while a few of the mid-nineteenth-century immigrants remained in cities already established, the heart of the colonization was in the midst of an uninhabited wilderness of south Ottawa and north Allegan counties in Michigan. It is indicative of the nature of the colonization that, within three years after the establishment of the first group at what is now Holland, Michigan, seven settlements had been formed, each bearing the name of one of the provinces of the Netherlands, and each center had a church. At least four of these congregations had their own minister, in every instance an ordained minister of the Gereformeerde Kerk of the Netherlands.

When Albertus C. Van Raalte broached his plan for a school of Christian education, and launched the campaign by donating a five-acre tract of land in Holland, he seems to have had the support of most of his brother clergymen. However, a goodly number of laymen were opposed. They could not see the value of "book-learning" in the tasks of their day. As one pious elder put it, "To get into heaven no learning is needed. For God has hidden his mysteries from the wise and prudent, and revealed them to children."

To what extent has Hope College realized and fulfilled the aims and purposes of the founders? If Dr. Van Raalte intended to establish a Netherlands in a new land — and he may have, for the United States at that time had not been integrated into a nation by the bloodbath of the Civil War — he failed. No doubt many of the settlers retained that idea for many years. Today all these settlements have been Americanized; I doubt whether 10 percent of the students at Hope College can speak the Holland language.

To their deeper purpose, the establishment of their faith, Hope College has made a substantial contribution, if not complete victory. For these men had perceived, perhaps somewhat dimly, that the great problem of mankind was not the conquest and control of the forces of nature, but the control of man himself, and that the key to good human relations was to be found in the teachings of the Prince of Peace.

CORNELIUS VANDER MEULEN, Hope — 1900
Grandson of the founder of Zeeland, Michigan

* The Honorable Cornelius Vander Meulen died February 27, 1968.

ACKNOWLEDGMENTS

THIS BOOK would never have been written without the generous assistance of many people. I owe a special debt of gratitude to the Reverend George B. Scholten of Wayne, New Jersey, for his constant encouragement and for inviting me to his home to examine his collection of papers from the pen of Philip Phelps, Jr. A hearty vote of thanks goes to the archivists of Calvin College, Hope College, and Western Theological Seminary, Dr. Lester DeKoster, Miss Janet Mulder, and Miss Mildred Schuppert. Others are Dr. Clarence De Graaf of Hope College and Drs. James O. Knauss and Willis Dunbar of Western Michigan University. The Reverend Gerrit ten Zythoff, Assistant Professor of History, Ohio State University at Mansfield, Ohio, gave me important information with reference to Albertus Christiaan Van Raalte. The Reverend Donald Bruggink of Western Theological Seminary read the manuscript and recommended its publication. Miss Metta Ross has reviewed the chapter on Dr. Edward D. Dimnent, and Dr. John Hollenbach gave me valuable information about the Great Lakes Colleges Association. Many thanks are due President Emeritus Irwin J. Lubbers for assisting with the outline and especially for writing the chapter on my administration. Thanks are due the Honorable Cornelius Vander Meulen, grandson of the founder of Zeeland, for the Foreword, and Dr. Calvin VanderWerf for reviewing the last chapter and the Epilogue. Mrs. J. A. Stryker assisted in the selection of pictures. Finally, credit must be given to Willard Chester Wichers of the College Board of Trustees for arranging the publication details with the William B. Eerdmans Publishing Company of Grand Rapids. I am especially indebted to my wife, Alyda De Pree Wichers, for her patient waiting and encouragement during the years of research.

CONTENTS

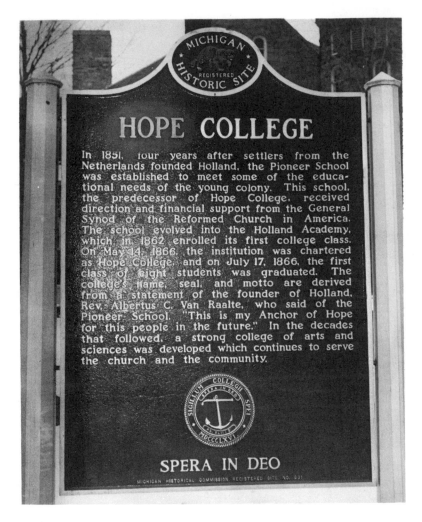

An official marker on the campus of Hope College, dedicated by the Michigan Historical Commission on May 24, 1963.

PROLOGUE

EARLY IN THE EVENING of February 9, 1847, in a sleigh drawn by
a team of oxen, six white men and one woman came to the end
of a forest trail in Section Three of Fillmore Township in Allegan County. Here was a small Indian settlement called Old Wing
Mission. Among these Indians lived two American families —
the families of Isaac Fairbanks and the Reverend George N.
Smith, both employees of the United States government. The
leader of this small company of newcomers was the Reverend
Albertus Christian Van Raalte, recently arrived with a vanguard
of Dutch emigrants who had been driven from their native land
by religious unrest, and were seeking a site in which to found a
Calvinistic colony for the hundreds of Hollanders who were
expected to follow. After much searching, the site which their
intrepid leader had already chosen lay in the forest at the mouth
of the Black River in Ottawa County, Michigan. On the south
shore of Black Lake, at the extreme end of what is now West
16th Street, Holland, Michigan, stood a village of about three
hundred Indians under their chief, Peter Waukazoo, all pen-
sioners of the federal government. Between this village and the
Old Wing Mission there was a zigzag trail winding through
swamp and forest.

In 1847 nearly all the western part of Michigan was inhabited
by Indian tribes, with here and there some white clearings in
the forest. Between the Kalamazoo and the Grand rivers were a
few small villages. The village of Superior, which had been
located on Black Lake in 1836, was deserted and lingered only as

11

a relic of a wild speculation in Michigan lands in the late twenties and early thirties. Such was the nature of the site that Van Raalte had chosen for his Dutch colony. One of those who came with Van Raalte on February 9 described it as follows:

> It was a strange sight that greeted us. With the exception of the families of Fairbanks and Smith, our neighbors were Indians. We beheld surrounding us on all sides a virgin forest teeming with wild life as yet wholly undisturbed. We viewed with astonishment the mighty giant trees which perhaps were a hundred feet tall and six feet in diameter, all growing on a terrain of various kinds of soil, and dense underbrush cut by streams and creeks fed by springs and bubbling waters, a desert wild and fit only for the timid creatures of the forest. Nevertheless, this is the place declared Domine Van Raalte where a city and a number of villages, and where an extensive Dutch Colony should be planted — where we and our children would enjoy an untrammeled existence, serve our God freely and without restraint.[1]

With characteristic vision and insight, the colony's first concern, after providing rude shelters and a place to worship, was the establishment of a school. This event and its evolutionary development throughout the ensuing century are described on a historical marker on the campus of Hope College in Holland, Michigan:

> In 1851, four years after settlers from the Netherlands founded Holland, the Pioneer School was established to meet some of the educational needs of the young colony. This school, the predecessor of Hope College, received direction and financial support from the Synod of the Reformed Church in America. The school evolved into Holland Academy, which in 1862 enrolled its first college class. On May 14, 1866, the institution was chartered as Hope College, and on July 17, 1866, the first class of eight young men was graduated. The name, seal, and motto of the College were derived from a statement of the founder, Reverend Albertus Christian Van Raalte, who said of the Pioneer School, "This is my anchor of hope for this people in the future." In the decades that followed, a strong college of arts and sciences was developed which continues to serve the church and community.

This volume is concerned with the persons and events involved in building the college and community on these significant foundations.

---

[1] "Egbert Frederiks' Pioneer Memories," *Memoirs and Related Pioneer Writings,* ed. Henry Lucas, I, 67-68.

BOOK I
COLONIAL ORIGINS

1: FROM HOLLAND TO HOLLAND

OUR STORY BEGINS in 1815, when the Congress of Vienna refused to restore the ancient Dutch Republic and set up in its stead The Kingdom of the Netherlands under William I of the House of Orange. Shortly after his accession, the King approved a new constitution and a set of rules for the State Church, which not only changed the name and character of the old Reformation Church, but also introduced practices that were contrary to those which the church had enjoyed for centuries. Many ministers felt that the changes would increase the trend toward rationalism which had arisen in the eighteenth century.

While these changes were taking place in the structure of the State Church, a new religious movement, known as the Reveil or Awakening, was sweeping over western Europe. To many leaders of religious thought, especially in the Netherlands, this was a fresh breeze against the current liberalism. Poets such as Isaac De Costa, and the historian Groen Van Prinsterer, were inspired by it and sought to promote it while remaining loyal to the church. However, some of the ministers saw no hope for reform, and sought refuge in secession rather than to submit to a church polity and discipline that seemed contrary to their standards of faith. Among them were the Reverends Hendrik C. De Cock, Hendrik Pieter Scholte, Anthony Brummelkamp, and Isaac Van Velzen. The first step was taken on October 14, 1834, when the pastor and congregation of the church in Ulrum, Province of Groningen, signed a document known as "The Instrument of Secession and Return." The pastor of this church,

15

De Cock, had already been suspended for his refusal to obey the new rules. The suspension and deposition of the others came quickly. Although the movement grew slowly, the schism progressed when the king took punitive measures against the separatists that further destroyed their freedom of worship. In March of 1836, a few of the seceding ministers held a secret Synod in Amsterdam and organized The Christian Reformed Church of the Netherlands.

It was this Synod that ordained Albertus C. Van Raalte into the ministry of the seceding churches. He was born at Wanneperveen in the province of Overijsel on October 17, 1811. His father was a minister in the State Church and was hopeful that his son would follow in his footsteps. After Albertus had completed his work in the Gymnasium, he entered the University of Leiden, from which he received his degree. Presenting a certificate of membership in the Reformed Church of Leiden, he became a candidate for the ministry. When he was examined by the Provincial Synod of South Holland in 1835, he was denied a license because he seemed hesitant in matters of ecclesiastical law. He tried again on August 5, but his petition was denied because he claimed that in certain respects the State Church was not Reformed. By letter, he asked the Synod to reconsider its action, but received no answer to his communication. Failing to win approval as a pastor in the State Church, Van Raalte threw in his lot with the separatists and was ordained by their Synod in 1836. A few days later, he married Christina Johanna De Moen, a sister of Mrs. Brummelkamp and Mrs. Van Velzen. His first charges were at Genemuiden and Mastenbroek, but in 1847 we find him associated with his brother-in-law at Arnhem, preaching, and teaching candidates for the ministry in the seceding churches. Like others of his group, Van Raalte began to suffer abuse and persecution. He was arrested, jailed and fined, and in addition was abused and scorned by those who remained loyal to the State Church. In 1872, the Reverend Christian Vander Veen described the nature of this abuse as follows:

The Reverend Albertus C. Van Raalte, D.D., 1811-1876, founder of Hope College.

If you were a hired man, you lost your position. If you were a merchant, you lost your clientele. They pointed the finger of scorn at you and public men spoke to you with great condescension. We brought with us as children from the Netherlands the memories of the abusive and disdainful expressions that were hurled at us in the school and on the street by children from whose parents our fathers and mothers received similar treatment. It was this senseless abuse more than actual poverty, the sense of which was certainly intensified by the former, which compelled our parents, twenty-five years ago, to seek in the new world the self-respect, the freedom and the influence which was denied them in the Netherlands.[1]

Although the persecutions were soon discontinued, Netherlanders began to leave the country in increasing numbers. In the years 1831-1847, eight thousand persons are said to have left the country. While the religious motives were dominant with those who came to Michigan and Iowa in 1847, there were many more who sought social and economic freedom in America. Following the era of Napoleon and the Belgian War, burdensome taxes were laid upon the people. The climax to the distress of the poorer classes came in a severe economic depression, and in the potato blight of 1844-1845 which destroyed their chief article of food. For all these and other varied reasons, agitation in favor of emigration increased and many made preparations to improve their lot in North America.

Now the leaders of the Secession churches became alarmed because they feared that this uncontrolled type of emigration would mean the dispersion of the emigrants among foreign populations and the possible loss of their language and their Calvinistic faith. Van Raalte said,

If the Hollanders are scattered among the foreign populations they will be too much left alone with the language in which the gospel is preached. Through colonization, those who leave will be able to remain to hear the gospel in their own native tongue, during the first few years at least, and may receive that spiritual sustenance which will confirm them in the faith, kindle them in love, and warn them against the cravings of the flesh which militate against the spirit.[2]

---

1 The C. A. Vander Veen Papers. Calvin College Library.
2 The Van Raalte Papers. Calvin College Library.

It was for that reason that the leaders began to plan emigration by colonies. But where would they go? Emigration to the Dutch possessions had become impossible. By the fall of 1846, Van Raalte and others at Arnhem published a pamphlet entitled, "Why do we advocate emigration to North America and not to Java?" Of this pamphlet Van Raalte said, "It did kindle the country like a prairie fire, and I was pressed into service to direct it." Although Van Raalte had not intended to leave his country, he soon found himself in a position where his own leadership would be essential to the success of the colonization movement.

In April 1846, a society had been formed and a constitution drawn up for the control of emigration by colonization. It provided for two committees, one in the Netherlands and one in the United States. The document was called "The Principles of the Society of Christians for the Dutch Emigration to the United States of America." One of the provisions clearly indicates that the religious motive was dominant in the reasons for emigration:

> The first consideration is to make the colony a Christian community, for which the Commission must take care in accepting candidates for emigration and helping them to reach their destination, in order that those persons may become a salt in the colony and form a Christian majority among the inhabitants. For that reason, only Christians will be accepted of whom we may expect that they gladly submit themselves to the word of God, in order that not only a Christian church government but also a Christian civil government shall be established. This will have as its task the execution of God's government which is the basis of every state.[3]

Following the formation of the society, money was sought to help the poor emigrants. Van Raalte and Brummelkamp addressed a letter "to the faithful in the United States." The letter was translated into English and published in the *Christian Intelligencer* of the Reformed Church in America in October 1846. By that time, a society had been organized in the Dutch Reformed Church in Albany, New York, called "The Protestant Evangelical Holland Emigrant Aid Society." A similar society was organized in New York City called "The Netherlands Society for the Protection of Emigrants from Holland." By the time that Van Raalte's letter appeared in the *Christian Intelligencer,* he

---

3 The Van Raalte Papers.

was already sailing the Atlantic with a vanguard of fifty-three followers.

The party left the port of Rotterdam on September 24, 1846, to begin the long and tedious voyage from their native land to found a colony somewhere in the United States, possibly in Wisconsin. Most of the colony travelled steerage in the three-masted sailing vessel, *The Southerner*. Van Raalte, his wife, their five children, and a maid were in cabin class. The children were Albertus Christian, age nine; Johanna Maria, age seven; Benjamin, age five; Dirk, age two, and Christina Catherina, age five months.

They arrived in New York on November 17, and were met by the Reverend Thomas De Witt, who showed Van Raalte the city and helped them aboard the Hudson River steamer bound for Albany. Here they were received by the Reverend Isaac Wyckoff and others from the Albany Emigrant Aid Society. From Albany the colony travelled to Buffalo by rail. On November 27, they left Buffalo by lake steamer for Detroit. While en route, Van Raalte wrote a letter to Brummelkamp in which he said that he would either spend the winter in Detroit or go on to Milwaukee. However, Mrs. Van Raalte preferred to spend the winter in Detroit. In any case, he had no choice since navigation on the lakes had closed for the winter. On December 14, Van Raalte wrote another letter to his brother-in-law in which he said:

> The steamships do not cross the Great Lakes any more during the rest of the winter because the narrow straits farther to the north are frozen over very quickly.[4]

In Detroit

Van Raalte arrived in Detroit with a letter of introduction to the Reverend G. B. Duffield of the Presbyterian Church. Van Raalte knew no English except for a few words taught him by the captain of *The Southerner*. Duffield's son spoke at the Hope College commencement in 1890 and recalled his impressions of his first meeting with Van Raalte. He said,

> Van Raalte presented himself at my office inquiring after my father. He was stout and short of stature, bright eyes, earnest

---

4 The Van Raalte Papers.

and resolute of manner, and in personal appearance the very personification of a Dutch Domine. He at once tried to make himself known and his wishes, but his speech being only in his native tongue, was too much for a fresh young lawyer. French failed, German too, and still he thundered at me the sturdy bullet-like words of his own dialect. At last, I ventured a remark in Latin. At once he responded and the "Open sesame" was found. On my father's return, the dead language was continued.[5]

Since the Michigan Legislature was still meeting in Detroit, Duffield was able to introduce Van Raalte to some important people who spared no effort to sell Van Raalte on Michigan as the place for his colony. Among them was Theodore Romeyn, a graduate of Rutgers and a leading attorney in Detroit. Others were the Honorable C. C. Trowbridge and the Honorable Lewis Cass, former Governor of Michigan Territory and now a United States Senator. Writing to Brummelkamp on December 16, 1846, Van Raalte said:

I feel oppressed by cares. Please pray for me that God may guide me in the matter. I have already heard much that makes me think ,seriously about remaining in Michigan. But I shall withhold the final decision until I have learned more.[6]

In December, Van Raalte came to Kalamazoo with a letter of introduction to the Reverend Ova P. Hoyt, who in turn arranged a meeting between Van Raalte and Judge John R. Kellogg of Allegan. Kellogg strongly urged the leader of the emigration to explore territory in Ottawa County, and on the last day of December 1846, Van Raalte and Kellogg travelled through the dense forests between Allegan and the Black River region in Ottawa County. In the evening, they reached the Old Wing Mission, and on the next day they set out upon the trail from the Old Wing Mission to an Indian village on the south shore of Black Lake. It was on this trip that Van Raalte arrived at his decision to plant his colony in Ottawa County. What remained was to convince his friends in Detroit and his followers in St. Clair that this was the place of opportunity and religious freedom. Until January 11, 1847, he was the guest of the Reverend George N. Smith at Old Wing Mission. From this base

---

5 Hope College *Anchor*, July 1890.
6 The Van Raalte Papers.

of operations, he explored the surrounding territory and made a visit to Grand Haven to examine some land titles. Here he was the guest of the Reverend William Montague Ferry, the founder of Grand Haven, and in whom he found a kindred spirit. Ferry was a graduate of Union College and had spent two years in New Brunswick Theological Seminary of the Reformed Church in America, and was intimately acquainted with the Dutch Reformed Church. He became a warm friend of Van Raalte and did much to help him in the founding of the colony and in the early days of Holland Academy. His son, William White Ferry, was for many years a member of the Board of Visitors at Hope College.

Van Raalte persuaded the Reverends Hoyt of Kalamazoo and Andrew B. Taylor of Grand Rapids, and Judge Kellogg ·to accompany him to Detroit for a meeting of church and civic leaders who had interested him in settling in Michigan. A committee of seven was appointed for the purpose of assisting Van Raalte in every possible way. They advised him in the purchase of state and federal lands, and proposed that the township where he was to settle be named Holland Township, and that he make an application to bring it about.

One of the reasons for Van Raalte's choice of Michigan was the fact that here was an abundance of land that could be obtained for very little money. In the winter of 1846-1847, he began to purchase land from the state, from the federal government, and from private parties. He bought tax titles to hundreds of acres. For example, on one day in January 1847, he purchased at Detroit 125 acres for $5.67; 600 acres for $11.68; 600 acres for $26.25, and 186 acres for $21.47. As late as July of 1854, he bought 377 acres for $54.17.[7] He also purchased hundreds of acres of public lands that were subject to sale. From the General Land Office in 1848 he bought seven parcels totaling almost a thousand acres. From Mr. Courtland Palmer of New York he purchased about 3000 acres and from Peter Schermerhorn of New York City, 320 acres. In the isolation of the forest of Ottawa County, not too far away from settled areas, Van Raalte had

---

[7] Albert Hyma, *A. C. Van Raalte and the Dutch Settlements in Michigan* (Grand Rapids, 1947), p. 126.

found an ideal place for his colony. Here was land enough to receive all who were bound to come — a place where they could preserve their own language and religion, at least until such a time as they could, in the words of Van Raalte, "become Americans by assimilation and not by absorption."

The Beginnings

As soon as Van Raalte's decision to locate in Ottawa County had been approved by the meeting in Detroit, he informed his followers in St. Clair and gave them directions for following him to the new site. They had been employed during the winter in the shipyards of St. Clair, about fifty miles northeast of Detroit. Six families left at once for Detroit, where Mr. Theodore Romeyn assisted them with their transportation to Kalamazoo; they arrived there February 5, 1847. The next day they went by sleigh to Allegan where they were received and cared for by Judge Kellogg. Van Raalte and his family seem to have arrived on the same day. Mr. and Mrs. Bernardus Grootenhuis, accompanied by four American workmen, went ahead to the Old Wing Mission to make preparations for the reception of the colonists. On February 9, Van Raalte, accompanied by Evert Zagers, Egbert Frederiks, William Notting, Hermanus Lankheet, Jan Laarman, and one woman, Mrs. Notting, arrived at the Old Wing Mission in a sleigh drawn by oxen furnished by Judge Kellogg. The other women and children remained in Allegan until some shelters had been built. By the end of the month, two log cabins had been erected on the so-called Vander Haar Farm, and on the edge of the Cedar Swamp a log cabin had been built for Van Raalte and his family. On March 5, 1847, Theodore Romeyn wrote Van Raalte as follows:

> The residue of our Holland friends from St. Clair are in the City and will leave tomorrow for Kalamazoo. They go on the railroad for two dollars for each person and half price for each child. There is no charge for goods. I hope that our friends from Albany reached you safely. They left Wednesday night. I am very busy and have no time to write as I would wish. Give my affectionate regards to your family.[8]

---

8 Letter in the Van Raalte Papers.

The reference to friends from Albany relates to ten Hollanders who left the Netherlands on October 13, and had spent the winter in New York State.

About two hundred Dutchmen arrived in St. Louis in February. Van Raalte invited them to join his colony. After a committee of three had come on a tour of investigation, the rest came by way of Chicago and Grand Haven and from there by wagon to the head of Black Lake. And so in March, the population of the colony was increased by several hundred. Rude shelters were built for them on the shore of Black Lake at Macatawa. The colony now grew rapidly, and by 1850 there were several thousand in the village of Holland and in other outlying communities that made up the colony. One of the largest groups to arrive in the summer of 1847 was a party of about 300 Zeelanders who left the Netherlands in three ships. One group of about 157 came as an organized congregation with a consistory and pastor, the Reverend Cornelius Vander Meulen. They selected a site about six miles east of Holland and called their village Zeeland. In 1848, a group of Frisians settled about six miles east of Zeeland and called their settlement Vriesland. The same year a group under the leadership of the Reverend S. Bolks, who had been a theological student of Van Raalte, came and settled in Fillmore Township, and named their settlement Overisel. Other settlements followed, and all were closely knit together by ties of race and faith and a common poverty. They had not left their native land to build a settlement in a virgin forest in order to exploit the resources of the territory, but rather to realize in the colony ideals of liberty and government, of education and religion. In this respect, the movement was much like that of the colonization of New England in the seventeenth century. The movement of 1847 seems to be cut out of the same cloth. In the reasons for the emigration, the poverty of the beginnings, in the majesty of the faith manifested, and in their results, these movements are much the same. The impressions made upon our American life by leaders such as Bradford and Brewster were made again in the nineteenth century by Vander Meulen and Van Raalte.

Hardship

For some years, life in the colony was bound to be cruel. The people were desperately poor, the winters were rugged, and the forests and swamps inhospitable. Provisions had to be brought in from other communities and they were always insufficient. In the first summer, there was a great deal of sickness. Diseases such as malaria, cholera, and smallpox took a heavy toll. When Van Raalte in 1872 recalled those evil days, he said:

> In the latter part of the summer our trials reached their climax. The whole colony was one bed of sickness and many died through want of comfortable dwellings and suitable and well-prepared food. Physicians were summoned from the outside and paid out of colony funds. The conditions were heart rending and discouraging. Never was I so near the point of despair as when I entered those crowded huts. I saw the constant mingling of household duties and sickness and death, and the dressing of corpses in huts, where each family was forced to accommodate itself to a limited space of a few square feet. But God granted a change. The sick were restored to health. The Fall was a most beautiful one. The winter was so mild that everybody could build and perform outdoor labors, and even partake of food in the open air.[9]

Some help came from surrounding communities and from the emigrant aid societies organized in Albany and in New York City. In the First Reformed Church of New Brunswick, New Jersey, the pastor, Dr. David Demarest, organized a group of women who met for the purpose of making articles of clothing and other necessities for the colonists. The *Christian Intelligencer* on October 25, 1851, published a letter of thanks from Van Raalte for the receipt of twenty dollars in cash, one hundred articles of clothing, and thirty-nine articles of bedding. There is another such letter dated August 15, 1852. The church in Albany made a loan of $1000 to Van Raalte as Trustee for the colony. Gradually, things improved as the cleared lands produced larger crops and some industries developed. The continued growth of the colony was now assured.

The central point of colonial life was the village of Holland. Among the first streets to be cleared were River Avenue and

---

9 Address by the Reverend Van Raalte upon the twenty-fifth anniversary of the founding of Holland. See Van Raalte Papers.

8th Street, and the first houses were built on these streets. The plat of the village was filed with the County Clerk on July 21, 1848, and the Township of Holland was organized March 16, 1847. With reference to the industry of the Dutch colonists, the *Christian Intelligencer* on December 28, 1848, said, "With these settlers, the first thing they do is buy a piece of land. Then they begin chopping, after which they plant and make fences, and then they build their homes."

The Christian Intelligencer, *official organ of the Reformed Church in America (then known as the Reformed Prot. Dutch Church). It began August 7, 1830, merged with* The Leader *in 1934, and was called* The Church Herald *in 1944.*

2: PIONEER SCHOOL

Since the colonists had left their native land to secure for themselves freedom of worship and of education, it is not surprising that plans were laid for a church and school even before sufficient shelters for the growing population had been erected. The first religious services were held in the open air, and in the first summer the settlers began the construction of a log church in the burying ground. By 1848, there were seven Dutch congregations in the various settlements, which formed an association known as The Classis of Holland, entirely independent of any higher ecclesiastical control. The first meeting of the Classis was held on April 23, 1848, in the parsonage at Zeeland. The Reverend Van Raalte was chosen President and the Reverend Cornelius Vander Meulen, Clerk of the Classis.

As to formal elementary education, there is no doubt that the settlers preferred religious day schools under their own control. But since this seemed utterly impossible until financial conditions in the colony were much improved, Van Raalte determined to make use of the American public school and proposed its use at the first meeting of the Classis. Van Raalte's good friend, Thomas White Ferry of Grand Haven, was the Clerk Pro Tem of the Board of School Inspectors of Ottawa County, and at his suggestion the School Inspectors served notice of their intention to organize a school district in the Township of Holland. At the first public meeting of the taxable inhabitants, Van Raalte became the Moderator and Mr. Henry D. Post the Secretary. On June 14, 1848, a public meeting was

27

called for the purpose of selecting a site for a schoolhouse. For this purpose, Van Raalte donated some lots in Block 46, the present site of the Van Zoeren Library of Hope College. While some money was voted for a building, several years elapsed before the schoolhouse was built. In the meantime, pupils were taught in the log church and in several rented places in the village.

The first schoolmaster was Mr. Ira Hoyt, brother-in-law of Isaac Fairbanks. During the winter of 1847/48 he gave some English instruction to adults and to children. Now he began a brief period of three and one-half months of teaching in the district school. One of his pupils in later years said:

> The first place where school was taught was in a little log cabin on the southeast corner of what is now the Vander Haar Farm. Mr. Hoyt, the teacher, moved to the log church. Our first book was Webster's Spelling Book. The Reverend Van Raalte came once a week to teach the Catechism.[1]

[1] Derk Broek, "Reminiscences," *De Grondwet,* Jan. 3, 1911.

The first log church in Holland, Michigan, 1847. An artist's conception.

The second teacher was Miss Elvira Langdon. She was sent to Michigan by a New England organization which sought to promote education in the West. She came to Holland from Allegan at the request of Mr. Post, secretary of the school district. Her stipend was five dollars per week plus expenses from Allegan. In a letter written August 29, 1910, she tells her story:

It was in the middle of the century that I was employed by Mr. Henry D. Post to teach the first school taught by a woman in Holland. In addition to this, I also organized the first English Sunday School. It was kept for six months and then dropped owing to sickness and an epidemic of cholera. I boarded in Mr. Post's home and at that time we were the only American residents. I was treated with great respect by man, woman and child for I was the school vrouw. My first journey to Holland was tedious. I went from Allegan to Singapore by stage where I stopped for a week until such time as I could get word to Mr. Post, twelve miles distant. When my escort arrived, we went in an open democrat wagon, travelling on the beach to Lake Michigan. The sleet and snow made slow travelling for the horses and they had to rest often. Finally we reached the mouth of Black Lake. We reached Holland safely about dark, thankful to be on dry land once more.

There was no school house in Holland but I had a small comfortable room in the District School. I adopted methods in teaching suited to children who were ignorant of the English language. I used oral teaching entirely at first as I perceived they retained ideas better than when they were requested to study.

I began to think of a change but how to get out of Holland was a query. Finally a farmer from Allegan came to take home a hired woman and I engaged passage with him. When ready to return to Holland, I learned from Mr. Post that the people had voted no money for school or town purposes but that there was money enough on hand to pay me for the winter term. As my baggage was still in Holland, I went back and taught til spring when I was relieved of my labors and my name stricken from the Pay Roll. That winter I taught in a lone house for orphans.[2]

MRS. COOPER (ELVIRA LANGDON)

---

[2] Elvira Langdon in ₁H. Lucas, *Memoirs and Related Pioneer Writings*, I, 396f. The orphan house to which Mrs. Cooper refers was built in 1847 to house children whose parents had died as a result of the epidemic of that year.

*On the left, the Orphan House, 1847-1851, which became the first build-
ing of the Pioneer School in 1851. On the right, the house built by
Adrian Zwemer in 1857.*

Much as Van Raalte regarded the importance of formal elementary education for all the children of the colony, there is
little evidence of similar concern on the part of most of the
settlers. The district school report in September 1849 reveals
the fact that although there were 191 pupils of school age in
the district, only 27 had attended in the preceding year. At
the annual meeting of September 9, 1850, the people refused to
vote taxes for the support of the school, "neither for the payment of rent for a building, for the payment of debts or for
any other purpose." When the School Board was warned that
it might lose its organization or face a law suit, it reluctantly
voted $25 for rent, $20 for wood and other expenses, and $50

It was never used for that purpose because orphaned children were cared
for in the homes of the colonists. It was located on two acres of ground on
the south side of 12th Street where Western Theological Seminary now
stands. Van Raalte had donated the site and personally collected $200 for
its erection. Taylor later taught district school in this building. Van Vleck
moved his Latin class into it in 1857, and later it became the home of
De Hope Publishing Company. It was destroyed by fire March 26, 1889.

for the payment of debts. One of the reasons was the general poverty in the early settlement. Parents were apt to keep their children at home to assist in the family chores. Van Raalte complained about the lack of interest in the public school and expressed regret that English instruction was neglected because the pupils did not realize its value and also because there was little money available for it. But there is also the suggestion that many of the colonists were distrustful of any system of public education and preferred their own religious day schools. At a meeting of the Holland Classis on September 27, 1848, it was resolved

> that the interests of the schools be discussed. The discussion takes place and the judgment is that schools must be promoted and cared for by the churches as being an important part of the Christian calling of God's church on earth. All lukewarmness and coldness must be condemned and rebuked.[3]

Van Raalte himself began to feel some dissatisfaction with the operation of public education in the district. As long as the colony was homogeneous and Calvinistic, the churches could exercise proper control; but as the colony grew, the church began to exercise less and less control, and frequent conflicts arose between those who favored public education and those who favored elementary parochial education. There was some experimentation with religious elementary education under the direction of the Classis of Holland, but it failed because it was not supported adequately by the church and strongly opposed by the Americans in the community.

Not only did Van Raalte feel the need for elementary education for all children, but he also was much in earnest about the need of a church-controlled secondary school. Himself a graduate of Leiden University, he could not overlook the need of his people for higher education. He was mindful of the need for educated ministers and teachers. He knew that the future leadership of a growing church could be met only by recruiting and training Western men for the Western church service. It was his conviction that higher education was a prime essential in the process of Americanization and for the preservation and extension of the Dutch church in the West. With this in mind,

---

3 Translation of the Minutes of the Classis of Holland, Sept. 27, 1848, p. 26.

he began to devote his energies to the task of founding a secondary school to prepare men for college entrance. This was a difficult task, because while there were some people in the colony who felt the need very strongly, there were many more who did not feel the need for higher education at all. To accomplish his purpose, Van Raalte would need the help and strong support of the Reformed Church in America, with which the Classis of Holland became identified in 1850.

At a meeting of the Classis of Holland on October 30, 1850, Van Raalte reported on the result of a journey which he had recently taken and said that

> he had taken the liberty, at a meeting of the Synod of Chicago, to give information with regard to the particular interests of this Classis by laying bare the real state of affairs among us, begging them earnestly to take a hand in the education of our youth, which, for years, we shall be unable to do ourselves.[4]

The need of such an institution in the West had been advocated by leaders in the Reformed Church long before Van Raalte came to Michigan. When he arrived in 1847, there were several Reformed churches in Illinois and in Michigan. The oldest was the church at Fairview, Illinois, founded in 1837 by a group of Dutch-Americans from the Classis of New Brunswick. These infant churches in the West had roused the interest and concern of the General Synod a decade before Van Raalte came to Michigan. In 1836, when the Synod was discussing the possibility of planting schools in New York, auxiliary to New Brunswick, the Classis of Schoharie had introduced a resolution calling for the establishment of a theological school and a preparatory school in the valley of the Mississippi. The resolution resulted in the appointment of a committee

> to visit the western states and the Territory of Michigan and report on the expediency of establishing missionary stations for the benefit of those formerly connected with our church and their children.[5]

However, the General Synod was not greatly concerned with the problem of education in the West until, in 1843, it heard an earnest appeal from the western Classis of Illinois and Michi-

---

[4] Minutes of the Classis of Holland, Oct. 30, 1850, pp. 39f.
[5] Minutes of the General Synod, R.C.A., for the year 1836.

gan for institutions of higher education in the West. And in the East, the Reverend James Romeyn began vigorously to champion the cause of such schools. In a sermon delivered on June 1, 1842, he called upon the whole church

> to devise some method for training under her influence western young men for the western service. This could be accomplished by the establishment of an academy of high grade somewhere near the head of the Valley.[6]

And then Van Raalte and his followers came to western Michigan. In this immigration, Dr. Romeyn saw the greatest meaning and he declared:

> This movement will not suffer on the score of its grandeur by comparison with any associated act of immigration in the history of our country.[7]

So earnestly did he press the matter of education in the West that the General Synod in 1847 resolved:

> We regard Christian education to be preeminent among the instrumentalities which God has put into our hands, and that we especially recommend it to the attention and fostering influence of all our churches in relation to the necessities of the West.[8]

The Synod then appointed a special committee to consider the matter and report to the Synod of 1848. This Synod adopted the recommendation of the committee,

> that an institution of high order for classical and theological instruction, under our influence, as long as necessary, be established.[9]

Now that Synod had determined the matter of need, the only thing left to be done was to find the proper location. Upon this question, Van Raalte brought to bear all the finesse of his acute mind. This was his opportunity and he was determined that an academy should be located in his Holland settlement.

In the accomplishment of his purpose, Van Raalte was given an assist in 1850 when the Classis of Holland joined the communion of the Reformed Church in America. In 1849, the Reverend Isaac N. Wyckoff of the Dutch church in Albany

---

6 Minutes of Synod 1842.
7 Hope College Catalog 1876/77, p. 76.
8 Minutes of Synod 1847.
9 Minutes of Synod 1848.

paid a visit to the Holland colony at the request of the Board
of Domestic Missions, R.C.A. He was to ascertain how the
colonists were faring, and to discuss with the leadership the
question of a possible union with the Reformed Church in
America. After visiting all the settlements, he held an informal
meeting with all the ministers and twenty elders and deacons
of the Classis. The conference said that the Classis felt itself
one with churches that had the same form of government, the
same liturgy, and the same expression of faith. They expressed
a desire to live in communion with other Dutch churches and
to send delegates to their church assemblies. After the Particular Synod of Albany had extended to the Classis a formal invitation for union, the Classis agreed to send Van Raalte "to
give and ask for all necessary information that may facilitate
the desired union."[10] In 1850, the Classis joined the Reformed
Church in America and was placed under the care of the Particular Synod of Albany. This gave Van Raalte the assurance
of financial help from the denomination in the establishment
of a secondary school in the colony.

Pioneer School — Walter T. Taylor

Of equal importance in influencing the Synod to open a
secondary school in the colony was a visit by the Reverend
John Garretson, Secretary of the Board of Domestic Missions.
The seed sown by Romeyn, the persuasive arguments of Van
Raalte, and the promising future Garretson saw in the Holland
colony completely won him to a plan for an academy. The
plan was laid before the Synod of 1851 and received approval,
with the suggestion that five acres of land be procured by gift
or otherwise, to be located in the town of Holland, for the
use of the academy, and that, as soon as possible, funds be secured for the necessary buildings.[11] Under this plan, the Board
of Education was to send a teacher who would be responsible
to a committee consisting of the President of Rutgers College,
the Senior Professor of Theology at New Brunswick, and the
Reverends Isaac Wyckoff of Albany and Thomas De Witt of
New York.

10 Minutes of the Classis of Holland, April 1850, p. 37.
11 Minutes of Synod 1851.

In 1851, the hopes of the founders were realized when Mr. Walter T. Taylor was chosen to become the first principal of the pioneer school. Mr. Taylor was the proprietor of a private academy in Geneva, New York, and a prominent elder in the Dutch church. First approached by Garretson in March 1851, he became interested and made a visit to the colony in September 1851. On October 4, 1851, Van Raalte received Taylor's acceptance and immediately wrote him as follows:

> Today received your welcome letter. God bless you in your intention. Upon receipt of your letter, I ordered the carpenter to finish the house. I am doing all I can to have it ready. In regard to your route of travel, I recommend that you come by steamer through the Great Lakes around Mackinaw to Chicago. From there a steamer leaves every two weeks for Grand Haven. If the weather permits, the steamer will stop at Black Lake to disembark passengers. This is the best, the easiest way. May the Lord make you a blessing among this newly planted people.[12]

On October 14, 1851, Van Raalte announced to the Classis that

> the prospects for an English Academy were getting more and more encouraging. That the hope was cherished of having found an exceptionally well-qualified instructor for this Institute, one whose good reputation as a teacher had been established for a number of years, to wit, Mr. Taylor of Geneva, who is known as an Elder and as a zealous advocate of the doctrine of free grace, and was for that reason considered to be exceptionally well fitted for this important position.[13]

Mr. Taylor arrived in Holland late in October with his wife, his son, Hugh Woodruff Taylor, and two daughters, Margaret W. and Anna B. Taylor. One of his pupils in his later years said, "I remember Mr. Taylor very well. He was an elderly gentleman with a long gray beard. I stood in awe of him as did all the boys who passed under his rod."[14] He met his first classes in the orphan house, which was the only building available since the district schoolhouse was in process of erection. His duties were to organize a class of boys in preparation for Rutgers College, and also to educate some of the daughters of the colonists. In the district school he found eighteen boys who were ready for secondary work. Most of the other pupils were

12 Van Raalte Papers.
13 Minutes of the Classis of Holland, Oct. 14, 1851, p. 63.
14 Cahill, "Old Colony Days," in Lucas, *op. cit.*, I, 373.

Walter T. Taylor, first principal of the
Pioneer School, 1851-54.

in the primary grades. Classification was impossible since "hardly six of them knew the multiplication table."

A question arises as to how Taylor became involved in the district school since his appointment came from the Reformed Church boards, his compensation was to come from these boards, and his instructions were to make his reports to a standing committee appointed by the Synod. One of his pupils, the Reverend C. Vander Veen, alumnus of the academy in 1854, discussed this matter in 1890 in an address made on the occasion of the quarter-centennial of Hope College. The title of the address was "The Genetic History of Hope College." According to Vander Veen, it never entered into the mind of Taylor that he would in any way be connected with the district school. It was his understanding that he was to be principal of the academy. But when he came to Holland, he discovered there had been no teaching in the district school for about six months. He then wrote a letter to Van Raalte in which he said:

> It is now six months that we have had no school in the District School. As this state of things, if it continues, must result in great evident injury to the Latin School both directly and indirectly, I propose to take the School for the remainder of the year, if nothing occurs to prevent, and to receive only the Mill Tax and Public Money, and this not for myself but on condition that it be devoted to the following objects: one-third to the fund for aiding emigrants from Holland, and two-thirds to a fund for boarding female students who may wish to attend the academy.[15]

---

15 Van Raalte Papers.

The arrangement was unfortunate in that it gave rise to many difficulties and led to a quarrel with Van Raalte. His connection with the district school made Taylor subject to several different authorities, all of whom claimed certain prerogatives. Instead of being subject only to a committee in the East, he became subject to the Classis of Holland, to the District School Board, to the consistory, "which had a high opinion of their general prerogatives and were never hampered in the ascertaining of them," and to Van Raalte, who had some well-formed ideas of his own. Mr. Vander Veen says:

> Mr. Taylor was a most sincere man, simple hearted and unselfish and by instinct a scholar, and unworldly but with a strong sense of duty and faithfulness to the charge entrusted to him by those who sent him and as he understood it.

At any rate, Taylor and his family now were in charge of a district school in which there was a Latin class of boys preparing for college. The first year passed favorably. There was real enthusiasm for the Latin class and Taylor's relations with the community were pleasant, especially with the Americans in the settlement. In his first report to the Eastern committee, he acknowledged his difficulties but expressed the hope that "the lowering seed time might be followed by a rich and sunny harvest." It was to this report that Van Raalte appended the words, "This is my anchor of hope for this people in the future." From this felicitous phrase were derived the name and the seal of Hope College.

The Latin Class Placed Under the Care of Synod

The colonial leaders knew full well that the Garretson Plan could be but temporary and that soon or later Christian higher education in the West would have to be placed on a firmer foundation. Since boarding houses were not available for outside students, the institution tended to become a purely local one, although the intent had been to confer educational benefits on all the colonial congregations. In a lengthy address before the Classis on September 1, 1852, the Reverend Vander Meulen made a strong appeal for funds with which to support boarding houses for pupils. At a Classis meeting on April 27, 1853, Van Raalte made the observation that the so-called English Academy would sooner or later need to have buildings of its own since the future of the institution required that it rest on its own foundation. He then offered to give property in Block 50.

> Trusting that with regard to the Classis, the gift in the interest of the education of the youth will be dear to her, and that she will feel herself obligated to accept the property for the said object, with the purpose of being willing to make sacrifices to meet the necessary expenses, and to begin to see to it that the necessary buildings are erected.[16]

Although there was some objection to the acceptance of the gift, when it was announced that Mr. Van Schaick of New York had offered $500 for the building on condition that the churches show that they have a heart for it, the Classis resolved to accept the gift and appointed a committee of three ministers and four elders as trustees. The brethren from Overisel offered to clear the grounds of the superabundant timber as soon as the transfer of title had taken place.

While sentiment was growing in the colony for a church-related academy, the Board of Education was taking action to solve the problem. In 1853, Synod's Committee on Education reported:

> It appears that the colony of Hollanders have an Academy, the object of which is to prepare sons of the colonists for Rutgers and also to educate the daughters of the colonists in the branches of study usually embraced in a female education in this country. The School has a Principal who employs three assistants. The number of pupils varies from 20 to 120. Of these about thirty have in mind a course of study in our college at New Brunswick. The proposition submitted to Synod is to make an entire transfer of the Academy to the General Synod. This your committee considers with favor. They have shown an interest and earnest desire to promote the cause of Christian education among themselves but their means are limited and out of their poverty they have done what they could. We have come to the conclusion that the Academy should be taken under the care of the Synod.

The report was adopted and the Board of Education was instructed to carry out the plan and to take immediate steps to raise the requisite sum to meet the salary of the teachers.

---

16 Minutes of the Classis of Holland, April 27, 1853, p. 112.

Change in the Administration of the School, 1854

At the meeting of the Classis on April 13, 1854, it was announced that Mr. Taylor offered to resign on condition of the payment of all monies due him. The Classis agreed to accept the resignation and resolved to petition the Synod to change the administration of the academy. They proposed that the Boards of Education and Domestic Missions unite

> to send us a faithful servant of Christ, who would be competent to give instruction to our children, and at the same time could preach among the American population, whereby, in such a case, the academy would not be too heavy a burden and at the same time there would be a supply for a great and many-sided need, namely, the religious education of the youth, work among the American population, and the gradual transition of our children to the American religious service.

The Board of Education asked the Synod to agree that "instead of trying to sustain an academy in its present condition, a Missionary be commissioned to the field who shall add to the duty of preaching the gospel, the special care of the academy." The Board of Missions concurred and said that the interests of the field justified the employment of a teacher in the Holland academy in the office of the ministry, and that a sufficient appropriation for the contemplated missionary services might be properly made.

The Synod agreed. The new plan meant not only the continuance of the academy on an independent basis, but also the beginning of English preaching in the Holland colony. The control of the academy was now in the hands of the boards of the Reformed Church. To fill the vacancy caused by the resignation of Taylor, the boards appointed the Reverend F. Beidler. He it was who began English preaching in the Holland colony. The first missionary teacher to be appointed under the new plan was the Reverend Cornelius Crispell. When he declined the invitation, the Reverend John Van Vleck was appointed.

Although Taylor resigned in the spring of 1854, he continued to teach until the end of the school year. Monies due him amounted to about $3000, which the Synod instructed the Boards of Education and Missions to pay. He left Holland on Septem-

ber 21, 1854. The Reverend C. Vander Veen said that Taylor
left because

> he was disappointed and disheartened. No more single-minded,
> simple-hearted, unworldly and sincere man ever lived. He had
> a genius for language and indomitable energy. He was sought
> out to undertake here what was to be a holy and solemn mission.
> He accepted it at the sacrifice of everything. He was sent out
> for only one purpose, in which he believed. He soon found
> himself thwarted in that purpose by evil influences in Holland.
> He did not find in Holland what he had been taught to expect
> nor was he permitted to do the work which he had come to
> carry out. He was left to fight the battle alone and he was
> crushed. He went away and died of a broken heart.

As was the case with Vander Veen, all of his students loved
Taylor. To them he was an able teacher and thoroughly devoted
to his task, even to the extent that at one time he taught his
pupils from his sickbed in order that there might be no delay
in their preparation for Rutgers. The hardships of the frontier,
the rugged winters, the death of his daughter, Margaret, in
July 1852, and the difficulties of an impossible task made it
necessary for him to leave Holland to return to his former associations in Geneva. He died in December 1856. Before he
left in 1854, he had succeeded in preparing four men for Rutgers — Cornelius Vander Veen, Jacob Vandermeulen, Henry
Courtney Taylor, and John Mokkelenkate. The first two graduated from Rutgers and entered the Reformed Church ministry.
John Vandermeulen entered Rutgers in 1855.

It is unfortunate that an estrangement occurred between Taylor and Van Raalte. On December 21, 1856, a few days after
the death of her father, Anna Taylor wrote the following letter
to Van Raalte:

> I have been thinking of those days of pleasant social inter-
> course between our families and regretting that anything should
> have happened to mar it. It has always seemed a great source
> of grief to me and I had hoped that all those misunderstandings
> which have crept in between you and father destroying your
> friendship for one another would pass away for he often spoke
> of you with great kindness and sympathy, and only the night
> before he died, he was wishing that he could see you and Mrs.
> Van Raalte and the children. You have doubtless heard of
> father's death. It was very unexpected. He was sick only a few
> days. Please write to me. Give my love to all the family.

3: HOLLAND ACADEMY

THE REVEREND JOHN VAN VLECK was born in Shawangunk, Ulster County, New York, in 1828. An alumnus of Rutgers College in 1852 and New Brunswick Theological Seminary in 1855, he was recommended for the principalship by the Reverend Charles Scott, who was his pastor at the time. As a young man, he came to Holland in the summer of 1855 with his wife, Cornelia Falconer, and her sister. The two women took charge of the district school, and Van Vleck began teaching in the academy and preaching in English. He taught his classes on the upper floor of the district school until 1857 when he moved into the orphan house. The separation of the academy from the district school in 1857 marks the real beginning of Holland Academy.

Mrs. Van Vleck and her sister also gave private instruction to Van Raalte's children. For this service, Van Raalte gave them title to two lots in Block 50, which he repurchased two years later. An interesting sidelight is the fact that Van Vleck came to Holland with a letter of transfer of his church membership from the Classis of Orange to the Classis of Holland in which he was to be ordained. His reception and ordination were postponed for more than a year since the ministers in the Dutch church were unable to examine a man who knew no Dutch. In the next year, Van Vleck learned enough Dutch so that he could answer questions put to him by the Classis. After examining him "for the space of three hours in theology and especially in the Five Points Against the Remonstrants"[1] he was received and immediately ordained.

When the General Synod adopted the academy in 1853 for a trial period of five years, it was confidently expected that by 1858 the academy would have a campus and a suitable building, and much larger financial support from the community itself. So far, little financial support had come from the colony. Some Eastern benefactors such as Samuel B. Schieffelin, James Suydam, Abraham Van Nest, Myndert Van Schaick, and William Mandeville had been generous in their support. The boards of the church were paying the salary of the principal and the second teacher. Van Raalte became very impatient with his followers for their failure to support his educational efforts, and upbraided the members of his own congregation for their efforts to amass farms and material goods while they neglected the more important duties in the field of education. On November 18, 1856, he called a meeting of his consistory and read a letter addressed to them and to all the colonists. He told of the urgency and the cost of a building for the academy, that the principal was willing to assume the duty of supervising students in the building and was making a personal donation of $500. He announced that he had received an urgent call to a church in Pella, Iowa, which he was inclined to accept. He said he was willing to withhold his decision for twelve days and that their silence would indicate they were unwilling to respond to his appeal. In that case, he would accept the call and try to work out his educational ideals in Iowa. The letter and the discussion had the proper effect. Some cash was donated at once and more was promised. And so Van Raalte stayed in Holland.

One year before the end of the trial period, the new Secretary of the Board of Education, the Reverend James A. H. Cornell, came to Holland to discuss the academy and its future. When mention was made of the possibility of moving the academy to one of the chief cities of the West, Van Raalte made it clear that, even if this would happen, an academy in Holland would be indispensable and would be continued no matter

---

[1] Minutes of the Classis of Holland, Dec. 17, 1856, p. 231.

The Reverend John Van Vleck, third principal of the Pioneer School, 1855-1859.

how difficult it might be to support it. The Secretary was convinced and recommended to the Board of Education, R.C.A., continued appropriations and its ultimate expansion into a college. This was the decision for which Van Raalte had long been waiting. The trial period was over and an academy in Holland assured. With characteristic vigor, he began planning the building and raising funds.

One of the first things requiring attention was the matter of a site and a building for the academy. Prior to 1857, the academy owned no property. It used the orphan house which belonged to the First Church in Holland. Beside it, on the south two acres, was the Zwemer House erected by Adrian Zwemer while a student in the academy. It was a one-story house about 18 x 24 feet with a lean-to in the back. On the outside were rough upright boards which shrank so much during the summer heat that swarms of mosquitoes came in.[2] Later it became the property of the college, and it was in this building that the first classes in Theology met. After the fire of 1871, a two-story addition was added and the entire house converted into a residence for Professor Scott, who had lost his home in the fire.

The General Synod of 1857 authorized the erection of a building and commended Van Raalte to the churches in his efforts to collect the necessary funds. The Synod suggested that

---

[2] Adrian Zwemer, "Life and Immigration to America," in H. S. Lucas, *Memoirs and Related Pioneer Writings,* II, 455.

it be located upon an elevated and healthy position in or near the town of Holland and that the Classical Committee already appointed by the Classis and approved by the Synod of Chicago, should regulate and manage the affairs of Holland Academy, and be requested to take charge of the property according to the legal form, or place the title in the General Synod, that the property may be secured to the object to which it is intended.[3]

It was not easy to raise the money. Little was contributed in the West except in the form of labor that could be employed in gathering materials and in actual construction. On June 1, 1857, Van Vleck wrote to Van Raalte:

> The building progresses slowly. The prospect of getting into it before winter is good. The incessant rains have made both the making and drawing of brick impossible. But it will probably not rain all summer unless the guilty comet should decide not to leave us. I tremble when I think how utterly dependent we are on your success. If the subscriptions here could have been paid, we might have come a little more smoothly. Not a cent has been paid as yet, probably not a cent will be paid. All depends on you. Be strong and may God strengthen and reward you.[4]

One may inquire why Van Raalte began the building of Van Vleck Hall before the Synod had given formal approval, and before any money had been raised in the West. The Dutch novelist P. J. Risseeuw gave a possible answer:

> When Van Raalte noticed that young Van Vleck, head of Holland Academy, had been thinking about the possibility of locating the institution in one of the chief cities of the West, he had the feeling that, without his knowledge, he had been stung by an adder. He did not let grass grow over it. Van Vleck's bad health was the main reason for the plan; the fact that he had to teach in the upper story of the District School and in the old wooden orphanage which was never meant to be used for such purpose, brought Van Raalte to the point. With the approval of the Classis, he undertook two long trips to the East to collect the money. The collections in the colony were disappointing. His own enthusiasm won over the doubters in the East and he came home with $12,000.[5]

---

3 Acts of the General Synod, R.C.A., 1857.
4 Van Raalte Papers; letter dated June 1, 1857.
5 P. J. Risseeuw, *Landverhuizers* (Baarn, The Netherlands, 1959), p. 374.

On June 27, 1857, there is another letter from Van Vleck to Van Raalte. He says:

> Last evening I received the letter sent by you from Geneva and another from Albany. Of course, I was grieved at your poor success in getting the money. You ask if I will come and help you beg. Now dear Domine, you know or ought to know that I would do almost anything to relieve you. But in this matter I cannot. I would not raise enough money to pay for my travelling expenses. I am serious and in dead earnest and I mean what I say when I say that I cannot beg money even though it be in a good cause. You can. Verbum sapienti sufficit. If you come home and the money is not raised, I will go and try and the result will probably be a serious failure. I am sorry to tell you this because it will add to your burdens and implies weakness on my part. But I had better speak the plain truth. The building progresses slowly. I hope that you will not neglect to send me cash as fast as you gather it. It will go from hand to mouth. I fear and tremble. Excuse my vanity, but I think decidedly that it is the best policy for me to stay where I am and for you to stick to it until we have the money. We can ill afford to have you miss the examinations but better than your presence this year is the presence of a new building next year. Be strong and patient. Remember that I love you.[6]

The academy report for 1858 indicates that the building was not finished and that only a part of it was ready for use. The

[6] Van Raalte Papers.

The first buildings of Hope College on property given by Dr. Albertus C. Van Raalte. On the right, Van Vleck Hall, built in 1857, and on the left, the Oggel House, 1860-1941.

On the left, Van Vleck Hall, 1857; on the right, the first chapel, 1862.

General Synod then resolved that every effort should be made
to complete and furnish Holland Academy and that the work be
commended to the earnest sympathy and liberality of the
churches. It was erected on the highest point on the campus in
the midst of a forest so thick that a road had to be cleared
before building materials could be brought to the site. It was
the most pretentious building in the whole colony. In the building were a residence for the principal, classrooms, dormitory
rooms, a reading room, and a refectory in the southeast corner
of the basement where Van Vleck boarded all the boys. The
Reverend Josias Meulendyke wrote:

> I was assigned a room in Van Vleck Hall. Furnishings and ap-
> pearances were of a kind to agree with the prevalent poverty
> of the students. Bare floors with nails protruding from wood
> boards, walls bare save as warmed by a picture from some maga-
> zine. Rising from straw ticks in the cold winter mornings, the
> student would wrestle with the contents of the wood box in
> the corner. A kerosene lamp helped him out in the preparation
> of his recitations.[7]

With a stove in each room, it is not surprising to hear President
Kollen say that by 1891 the building had been on fire at least
eight times. No furniture was provided until the General Faculty
of the college in 1872 decided that each room was to be equipped
with bedstead, table, two chairs, wardrobe, wash stand, and a

---

[7] Hope College *Milestone,* 1930, p. 277.

bed tick or mattress. The building marked an epoch in the history of the academy. Up to 1857 the character of the institution was tentative. Now it had a permanent home and the founders were free to give thought to its expansion into a college.

At a meeting of the Classis of Holland on April 23, 1853, Van Raalte offered to give the Classis certain lots in Block 50 which lay between 11th and 12th streets. However, no property was conveyed until May 1858, when title to certain lots in Block 45 was given to the General Synod. It is interesting to note that this is not the property he offered to donate in 1853. The campus was expanded from the original five acres to approximately sixteen on May 13, 1860, when the Rev. and Mrs. Van Raalte gave the General Synod title to the remaining lots in Block 45 and all of the lots in Block 50. Eleventh Street between College and Columbia Avenue was closed. It is conjectured that the court order closing the street was not recorded and was lost, and in consequence, the street was not formally closed until 1958.

There was some growth in the Van Vleck period. On April 6, 1857, the Classis discussed the necessity of increasing the staff "because Van Vleck could no longer take care of the work alone on account of the increasing number of students which probably will soon have grown to more than forty."[8] In 1857, the church boards sent an additional teacher in the person of Abraham Thompson, just graduated from Rutgers. After serving for one year, he entered New Brunswick Seminary and was succeeded by the Reverend Giles Vande Wall, who assisted in preaching and teaching until 1861, when he accepted a call to do missionary work in South Africa.

Although the academy was the property of the General Synod, and under the control of the Boards of Education and Domestic Missions, the actual day-by-day administration was, to a large extent, in the hands of the Classis. Upon the organization of the Particular Synod of Chicago in 1856, the Classis began to share control with the Synod. At a meeting in 1857, the Particular Synod expressed its confidence in Holland Academy and appointed a commission to attend the annual examinations of

---

8 Minutes of the Classis of Holland, April 8, 1857, p. 237.

the academy. These began in 1857 and continued until the appointment of the Board of Superintendents in 1863. The first examining committee reported that they examined eighteen men ranging from thirteen to thirty-seven years of age in the Classical Department of the academy. They noted that in addition there was a primary department of twelve boys and two girls. This sharing of control served the useful purpose of broadening the base of financial support, and extending the horizons of the school, making it much less provincial than it had been. In 1857, a committee of the Chicago Synod prepared a publication emphasizing the needs and purposes of the institution, and proposing to extend its purpose and to enlarge it in order to serve the American population as well as the Hollanders.

In 1858, the Chicago Synod organized a Board of Regents to assist the principal in administration. In 1863, the name was changed to the School Board of the Classis of Holland. The Board of Superintendents became responsible for the actual administration, while the School Board continued to serve in the recruitment of students and giving them financial support. In 1852, the Classical Board of Benevolence was organized following a dramatic and pathetic appeal by the Reverend Cornelius Vander Meulen, who said:

> The performance of this the primary duty of each of us is a burden not too heavy for us, since it requires from each of us but a small annual contribution in proportion as God has prepared him. Should not a man be able to dedicate to this end a thousand barrel staves or a couple of cords of bark, or a farmer some ten bushels of corn or potatoes, or some pork or butter, or a day laborer his wages for a couple of days? If all will act in this way, the work can take its course, and the unanimity will lighten the burden.[9]

As a result, the Classis organized the Board of Benevolence. The Board planned to house all students in boarding houses for proper supervision. Overseers were appointed to collect contributions, from house to house, in order to provide food for the pupils. A commission was appointed to find boarding houses and to keep good order in them. All of these efforts to assist students were important at a time when the finan-

---

[9] Minutes of the Classis of Holland, Sept. 1, 1852, pp. 100f.

cial conditions were still precarious. An old account book shows that in the years 1851–1861, the churches in the colony contributed over $7000 for student support, much of it in the form of grain, dairy products, or produce. In 1855, the Overisel congregation surprised the principal by sending three wagon loads of provisions for the students. In 1854, the Board of Education, R.C.A., began to assist students in Holland Academy studying for the ministry by relaxing the old rule requiring them to study at Rutgers. Three students received some assistance in 1854, beginning a practice that continues to the present day.

The campus was a virtual wilderness, described by an early student as follows:

> How dreary was the view of Holland as we drove into it. We strained our eyes through the trees when a turn of a very sandy knoll opened the town to view. Around the edge was a tangle of fallen hemlock branches and trunks charred and black. No beautiful shade trees. All was bleak sand. A walk led up to the Hall on each side of which were unhealthy pines.[10]

Student life in the academy was simple in the extreme. Students cut the wood for their own fires. Principal Van Vleck boarded the students and heard their prayers morning and evening. There were no school colors, no yells, no athletics, and few alumni. By the end of the Van Vleck period in 1859, there were nineteen alumni, of whom fourteen entered the ministry. The quality of work done impressed the examining committee of the Chicago Synod, who reported in 1857:

> We examined classes in Vergil, Greek Reader, Arithmetic, Cicero, Greek New Testament, Algebra, Homer, Geometry, and English Grammar. We were surprised at the extent and the accuracy of the information acquired. It is not often that so much is achieved in so short a time, and among such difficulties as those young men have to contend with. The larger part have studied only one year.[11]

Van Vleck was a Regent of the University of Michigan for a few months. He was elected on the Republican ticket in 1858 and took office January 1, 1859. Hinsdale in his history of the university says, "Van Vleck was a teacher of superior qualifications and power, and his work in Holland amid the privations

---

10 Henry J. Brown, "Recollections," in Lucas, *op. cit.*, I, 368.
11 Minutes of the Particular Synod of Chicago 1857.

of pioneer life was an influence for good, the lasting effects of which are felt today."

John Van Vleck resigned because of ill health in 1859. The Chicago Synod expressed regret, "as he had endeared himself to his colleagues by his faithfulness in the discharge of his duties." There is this fine tribute to him in the Minutes:

> The examining committee said that we believe that the methods of instruction used by Van Vleck are the right ones. He has endeavored not to produce scholars, so-called, who make an ostentation of learning without having real knowledge, but such as will understand the philosophy of the matter learned. In the midst of a wilderness, surrounded by the stumps of great trees and the prostrate monarchs of the forest, we have heard in a little building, ceiled with boards, such recitations in English, Latin, Greek, Mathematics, and witnessed such an exhibition of Christian manliness as would be an honor amid the advantages of a well-developed civilization.[12]

Dr. Henry Dosker in his life of Van Raalte says of Van Vleck,

> He was an optimist and ... this resulted in financial mistakes but ... at the same time, this was a virtue which gave birth to his students. He was the real father of the Academy and the love of his pupils was the crown of his work at Holland.[13]

As was the case with Taylor in 1854, the Van Vlecks left Holland unhappy and disillusioned. Salary was in arrears and Mr. and Mrs. Van Vleck were both ill. And it appears that serious differences had arisen between the Van Raalte and Van Vleck families. In a letter written by Van Vleck to Van Raalte July 5, 1859, he answered certain charges which he claimed Van Raalte made against him. Among the charges were that, in his writings, Van Vleck had abused the Hollanders, and that he had tried to persuade two boys to leave the academy and go East with him. There had been a difference over a small academy account and Van Raalte had evidently not forgotten that Van Vleck had discussed with James Cornell the matter of a relocation of the school. All of these charges are answered in the letter of July 5. Van Vleck admits that he may on occasion have criticized the Hollanders for some of their faults, but said:

---

12 Minutes of the Particular Synod of Chicago 1857.

13 Henry Dosker, *Levensschets van Rev. A. C. Van Raalte, D.D.* (Nijkerk, 1893).

I never expect to find in the world a better people. If there is any people that I love en masse, it is your people in Michigan. Were it not for the gulf which a strange language imposes, I should hope again to live among them or at least visit them. I do not know how many people in Holland have a personal affection for me but I really love them personally.[14]

As to the charge that he was attempting to persuade two boys to accompany him East he says,

I conceived the project of taking these boys with me. My reasons were that they might continue their studies so as to enter the Sophomore Class, which they could not do with Vande Wall (for they could teach him), that they might become a little more refined by contact with good society for a few months, that I might prosecute my studies in Dutch, that they might aid me in teaching. I made the project known to them and they rejoiced in it. I love both of the boys. I loved one of them as my own child. I did not know the bitter pangs with which I parted from them. Having so long and earnestly endeavored to sweeten the lives of them all, could I not have my life sweetened after leaving them?[15]

He acknowledges that he may have made a mistake when he did not tell the boys to get the consent of the Board, but that the thing was not done in a corner and that the Board should have offered objections if they were opposed. Van Vleck says:

Any unkindness that cut very deep was done then — an unkindness that I can and do forgive but can never forget. And my dear friend, never wound a sensitive nature unless there is necessity. It is never wise to break that which cannot be bent. I wish that you would let Brother Oggel read this. I know that he has a heart that can sympathize with my feelings. His feeling also became alienated from us. Surely it was the work of the Devil — perhaps it was divinely sent punishment for my worshipping him.[16]

Van Vleck was even more hurt that Van Raalte questioned his management of the school account. He says:

When I wrote you that my honesty was distrusted, you disavowed this and gave as your reason that you were in confusion about the item in question. How am I to understand such deal-

---

14 Vander Veen Papers, "Genetic History of Hope College."
15 *Ibid.*
16 Vander Veen Papers.

ings? While in Holland my books were continually open to inspection. I never made any effort to keep anything in the dark. Further I am honest. I have my failings but the love of money is not one of them. I spurn any insinuation of my being guilty in these respects. My dear brother, I have nothing more in the business line. If I have blamed you too severely, do not be angry. I have not written in a fault-finding spirit because I thought it was my duty to speak out, may the past make us both wiser. And may the Lord make us both better. May the Lord be with you and bless you. Please write me as soon as possible at length. Our united love to Mrs. Van Raalte.[17]

Philip Phelps, Jr.

In February 1859, Van Vleck informed Van Raalte of his definite decision to resign and that he had already asked the Board to appoint a successor. On his way to Pella, Van Raalte stopped at the home of the Reverend Mason Ferris in Chicago. After conferring with Ferris, Van Raalte on February 17 wrote a letter to the Reverend Philip Phelps at Hastings-on-Hudson. He said:

> Being very anxious over a successor, I take the liberty to suggest your coming in his place because I believe you are the man for it, not only as a teacher but also as a laborer to gather the Americans and the young Americanized people. It is a noble field and I have a deep conviction that you are the man. You have enough of the missionary spirit in you which is wanted in this situation. Your dear companion, I hope, has a heart for it, and the fact that she is able to converse with the Dutch would be a blessing to this community and could have a precious influence over the female portion. I hope her heart is willing. I wrote about this to the Board. I hope sincerely that the Lord may lead you and make you willing to go. Brother Ferris will write about it also. Please drop me a line about the matter in Pella.[18]

Van Raalte had met Phelps while on one of his financial missions to the East, and the Van Raalte family had met Rev. and Mrs. Phelps in September of 1856 when they made a visit to the colony. They were on their way to Davenport, Iowa. They had planned to go from Buffalo by steamer through the Straits of Mackinac. On account of the late severe storms, they aban-

---

17 *Ibid.*
18 Van Raalte Papers.

doned this idea and took the railroad to Chicago. Since there were no sleepers on the train, the family decided to stop in Kalamazoo overnight. Here they decided to pay a visit to the Holland colony and especially to call on Van Raalte and Van Vleck. They took the stagecoach to Grand Rapids and the next day took another stage to Holland. Mrs. Van Raalte made them feel at home. They called on Van Vleck, who lived in a small house in the village. Phelps preached in Holland on September 28, 1856, and the next day they took the stage to Grand Haven.

As soon as the Secretary of the Board of Education, R.C.A., had heard from Van Raalte and Mason Ferris, he made a personal call on Phelps urging his acceptance of an appointment as missionary teacher in Holland. He made a good impression, especially upon Mrs. Phelps, and convinced her that the Lord had prepared her to go to the Hollanders because she knew so many of them, knew some Dutch, and had worked with the Dutch immigrants in Albany.

Philip Phelps was born in Albany, July 12, 1826, the sixth child of Philip Phelps, Sr., who for fifty years was a Deputy Comptroller of the State of New York. He received his elementary and secondary education in Albany Academy and entered the Junior Class at Union College in 1842. He graduated in 1844 with Phi Beta Kappa honors. After teaching for two years at Mansion Hall, Greenburgh, New York, he entered New Brunswick Seminary. Ordained in 1848, he served the old Greenburgh Church in Westchester County for two years. He organized a mission church at Hastings-on-Hudson and became the first pastor in 1850. He came to Holland in 1859.

Mrs. Phelps was the former Margaret Ann Jordan, born in New York City, February 19, 1828. Her father was of Irish descent and educated at Dublin. She graduated from Albany Academy in 1842 and taught in the Rensselaer Street Mission School. In the First Presbyterian Church, she organized the first women's prayer meeting, and became deeply interested in the spiritual and physical welfare of the Hollanders when they reached Albany. She married Philip Phelps September 21, 1853.

After his arrival in Holland, the principal suspended theological studies in the academy and classified all the students either as Classical or Primary. He found classification difficult because of various degrees of attainment on the part of the students. Some were advanced students and some were without any knowledge of English. He said that the classes were so intermingled that no two could be found whose instruction could be conducted at the same time by different teachers.

Van Raalte in the East in the Winter of 1859/60

In the winter of 1859/1860, Van Raalte spent three months in the East in an effort to raise $3,000 for three objects — to clear the debt on Van Vleck Hall, to erect a house for a second teacher, and to purchase the necessary lots to complete the campus. The General Synod had title to five acres of ground upon which Van Vleck Hall had been erected. In 1859, the principal and the Secretary of the Board of Domestic Missions suggested to Van Raalte that a possible opening of 11th Street, between Cedar and Fish streets, would make the future expansion of the campus difficult. Van Raalte agreed with them that the entire block of sixteen acres ought to be secured and 11th Street closed. It could take about $700 to make the necessary purchases. In the meantime, the Board of Regents on October 4, 1859, resolved that Van Raalte in his proposed journey East should try to raise an additional $800 to erect a residence for the Reverend Giles Vande Wall and his successors.

Van Raalte raised the money with great difficulty. An article in opposition to his plans appeared in the *Christian Intelligencer* December 1, 1859. It was written by someone who signed himself "W." The writer asked the following questions:

> First, have we not been deceived in respect to what Synod voted in 1853 to transfer to the Board of Education the care of the Academy? Who would have supposed that this vote would transfer to the Reformed Church a debt and a Free School to be supported for years to come? The Committee was of the opinion that in five years it would be self-supporting. What efforts have been made in the West to make it so? Had I known the secret objects of the movement, I would have voted against it. Why bestow upon the Hollanders in Western Michigan a privilege which the members of our Eastern churches have never needed or asked for? Secondly, have we not done all that was asked for? The Boards employ two teachers and give them a competent salary. An edifice has been erected such as is enjoyed by few communities in the East. Several academies would be

glad to exchange properties with Phelps and Van Raalte. Thirdly, have ·not the Holland brethren been allowing themselves to walk too much on crutches? In 1851, they began without help. In 1853, they shifted the burden to the Board of Education. They themselves invested less than $1,000 in brick and timber. Now the title is vested in General Synod. Such gifts are Trojan horses. How many repair bills will it take to open the eyes of the Synod? Fourthly, why are these improvements needed now? There are accommodations for forty students. A Refectory was installed and now the new Principal declines to board the students. Then let him find a residence elsewhere. The Hall was not built to furnish a free residence for a principal, but to house a man who would take personal oversight over the pupils, the burden of boarding them as well. Mr. Van Vleck always paid rent or its equivalent. I see no necessity of a second teacher in the building.

Van Raalte was of the opinion that Van Vleck had written the article. In a letter to Phelps dated December 1, 1859, he charges Van Vleck with the writing. On December 17, he says,

> Let us not trouble ourselves with Mr. V. V. He says he did not write it, but it is his spirit. But I pray you let him alone. He is suspected in the East and they all say it will damage him very much. I wish his students would give us copies of his bitter expressions. There may be a writing against him on some future occasion.

The *Christian Intelligencer* editorially supported Van Raalte and the work of the academy. So did the Executive Committee of the Board of Education, R.C.A. Phelps answered "W" in two long articles to disprove the charges made against him. In the issue of January 25, 1860, "W" closed the controversy by saying, "Van Raalte is urging his appeal with success. The services of Phelps are too valuable to be lost." In spite of ill health and many disappointments, Van Raalte was able to accomplish his mission. On December 26, 1859, he writes Phelps as follows:

> You say that I must strike while the iron is hot. You are always right, but I wish you were the striker and I were the writer. Three months away from home for a man with an eating cancer of homesickness. Now, gentlemen and professors, will you allow me to come back at the end of January?

As a result of Van Raalte's efforts, a residence for Vande Wall was built on the northeast corner of the campus where Phelps Hall now stands. When Vande Wall left Holland in 1861, it became the residence of the Reverend Peter Oggel and became known as the Oggel House. The lots for the enlargement of the campus were purchased, and on May 12, 1860, Van Raalte gave a deed to the General Synod of the Protestant Dutch Church for the following property: Lots 1, 7, 8, 9, 10, 16 in Block 45 and all the lots in Block 50. The deed was recorded May 25, 1860.

The Gymnasium in 1862

In 1862, another building was erected. This time it was a frame structure to be used as a gymnasium and general assembly hall. It was erected by the students themselves under the supervision of the principal. As the story goes:

> The Principal proposed to the students that every man should take his axe and go to the forest and prepare lumber for the erection of a gymnasium that also might be used for commencement purposes. The work was distributed among the different committees, and after logging about 11,000 feet of lumber, the lateness of the season necessitated procuring the rest from the Mill. Meanwhile, they prepared and put together the material under the supervision of a carpenter, and when the April vacation came, the work was driven in all weathers. It was privately dedicated by the hoisting of the Stars and Stripes, the reading of a Psalm, the singing of a hymn, the offering of a prayer, and the concluding utterance of three rousing cheers. It was publicly dedicated at the Commencement in July 1862, when the pioneer class, having fulfilled their preparatory course, were ushered into the Freshman Class of the nascent college.[19]

This program on July 17, 1862, was made up of forty-one numbers. The class sang eleven songs including two anthems. There were eighteen recitations, three dialogues, an essay on the new gym by William Shields, and addresses by the Reverends Oggel and Kershow.

It is well to remember that students in those days were adult men. Among them were artisans experienced in several trades. The principal had to use some of his own money to finish the project but was later reimbursed by donations from Mrs. Few Christie of Hastings-on-Hudson, and by John L. Smith of New York. The original building was a simple structure with the entire framework visible from the interior. In 1878, the building was completed with ceiling, a hardwood floor, platform, and a

---

[19] First catalog, Oct. 1865, p. 40.

The original gymnasium and chapel, built in 1862 on the present site of Carnegie Gymnasium.

walnut balustrade, and was papered and painted. At that time, the building was raised from the ground on a brick foundation. Chairs replaced the old wooden settees. There is a model of the old building in the Netherlands Museum. It was made from the original timber by Philip Tertius Phelps and presented to the college in 1916 in connection with the semicentennial celebration.

The Civil War and Holland Academy

It is difficult to make an exact judgment of the impact of the war upon the institution. It was still in its infancy, with a handful of students, and financially unstable. However, there is no question about the loyalty of the founders and the students to the Union cause. Van Raalte himself was extremely patriotic and provided exceptional leadership. The best proof of his loyalty is the fact that his two sons volunteered and served in Company I of the 25th Regiment of Michigan Volunteers. When recruiting for this regiment began in August of 1862, there was great excitement among the students. D. B. K. Van Raalte, John Huizenga, William Ledeboer, William Walker, and William Van Putten enlisted in Company I, and Alec Eckerman, Charles E. Clark, and K. Drost enlisted in other units. Company I fought in many important battles — at Kennesaw Mountain, in the siege and capture of Atlanta; and they marched with Sherman to the sea. There were casualties among them. K. Drost was wounded, William Ledeboer died of disease, Charles E. Clark was killed in action, and D. B. K. Van Raalte came home without his right arm. Riding through the woods while carrying a message to headquarters, he was ambushed and wounded, and his right arm was amputated at the shoulder. Students A. Buursma and William Visscher enlisted as late as 1865. Visscher was thirty years old but volunteered to take the place of a draftee. The academy was proud of the students and carried their names on the class rolls as if they had been actually present. Some returned to the institution to complete their work and received A.B. degrees from the nascent college. Among them were D. B. K. Van Raalte, John Huizenga, A. Buursma, and William Visscher. Students in the service often showed their impatience with other students who remained in the academy. On December 20, 1863, D. B. K. Van Raalte wrote his father as follows:

> You asked me and Benjamin to give some money to the college or to the students. As far as I am concerned, I do not want to pay one penny for that purpose. . . . I think that the students had better come here and take up a gun and knapsack. I think we need them more here than anywhere else. We have to bleed and suffer while they stay at home and live at our expense. And they make fun of us. . . . It would be better if half of the students would join our ranks instead of staying at home like cowards and wait to be drafted. . . . We are more in need of soldiers at this time than they are of students. I think that if everyone would do as much for the college as you have done, things would be better.[20]

Lt. Col. Cornelius Gardener, a graduate of the academy and the first career soldier among the alumni, spoke at the quartercentennial exercises of Hope College in 1890. He had high praise for the patriotism and loyalty of the academy boys. Naming twelve of them, he said:

> During the course of the war, the excitement of the times also stirred the boys at the Academy. Some of them were still in their teens but full of enthusiasm, patriotism, loyalty, and were already imbued with love for their adopted country.[21]

20 Van Raalte Papers.
21 Hope College *Anchor*, July 1890.

A letter to Dr. Albertus C. Van Raalte from his son, D. B. K. Van Raalte, written during the Civil War.

Eerw verzoekt mij en Ben om geld te geven voor de College of voor studenten, wel ik voor my part gef er geen cent aan, als het voor en kerk was dan wel; maar ik denk dat het beeter was dat die studenten hier kwamen en er geweer en knapsack op hun rug deeden. Ik denk wij hebben die hier zoo groot nodig als ergens anders

Wij zullen bloeijen en lijden voor onze country en zullui zullen daar te huis blijven en op onze Zak teeren, en ons op de hoop toe bespotten, na belangen na niet daar zal ik ze geen kans toe geven. Wij moeten te veel lijden het welk wij doen voor onze country's sake met blijdschap, en dat bietje geld dat wij nog verdiennen kan ik to goed gebruiken. Het zou wij wat beeterlijken dat de helft van de studenten die in de ranks waren; dan daar als cowards te huis te blijven, en te wachten tot dat he gedraft worden, en als ze gedraft worden dan gaan ze nog beddelen om geld om hun zelven vrij te kopen, Ik zeg elke een van de studenten die zijn eigen kost niet kan betalen om school te gaan die moet maar voor zijn kost gaan werken of maar enlisten. Uw zult mischien wel zeggen dat dit selfishness of domheid van mij is, maar zoo denk ik er niet over want wij hebben solda hoger nodig dan studenten op het oogenblik zoo denk ik er over voor mij part, en ik denk het zal wel zoo weese met al de andere jongens, Dit schrijf ik uw niet in kwaadheid maar in vriendschap, en ik denk als ze allemaal zoo veel aan de school deden als uw gedaan hebt, dan zal het wel schikken.

Early Efforts at Foreign Missions

When Dr. Jacob Chamberlain visited the colony, the Holland Classis resolved that the pastor and leaders of each church should attempt to raise three dollars per member for missions and education. In 1860, the Classis resolved to send a missionary to Africa, and Van Raalte offered his services. On August 31, 1860, he wrote to Principal Phelps:

> Several weeks ago I did write to the Cape, and did explain my peculiar circumstances and my desires, but I did not send it away, desiring to consider and to bring it yet before the throne of God. My common sense seems to dictate my removal and all my desires are stirred up to preach in the destitute regions of Africa. There is here too much opposition against me. I think it is well to take Dr. De Witt's counsel about my peculiar position and my thoughts about Africa. A call would be necessary. It would be impossible for me to defray the expenses of the journey. P.S. Can you find opportunity to gather information about South Africa from the Reverend D. Lindsey who is a missionary of the American Board and now in this country? I am anxious to hear from De Witt and will not write to the brethren at the Cape before that time.

Van Raalte and Phelps were missionaries at heart. Phelps's first full-time pastorate was in the mission church at Hastings-on-Hudson. He proposed that the first Chair in the projected seminary should be a Chair of Missionary Training. In 1864, he brought to Holland a noted missionary, Dr. John Talmage. His addresses resulted in a great revival of missionary interest in the colony. Phelps took advantage of this to propose the building of a missionary ship whose point of departure should always be Black Lake. The plans were approved by the Chicago Synod, which resolved:

> We regard with pleasure and devout thanksgiving to God the determination of the Missionary Committee of the Classes of Holland and Wisconsin to build a missionary ship, and we commend the enterprise to our congregations for their free will offerings, as another potent auxiliary for the publication of the Gospel in foreign lands.[22]

The idea was not original with the Holland settlers as the missionary ships of the late eighteenth and early nineteenth centuries had been brought to their attention in the Nether-

---

[22] Minutes of the Particular Synod of Chicago 1864.

lands in 1845. Phelps secured the model of the ship through Captain Samuel J. Waring of the Atlantic Insurance Company of New York. The ship was to be built in a large building on Black Lake which had been leased for ten years for this purpose. The keel was laid with great ceremony on June 24, 1864. Dr. Van Raalte was the chairman of the event. Professor Beck read the Scriptures from Isaiah 60. The Corresponding Secretary of the Board of Foreign Missions, R.C.A., the Reverend Philip Peltz, gave an address in English, which was translated and repeated in Dutch. The Reverend John Van Nest Talmage gave the main address. This was also repeated in Dutch. Other ministers of the colony followed. A missionary ode was composed by Phelps and sung by the academy choir. One verse reads:

> Hasten on the work of Hope
> Hope will soon be sight;
> In expectant vision's scope
> There is full delight.
> See the strong ribbed sides outstand,
> See the masts arise,
> See the eager sails expand
> Beauteous to our eyes.

But the ship never sailed. In the words of Samuel Zwemer, "The laying of the keel of the ship that never sailed was indeed a potent auxiliary for the publication of the Gospel." To Phelps and Van Raalte, it was tragedy. The Reverend Philip Tertius Phelps in a biography of his father says, "While the old oaken keel lay wasting on the ground, its soul went marching on. Today the number of ships which really sailed to every port of the world in the persons and lives of the young men of Hope College approaches the two hundred mark."[23]

---

23 1941, in College Archives.

BOOK II
HOPE COLLEGE
1866-1966

4: THE ORGANIZATION OF HOPE COLLEGE

It is clear that Philip Phelps came to Holland with a definite determination to reorganize Holland Academy into a preparatory school and to elevate it, as soon as possible, into an institution of collegiate level. In his later years he said:

> I started out with the simple idea that as a college in the West was indispensable to church extension, such a college should by the grace of God be planted.[1]

He felt certain that the Reformed Church in America would, at no distant date, organize a college, since Rutgers College was too far removed to recruit and to train the necessary teachers and ministers for the growing needs of the West. As a matter of fact, the General Synod had already been overtured to organize a college in South Bend, Indiana. And in 1857, the Classis of Illinois had instructed its delegate to the meeting of the General Synod to offer, for college purposes, a large parsonage that had recently been erected for the church in Fairview. However, the General Synod was not inclined to take any action until Western leaders had agreed among themselves where a college should be located. At an informal meeting of representatives of the Classes of Holland, Illinois, and Michigan, it was agreed to support a plan for a collegiate institution in connection with Holland Academy. Now that the West was in agreement, Phelps and Van Raalte were prepared to seek the approval of the General Synod.

As early as 1862, Principal Phelps wrote the Board of Education, R.C.A.:

---
[1] Hope College Catalog, Oct. 1865, p. 45.

As long as Holland Academy is but an appendage to New Brunswick, it can exert but little influence anywhere. Here is the field and here are the necessities. We did not create them, and they exist independently of east or west. We cannot ignore them and we ought not to retire from the field.[2]

With the active support of Van Raalte and the Classis, the principal recruited his first Freshman Class in the autumn of 1862. He had been encouraged to take this step by the Synod of Chicago, and by a resolution of the General Synod which expressed the hope that the curriculum of the academy would soon be of such an elevated grade as to make it unnecessary for graduates of the academy to enter other institutions of higher learning. At the same time, he had received assurance that the Michigan Legislature would, at its next session, authorize the Board of Direction, R.C.A., to hold property in Michigan.

In the spring of 1863, at the request of the principal, the Synod of Chicago appointed a Board of Superintendents to manage the affairs of Holland Academy, and authorized the college plan. At its June session, the General Synod approved these arrangements on the recommendation of the Boards of Education and Domestic Missions, R.C.A. When this had been done, the Board of Education, R.C.A., resolved to send the Vice President and the Secretary of the Board of Education, R.C.A., to attend the commencement exercises of the academy on June 23, 1863, in order "to welcome the nascent college into the sisterhood of American colleges."

The exercises in 1863 were joyous, and a large audience filled the gymnasium. The program was the longest in the history of the academy and consisted of forty-two different numbers — essays, recitations, dialogues, music, and addresses by representatives of the Classis of Holland and the Board of Education, R.C.A. An account of the program reads as follows:

> The exercises were begun at a quarter before eight o'clock in the evening and continued with unflagging interest, before an audience of six hundred persons packed into the Gymnasium, until one o'clock in the morning when Mr. Taylor rose to make his congratulatory remarks. The supplementary speeches occupied an hour longer and then a huge bonfire lighted the people to

2 University Circular, 1876, p. 93. College Archives.

their homes. The last speaker said, "Since I cannot bid you goodnight, I wish you good morning."[3]

The General Synod also endorsed a proposal of the Synod of Chicago that an endowment of $85,000 be raised and that Philip Phelps be recommended to the churches to raise this amount. Phelps was able to raise about $40,000 in the Eastern churches, while the Reverend Peter J. Oggel obtained subscriptions in the Western churches. In his appeal to the General Synod of 1865 for speedy completion of the endowment, Phelps observed that the academy had educated the Eastern churches to the conviction that a college in the West was necessary for church extension, and the Western churches to the conviction that colleges were necessary for their gradual Americanization and for the sake of the perpetuation of their own church.

The General Synod of 1864 officially endorsed the college plan, and referred the matter of arrangements to the Board of Superintendents, and resolved:

> That in order to enable the Board of Holland Academy to obtain a charter under the laws of Michigan, as soon as they shall have obtained subscriptions in the amount of $30,000 with twenty percent thereon paid to the Board of Direction, R.C.A., they shall obtain a proper instrument from the Board of Direction donating $30,000 to the Board of Superintendents.[4]

When the Board of Superintendents met on October 27, 1865, it was reported that sufficient funds had been subscribed to meet the Charter requirements. The Board proceeded to draft Articles of Association for a college to bear the name of Hope College, and to be governed by a Council as a Board of Trustees. It was decided to delay actual incorporation until the close of the school year. The General Synod of 1865 empowered the Board of Education, R.C.A., to continue appropriations for salaries "as the interests of the institution may, in their judgment, require until the securing of sufficient endowment may release the Board from this necessity." The Synod of 1866 gave its final approval to all the arrangements and resolved:

> That the Synod and the whole church should rejoice and join in a sacrifice of praise and thanks for this our college in the

---

[3] College Catalog, 1876, p. 89.
[4] Acts of the General Synod 1864.

West, which has just been incorporated by the State of Michigan.[5]

The Inauguration and the First Commencement

On May 14, 1866, Hope College was incorporated under the terms of the Michigan General College Law. The Reverend Van Raalte was absent, since "he has been constrained to spend some time in Europe on account of the health of Mrs. Van Raalte and himself."[6] Philip Phelps was formally inaugurated as the first President of Hope College on July 12, 1866. There were formal addresses by the Reverend Mancius Hutton, President of the Board of Education, R.C.A., and by the Reverend Isaac N. Wyckoff, who had been Phelps's former pastor in Albany. The chairman of the inaugural committee gave a brief address in Latin, and the new President was invested with the academic regalia presented by the women of the community. In his inaugural address, the President praised the Reformed Church in America for its historic interest in education, but claimed that the program had been kept within narrow limits because it had refused to use the English language in its church services and had "interposed a national sentiment between the gospel and the souls of men." Appealing to Hollanders in the community for a broader nationalistic viewpoint, he urged them to provide full equipment to make Hope College a first-class college. As for himself, he pledged all his strength and influence to make the institution useful and practicable to the Christian church by whose men and money it had been established.

On July 15, President Phelps preached the baccalaureate sermon on the text, "Behold, the fear of the Lord, that is wisdom, and to depart from evil is understanding." Addressing his first class, he said:

> You are my class. I have been to you a preacher, preceptor, counsellor, friend and companion. Together we have been compelled to touch, however lightly, on almost every division of the curriculum. Together we have gone into the woods and there on our own ground have labored with our own hands. We have worshipped together, morning and evening, at our academic altar, and on the Sabbath in the Sanctuary. We have passed

5 Acts of the General Synod 1866.
6 *Remembrancer*, July 17, 1866, p. 6.

*The Reverend Philip Phelps, D.D., who became the fourth principal of the
Academy in 1859 and was the first president of Hope College, 1862-1878.*

together through the varied experiences connected with the
infancy of the college. You have been not merely recipients
but co-workers.[7]

The first commencement exercises of the nascent college were
held in the gymnasium on July 17. Bachelor of Arts degrees were
conferred on William B. Gilmore, Gerrit Dangremond, Peter
Moerdyke, William Moerdyke, John W. TeWinkle, Ale Buursma,
Harm Woltman, and William A. Shields, and an honorary
Master of Arts degree was awarded to Dr. Arend VanderVeen of
Grand Haven, Michigan, an alumnus of Holland Academy. Each
member of the class delivered an oration. Among the orations
was a salutatory in Latin, the valedictory, and an oration in the

---

[7] *Remembrancer*, p. 30. College Archives.

FIRST COMMENCEMENT

O F

HOPE COLLEGE.

IN THE GYMNASIUM, JULY 17th, 1866.

ORDER OF EXERCISES.

Prayer.

Music.

PETER MOERDIJK—*Kalamazoo, Mich.*

ORATION.—Latin Salutatory.

Music.

WILLIAM F. GILMORE—*Fairview, Ill.*

ORATION.—Hope.

Music.

HARM WOLTMAN—*Holland, Mich.*

ORATION.—Public Opinion.

Music.

WILLIAM MOERDIJK—*Kalamazoo, Mich.*

ORATION.—Trial and Triumphs of Liberty.

Music.

WILLIAM A. SHIELDS—*Fairview, Ill.*

ORATION.—Man, as he was, is, and is to be.

Music.

JOHN W. TE WINKLE—*Clymer, N. Y.*

ORATION.—*De Pen is machtiger dan het Zwaard.*

Music.

ALE BUURSMA—*Holland, Mich.*

ORATION.—Skepticism.

Music.

GERRIT DANGREMOND—*Overijssel, Mich.*

ORATION.—Valedictory.

Music.

CONFERRING OF DEGREES.

Benediction.

The program of the first commencement, 1866.

The first class of Hope College, 1866.
Upper row from l. to r.: H. Woltman, Peter Moerdyke, G. Dangremond, and A. Buursma.
Lower row from l. to r.: W. Moerdyke, W. B. Gilmore, W. A. Shields, and J. W. Te Winkel.

Dutch language. The whole class sang a commencement ode composed by the President and set to music by William B. Gilmore.[8]

The men of this class are held in high honor because they were the firstfruits of Hope College. Some wore beards and all of them looked much older than their years, but they were no different from alumni of later years. The writer knew some of them and remembers them as men of average intellect, of serious purpose, and of deep religious faith, in every respect real men and very human. President Phelps wore academic regalia, and, in a letter to the Council in 1894, he said:

> Both the gown and the hat were made of rich materials after the style adopted by the Chancellor of New York University. At the first commencement, and I think at the second, I wore them but afterwards discarded them as not being consistent with the simplicity of the institution.[9]

---

[8] See text in Appendix.
[9] Letter to the Council. In the Diekema file, College Archives.

Another interesting feature was the lighting of a high chandelier of ninety kerosene burners so arranged as to form the letters H O P E. The chandelier had been made in the Netherlands several centuries earlier and hung in the old Middle Church of New York City until the building was abandoned in 1844. Mr. Phelps secured possession of it and brought it to Holland when he came in 1859. It was used at several commencements, and in the intervals between commencement, hung in the President's study in Van Vleck Hall.

The Articles of Association

Articles of Association were drawn up with the help of the Hon. Theodore Romeyn of Detroit. The Articles provided for the following departments: Grammar or Preparatory School, Academic, and Theological; and they authorized the Council "to institute such other departments as are in harmony with these Articles." All the real estate formerly known as Holland Academy was set aside for the use of the institution, and entire control was vested in a Council or Board of Trustees consisting of nineteen members, of whom thirteen were ministers and six were laymen, one of whom was the Honorable Schuyler Colfax, soon to become Vice President of the United States. Each of the four Classes or Presbyteries in the Particular Synod of Chicago nominated four members for a term of four years, while the Chicago Synod itself nominated one member to serve for a term of thirty years or for the life of the Charter. This honor went to Van Raalte, who was also named President of the Council, an honor which he held until his death in 1876. The President of the college and the Secretary of the Board of Education, R.C.A., became members *ex officio*. The General Synod had ultimate control and jurisdiction because it had the power to accept or reject the nominations of the members of the Council. The Articles could not be amended without the approval of the General Synod.[10]

The Department of Theology

The advocates of higher education in the Michigan colony had never been interested in an institution of higher learning that

10 See Articles of Association in the Appendix.

did not have a Department of Theology. In this respect, they were like the founders of Rutgers College and like the founders of many of the pioneer church colleges in the West. As early as 1857, a circular prepared for the Chicago Synod declared that the purpose of the institution was to train teachers and preachers, and to prepare missionaries for the foreign field. In 1864 the Synod of Chicago asked the General Synod to lay the foundation of a theological seminary by: "Establishing at once a Theological Professorship of Missionary Training, and then according to need and opportunity, the usual departments to be added." The General Synod did not approve this request but promised that the institution should have a theological character as soon as possible. The Synod said:

> With respect to the proposed connection of a theological depart-
> ment, this will grow out as the wants of the Church require, yet
> in the midst of so many other important enterprises, this is not
> the time to propose it or to press for it.[11]

But the West was not to be denied. In his inaugural oration in 1866, the Reverend Isaac N. Wyckoff urged the promotion of a Department of Theology and said that "it was intended and hoped that the college be a seminary of evangelical religion." The matter came to a head when seven members of the first graduating class sent a memorial to General Synod praying the Synod to take such measures as might enable them to pursue their theological studies at Hope College. The committee to which the matter was referred said:

> The matter should receive the careful consideration of Synod
> because the establishment of a seminary in the west is an old
> and cherished sentiment of the Dutch church. Your committee
> recommends that the subject be referred to the Board of Educa-
> tion and to the Council with instructions that leave be granted
> to pursue their studies at Hope College, provided that no meas-
> ures be taken by which additional expense shall be thrown upon
> Synod or upon the Board at this time, and provided that the
> Synod reserve the right to withdraw the permission at any time
> that may seem expedient.[12]

It was further provided that a committee should visit the West-

---

11 Acts of the General Synod 1864.
12 General Synod 1866.

ern churches and make a recommendation to the next Synod. In 1867, this committee suggested that there was a great need for a Theological Department at Hope College. Thereupon the Synod elected Professor C. E. Crispell as Professor of Theology, without extra compensation, and invited other members of the faculty to serve as Lectors in teaching the cognate subjects. Professor Crispell immediately raised the question whether the School of Theology was merely a department at Hope College, or a theological seminary under the control of the General Synod. The Synod made it clear that it had not recognized a seminary but merely a theological class under one Professor, and defined his title as Professor of Didactic and Polemic Theology at Hope College. This arrangement was satisfactory neither to Crispell nor to the Council. In 1868, the Council requested the General Synod to terminate the previous arrangement and appoint the Council of Hope College a Board of Superintendents of the Theological School at Hope College, with the same duties and prerogatives as those of the seminary at New Brunswick. The Synod agreed, and instructed the Council to complete the organization of the department according to the provisions of the Charter and the original design of the Synod. And so, the first seminary class was graduated in 1869.

The Faculty

In the year 1866/67, there were sixty-four students — seven in Theology, nineteen in the Academic Department, and the remainder in the Grammar School. The faculty numbered six, including the President. All of them were gentlemen scholars with a broad liberal training, and all were ministers except Mr. Cornelius Doesburg. They held chairs with high-sounding titles, but all taught a variety of courses. For example, President Phelps was Professor of Moral and Intellectual Philosophy, but remarked that at one time or another he had taught every subject not definitely assigned to someone else. Cornelius Eltinge Crispell was called to be Professor of Mathematics, Natural Philosophy and Astronomy, but began to teach Theology in 1866. Professor T. Romeyn Beck was Professor of Greek and Latin and was also appointed a Lector in Theology. He was a man of wide experience. Upon his graduation from Rutgers, he practiced law in the city of Chicago for a number of years. He was Acting Professor of Greek and Latin at Rutgers while pursuing his theological studies at New Brunswick. After his ordination, he served as a Chaplain in the United States Army, before coming to Hope in 1866. Professor Charles Scott taught for four years in South Carolina following his graduation from Rutgers. Having been converted there, he entered New Brunswick Seminary, and upon his ordination, served the church at Shawangunk, New York, before joining the faculty in 1866. Mr. Doesburg was a Dutch schoolmaster who emigrated to the Van Raalte colony. After serving as principal of the Union School in Holland, he began his long career as Tutor and Professor of Modern Languages. The Reverend Peter J. Oggel was Professor of Sacred Literature and Lector in Theology until his death in 1869. William Shields, of the Class of 1866, joined the faculty in 1867. Indicative of the teaching loads carried by instructors is the fact that Shields taught thirty hours per week, and in addition was in charge of the textbook account. An important addition to the faculty in 1871 was Gerrit J. Kollen, who was destined to bring distinction to Hope College as a Professor and President.

The First Formal Constitution

Until 1871, the college was loosely organized under the Articles of Association. As early as 1868, a committee of the Council had been appointed to draft a formal constitution and by-laws. Nothing was accomplished until 1870 when General Synod's Committee on Education requested the Council to prepare a draft for presentation to the Synod of 1871. Adopted in 1871, the constitution spelled out the duties of the faculty and officers of the Council, prescribed the manner of election of the President, and required that all members of the Council be communicant members of a Reformed church. It made provision for three departments of instruction and laid the basis of a future scientific department by stipulating that the income from the James Suydam Farm be devoted to the establishment of a scientific school, whenever the farm had produced sufficient revenue for it, in which case the scientific school was to be included as one of the departments of instruction. Under the terms of the constitution, the General Synod was given one seat on the Council.

Mr. Arend Visscher, the only member of the Class of 1872. A prominent Holland attorney who served as a member of the Council of Hope College, 1885-1921.

General Faculty

The 1871 constitution provided for the organization of a faculty for each department, and in addition made provision for a General Faculty composed of a representative from each instructional department. The duties of the General Faculty were described as follows:

> To it shall be submitted all proposals for changes in the course of study, or in textbooks in any department. It shall have the care of students in the general hall and in the dormitories, which shall hereafter be occupied by none other than those preparing for the ministry in any of the departments. It shall have charge of lecture rooms, dormitories, boarding houses used in common by more than one department. It shall make arrangements for chapel exercises in which all students in all departments shall participate.

The Minutes of the General Faculty throw light on some of the early concerns of the faculty. This faculty discussed the obligation of theological students to attend the chapel exercises, voted on changing hymnbooks and textbooks, and made arrangements for the commencement exercises. It appointed students to ring the chapel bell and to lead the singing at Chapel. They investigated boarding houses and exercised student discipline. In 1872, they passed a rule requiring all students to be in their rooms by 10:00 P.M. and forbade all social visiting and musical exercises after that hour. In 1878, it published a set of rules for all students, a paragraph of which reads as follows:

> Between eight and twelve o'clock in the forenoon and between one and three in the afternoon, there shall be no singing nor practicing musical instruments except such as are used in regular instruction, nor any playing or unnecessary noises of any kind, nor any sawing or splitting of wood. All ball playing, quoits, leap frog, or any kind of outdoor games are limited to the open space in the southeast corner of the campus. No playing or disorder in any of the buildings at any time. No defacing of property or marking with chalk except on the blackboards, damage to be paid by the student offending. No student shall be permitted to bring any gunpowder or any deadly weapon on the premises. Students shall not invite or bring any lady visitor to the building except by special permission of the President.

The Academic Faculty

At the first meeting of the Academic Faculty, Gerrit John Kollen was welcomed as a new Tutor. In April 1872, the faculty discussed the importance of granting diplomas to members of the graduating classes. President Phelps had planned to give diplomas to the Class of 1866, but the certificates did not arrive until after the class had left the campus for the summer. There was no academic commencement in 1872 since the class had only one member, Mr. Arend Visscher. Other considerations interfered with the practice until 1873. In a letter dated June 17, 1885, to the Council, Phelps explained the circumstances and his attempt to rectify the omission. He explained that all members of the early classes were finally given diplomas, some with the actual signatures of faculty and trustees, and some with facsimile signatures "so skillfully executed that even an expert could not have told" whether the signatures were actual or facsimile. Not until 1873 did graduates receive diplomas at the commencement exercises.[13]

At a meeting of the Academic Faculty in 1876, Professor Crispell complained that his entire class, with one exception, had been absent because they claimed that the bell had not been rung. At another meeting, a student was charged with smoking on the campus. And, at one meeting, there was a long discussion about a rumor that some students were attending private parties whose object it was to cultivate dancing.

Publications

The constitution of 1871 made provision for a Department of Publication which was to have oversight over the several publications of the college. One of these was *The Searcher*, "a periodical designed and devoted to the investigation and illustration of the Scriptures, especially the more difficult portions." Three numbers had been issued by October 1865, and it was expected that the first volume would be complete in twelve numbers. Another contemplated publication was *The Remembrancer*, designed to preserve Hope College commencement literature. The only number published contained the addresses delivered at the inaugural and first commencement. It was dedicated to Samuel B. Schieffelin, "whose sympathies and liberalities have been enlisted in behalf of Hope College from its germinal to its present condition."[14]

The most important publication was a Dutch religious weekly known as *De Hope*. Van Raalte had planned a weekly of this nature as early as 1848 in order to instruct his people in the history and character of the United States. An early venture was unsuccessful, but in 1862 Mr. John Binnekant, who had been associated with a Dutch weekly *De Hollander*, began the publication of the *Verzamelaar* (Collector). In 1865 this became known as *De Hope*, the official religious weekly of the Hollanders in Michigan. Members of the faculty made up the editorial board, and it was printed in the orphan house until 1876, when a new brick printing plant was erected on the site now occupied

---

13 See letter in Appendix, p. 280.
14 College Catalog, Oct. 1864, p. 41.

by Graves Hall. Upon the erection of Graves Hall, the printing plant was moved to the east end of the campus facing 11th Street. Subsequently, this building was rebuilt and enlarged for the use of Hope High School. For almost seventy years *De Hope* was a most important weekly, and assisted in the preservation of the Dutch language and culture until such time as the Dutch had become Americans "by assimilation and not by absorption." Although the circulation was never large, it filled a responsible place in the history of Dutch-language journalism. Finally, the time came when there was little need for a Dutch press. It has been said that by the year 1900, two thirds of the constituency of Hope College no longer read Dutch. Circulation was suspended in 1933 and a new religious weekly known as *The Intelligencer-Leader* took its place.

Such is the story of the early organization of Hope College. The 1871 constitution remained unchanged until 1878. Two literary societies were organized — the Meliphone Society founded by John Van Vleck in 1857, and the Fraternal Society founded by President Phelps. The Minutes of the Meliphone Society indicate that on October 15, 1863, a motion was passed "to form a collegiate society whose members will for the present remain members of the Meliphone Society." The principal, the Reverend Phelps, then obtained the archives of the Fraternal Society of Union College of which he had once been a member and which had since been discontinued. He initiated the college students in the academy into the new society in the fall of 1863. Since the number of men in the college was very small, the existence of the society was often in jeopardy.

Financially, the institution was on the verge of bankruptcy. The original endowment of $30,000 given to the Council by the Board of Direction consisted largely of notes and pledges. Less than one half of the amount was realized. The same was true as to the endowment raised by Phelps and Oggel. In 1870, the Board of Direction reported that Hope endowment receipts amounted to a total of $48,708, of which $30,000 had been paid to the Council. In 1865, Phelps reported to the Synod that he had received one gift of $5,000 from James B. Schieffelin to endow a scholarship of the General Synod, and $2,500 to endow two scholarships of the Theological Seminary. He also reported

The Oggel House.

a gift from elder James Suydam for a scholarship bearing the name of Rutgers College.

The first catalog, October 1865, also gives information concerning the Classical Board of Education of the Classes of Holland and Wisconsin. The purposes of this Board are defined as follows:

> This Board was organized to provide students for the Institution, within the bounds of the Classes represented, and to obtain the means of supporting them. Its supervision over the students or its funds is similar to that exercised by the Board of Education of the Church in relation to its students. Of the whole number of graduates, between forty and fifty (including those sustained by the Classes before the formal establishment of the Board) have been carried through their course at the Academy, and thus far through the College, by means of this Board. In the absence heretofore, of contingent fees, it has also met the contingent expenses of the Institution. The ministers of the Classes are ex-officio members of this Board; and each Classis chooses representative Elders.[15]

---

15 College Catalog, Oct. 1865.

According to the first catalog, the school year was divided into three terms, and all recitations were held in the forenoon. This remained true until early in the twentieth century. It appears that tuition fees were never charged and that a contingent fee, ranging from four dollars to eight dollars per term, covered all expenses. This was true until the Dimnent administration, when contingent fees were removed and a tuition was charged. The catalog remarks, "All that is claimed is that a good foundation has been laid, and is in suitable shape for permanency, enlargement and usefulness." Discussing the denominational aspect of the college, President Phelps says,

> There has been no concealment of the denominational nature of the enterprise. Why should there be? A college is not injured by denominationalism but by the failure on the part of its ecclesiastical parent to provide what may be essential to render it respectable and attractive in the eyes of strangers. However, the design in planting this institution has been to promote that sound, Christian Education by which alone the Church and the Nation are maintained, and as it exacts no sectarian tests, it makes its appeal to Christian patriotism and philanthropy in general.[16]

---

[16] *Ibid.*

5: THE UNIVERSITY IDEA

THE INTRODUCTION of a Department of Theology at Hope College was the first step in the President's dream to elevate the college into a university, to be called Hope Haven University. The name was derived from the fact that the region around Black Lake had been a haven of refuge for the Dutch colony in 1847. Introducing the idea of the Council of Hope College in 1867, President Philip Phelps claimed that

> the name Hope College was significant only because it was a transition name, which was placed in the charter for want of a permanent name, and that the term University is the only one that fits the Church's theory of Education.[1]

The Council approved the idea, and sent a communication to the General Synod which proposed the adoption of a university status and name for the whole school. In laying the proposition before the General Synod in 1867, the President argued that

> the continuous development of the school now called for the status of a university. There was first a semi-parochial school, which expanded into an academy, which was elevated to a college, and which has just become a theological school that is a university.[2]

The catalog in 1867 announced:

> A proposition was sent to the General Synod at its November session to recognize the position of the institution as a university in consequence of its having attained the highest professional status, the theological, and that a special committee had been appointed by the General Synod to report on the matter in 1867.

---

[1] Report of the Council to the General Synod 1867.
[2] *Ibid.*

Hope College.

Holland, Ottawa Co. Mich.

18

A letterhead used by President Philip Phelps. A growing tree with the words, "Hope Haven University." The Dutch phrase "Eendracht maakt macht," still the motto of the Reformed Church in America, means "Unity produces strength."

The question of university status for Hope College further alienated many church leaders in the East. The introduction of a Department of Theology and the request for university status seemed unrealistic in the light of the poverty and infancy of the college. In 1868, the Committee on Professorate of the General Synod took up the report of the Council requesting that

> Hope be expanded and called Hope Haven University, and recommends certain changes in the Articles of Association. Phelps will resign as President of Hope on the day in which Synod should confirm the university status. The plan is opposed by Professors Crispell, Beck and Scott who favor an independent Theological School. The Committee recommends that the Council be authorized to publish in the catalog that the theological school is the first professional department in the university. That the Synod consent to the university plan and to the name Hope Haven. That the Council be empowered to elect a President of the university and that the theological school be organized as the theological seminary of the Reformed Church at Hope Haven.[3]

Action was deferred to the General Synod of 1869. In that year, the Committee on Professorate reported to the General Synod:

> The college is now sustained by the Hollanders but the Hollanders have no sympathy with a merely literary institution and

---

[3] Minutes of the General Synod 1868.

will not support it. They say so and reiterate it in the various communications to Synod. It is a theological school they principally want, hence the university idea. The committee does not approve of the university plan. We are of the opinion that unless under State control or with the prestige of a large endowment, a university is a thing of time and growth. A university of fifty students, no funds, and paper professorships can command no respect and does not meet the proper idea of that term. Therefore, be it resolved that we rescind the action of the Synod of 1867.[4]

However, the General Synod approved the following clause in the constitution of 1871:

As soon as the possession of sufficient endowment shall have relieved the Board of Education and the Synod from the support of the President and Professors, the Council shall adopt the name Hope Haven for the whole school, and shall proceed at once without further reference to previous stipulations to complete the requisite amendment to the First Article.[5]

This was not likely to occur in the foreseeable future, but the President was determined, and refused to give up the idea. When the plan had been approved by the General Synod, the President placed in the hands of the Council his resignation as President, to be effective at such time when he should become Chancellor of Hope Haven University. In the endowment circular of 1878, Phelps was still listed as Acting President of Hope College, and announced:

Development of Hope College into Hope Haven University — which is the future name adopted for the institution by the General Synod — would be wild and visionary except for such faith as is inspired by its past history — but is anything too hard for the Lord?[6]

The President's resignation in 1878 brought his dream to an end.

Postgraduate Science

As a part of the university idea, President Phelps had plans for a postgraduate School of Science. The catalog of 1872 announced:

One of the important features of the school is apparent in the basis furnished through the beneficence of Elder James Suydam.

---

4 Minutes of the General Synod 1869.
5 Constitution of 1871, p. 8.
6 College Catalog, 1876, p. 17.

Although the relations are as yet only general, it may be added here that since nothing ought ever to supersede the old classical course so essential to mental culture and discipline, it would seem that, in the present advanced stage of knowledge, the scientific course should be a post-graduate course and not a parallel one.

It was contemplated that the School of Science would be supported by income from the Hope Haven Farm. This plan originated in 1862 when representatives of the Classes of Holland, Wisconsin, and Michigan decided to purchase and cultivate a tract of land and to use the proceeds for the benefit of the academy, a plan which had the approval of the General Synod and the Synod of Chicago. However, it became clear that a much larger tract would be needed to make the venture a success. As a result, in 1867, a tract of 830 acres was purchased at Point Superior on Black Lake at a price of $9400. The Council borrowed $5000 from the endowment funds to make the down payment and announced that the tract of land was suitable for fruit culture and for the establishment of a scientific school. The faculty did not agree with the President and Council. Professors Beck, Crispell, and Scott sent a communication to the General Synod expressing their strong opposition. They objected to the fact that endowment monies had been used to make the initial payment, and argued that a great deal of additional money would have to be invested before the land could be prepared for its only suitable use. Land had to be cleared, orchards had to be planted and the taxes paid. They raised the question whether the church was prepared to assume further financial responsibilities in connection with the project. Closing their statement, they said, "The undersigned would express their conviction that the true interests of our western institutions demand a vigorous prosecution and speedy completion of the endowment of Hope College."

In October and November of 1869, Van Raalte spent two months in the East in his attempt to raise $10,000 to restore the money borrowed and to complete the contract payment. He met with great difficulty and discovered that some of the early benefactors of the college were beginning to question the financial acumen of a Council composed almost entirely of ministers. Schieffelin and Suydam did not look with favor upon the Theo-

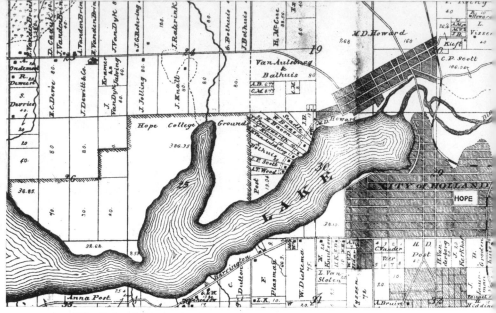

The Point Superior land on the north side of Black Lake intended to be the site of Hope Haven University.

logical Department and the university idea, and considered the purchase of the Point Superior lands an unwise investment. In November 1869, Van Raalte wrote Phelps as follows:

> I saw Suydam again. I found him under an influence by which he is anxious to be released from Hope College. I could see that in his whole manner of conversation. He said even if I give you $10,000 it would not better the case, for you would run into debt again in the first six months. Then he asked me if I would go home if he gave me some money. I proved to him that I had to keep on with my work. At last he promised to send some money, but he forbade me to speak about it. Now if it is possible, write him a line before he sends the money to prove to him that Hope College is not a hopeless case.

Suydam sent $5000 to restore the monies borrowed from the endowment funds. Van Raalte kept pressing him for another $5000 to clear the floating debt and Suydam finally agreed. At a special meeting of the Council

> warmest thanks were tendered Elder Suydam for his most timely interposition in behalf of Hope College, and in order that there might remain a lasting memorial of their gratitude, it was resolved that the tract thereafter be called the James Suydam Farm of Hope College, under which designation it will appear.[7]

----
[7] Minutes of the Council, 1870.

Mr. William H. Moore, a classmate of Phelps at Union College, established the Helm Trust in the amount of $4000 for the improvement of the farm. When the financial crisis came to a head in 1878, a special committee of the Synod examined the farm and in their report said:

> The Hope Farm was examined in person, crossing it by carriage and passing along its entire water front by boat. It is pleasantly located and has some fertile soil. In the hands of an energetic person with sufficient means at his disposal, it could be made a paying investment. But managed as it is, and must be, while it remains in the hands of the Council, its agricultural prospects will hardly pay expenses. To depend upon it as a source of income is, in our opinion, very much like looking to the lottery for a prize. The prize is among the possible but not among the probable.[8]

The plans for the cultivation of the farm and for the establishment of a scientific school were never realized, but President Phelps never lost faith in the venture. After his resignation, he took an option on a part of the farm and drew up Articles of Incorporation for a society to be known as the Hope Haven Unity Association. It was a scheme to secure additional endowment for the college by selling lots to members of the Association. He found the pattern in a similar association at Ocean Grove, New Jersey. In a letter to the Council on May 1, 1884, he said, "Our place can never become an Ocean Grove financially but I do not see why, by the grace of God, it may not be one morally."[9]

Primary and Female Education

The university idea of 1868 also embraced the resumption of primary and female education. In defense of his plan, the President said:

> Is it not simply true that the more numerous and stronger the Church makes all the departments, the more certain she will be of having a supply for her theological school? For the union of all departments gives influence and reputation to the whole institution, arouses greater interest in the Church, and affords encouragement to liberal benefactors.[10]

---

8 Minutes of the General Synod 1879.
9 See printed document in the Diekema files, College Archives.
10 College Catalog, 1876/77, p. 17.

Primary education for boys and girls was available in the pioneer
school and in the early days of the academy. Van Vleck was
forced to give up female education because of housing difficulties,
and Phelps had continued primary education when he began
the classification of students. Phelps was greatly interested in
female education and had tried to restore it in 1866 by·giving one
hour a day to that task in addition to his other duties, and this
he reported to the Board of Education and to the Synod. Van
Raalte was deeply interested in both primary and female education, and donated to the Council a large tract of land on the
south side of Black Lake for the education of both sexes. The
Executive Committee on July 29, 1867, agreed that the east half
of this tract was to be sold in lots and the proceeds devoted to
the grammar school of the institution, chiefly for the female
department. The female department, including both higher and
lower branches, was to be called Hope Female Seminary, and it
was expected that out of this would grow a Ladies' Collegiate
Department. As a site for the female seminary, Van Raalte gave
a large plot of ground bounded on·the north by the channel of
Black River, on the south by 7th Street, on the west by Cedar
Street (College Avenue), and on the east extending nearly to
Fish Street (Columbia Avenue). It was agreed that a small portion of the proceeds of the land, to be sold in lots, might be used
for the founding of a primary department as preparatory to the
grammar school. The primary school was to be a free school,
while in the female seminary tuition and contingent fees were to
be charged. As to female education, the Council said:

> The higher education of females seems to furnish the proper
> medium between the spirit of oriental barbarism which regards
> women as fitted to be only mother and housekeeper, and the
> infidelity of women's rights, falsely so called.[11]

In 1868, the President informed the General Synod that primary and female education would be resumed unless discouraged
by the action of Synod. Although several attempts were made
to resume primary and female education, very little was accomplished until the Executive Committee, on October 29, 1872,
directed President Phelps to secure a suitable teacher or teachers
without delay. The Committee resolved:

---

[11] University circular, 1876, p. 91.

Whereas it is important that primary and female education be, for the.present, combined, and formal separation of the two being reserved for future growth, that William B. Gilmore and Mrs. Van Olinda be appointed teachers in the combined department, the former at a salary of $1000 and the latter at $600. That the building recently used as a Refectory be set aside as the place of instruction. That the school be open to all who may be admitted on examination by the Faculty.[12]

Four years elapsed before Phelps reported that the combined departments had been organized with William B. Gilmore and Mrs. Van Olinda as teachers. According to the 1876 catalog, the primary department consisted of five classes below the grammar school level, the lowest "I" and the highest "E" Class. The Reverend William B. Gilmore was Van Raalte's son-in-law. He had been a teacher before he entered Holland Academy in 1861 and was a member of the first Senior Class at Hope College. While studying Theology at Hope, he was a Tutor in Music. For a brief time he had been connected with Amelia Institute in Virginia and more recently had been a pastor at Spring Lake, Illinois. Mrs. Van Olinda had taught in the Union School in Holland.

The experiment in primary education for both sexes in connection with the college was short-lived. Most of the faculty were opposed to it. Aware of the need of primary education under church control, they felt that some other agency ought to be created to bring it about. On October 5, 1875, the grammar school had already sent a communication to the Council asking them to sanction an arrangement whereby the lecture rooms in the grammar school would be opened to both sexes, provided that suitable facilities be furnished, especially through the appointment of a Rector. The Council authorized the faculty to receive women at the opening of the new school year. In the next year, sixty pupils were enrolled, of whom five were women. Women were admitted to the college in the year 1878. By this time, the President had resigned, the university idea was forgotten, and coeducation had become a reality. The first women to receive the A.B. degree were Sarah Gertrude Alcott (Whitenack) and Frances F. C. Phelps (Otte) in 1882. Mary

---

[12] Minutes of the Executive Committee, 1872.

E. Alcott (Diekema) and Eliza Phelps followed in 1885. Cornelia Cappon (Brusse) and Emma Kollen (Pieters) received their degrees in 1887. Fannie A. Steffens (Gleysteen) (1891) had the distinction of being the only female in her class during four years of college. Hope College was still very much of a man's college until the erection of Voorhees Hall. After that, the number of women increased rapidly, and sixty-three women graduated by 1916.

The Suspension of Theological Education

It is clear that the General Synod consented to a theological seminary in Michigan with great reluctance. Although it had refused to assume any additional burden, it soon agreed to pay the salary of the Professor of Theology, and to give formal appointments to Professors Beck and Scott as Lectors and pay their salaries at the rate of $1500 per year. President Phelps discovered that the Theological Department was expensive, and in 1873 complained to the General Synod:

> The aggregate liability against the treasury of the college, purely on account of theology, is $9500, of which the greater part is still owing the President and teachers.[13]

This caused great hardship and forced the teachers to borrow money for living expenses at rates as high as 10 percent. By 1878, the Synod itself was in arrears to the extent of $4000 for the salaries of theological instructors.

By 1877, the financial plight of the college was so great that the Synod found it necessary to suspend theological instruction, until such time as an endowment could be raised for it in the Western churches. The Synod of Chicago considered this a hostile action, and charged that the Eastern churches were not fulfilling their obligations to the college, and that promises made in 1850 were not honored.

On June 22, 1877, the Holland *City News* said:

> It is said that theology has been suspended. It will be looked upon as a backward step. We have yet to hear one good reason from the rich descendants of our forefathers in the East. Why will they not put their hands in their pockets and help the institution as an organization of the church in the West as well

---

13 Minutes of the General Synod 1873.

as Rutgers College in the East? We venture to say that if Van
Raalte had lived, it would not have been done.

The Classis of Holland, meeting in June 1877, believed that the
suspension of Theology would be fatal to the college and to
the church in the West. At another meeting, in September 1877,
it was reported that the members "came with the lamentation
of ancient Israel that the Ark of the Lord had been taken and
that the crown of their educational efforts had been lost."[14] The
Classis and the Synod of Chicago carried their case for the immediate restoration of Theology to the General Synod of 1878.

However, four ministers filed a minority report and gave
reasons why the action of the Synod of 1877 should be sustained.
Their report reads as follows:[15]

> The financial bases of the lower departments are still so incom-
> plete as to require the concentration of the most earnest ef-
> forts of the Church to secure their permanency. Until this is
> secured, the educational efforts of the General Synod in the
> West must, in a most serious case, still be called an experiment.
>
> The present financial difficulties of the college, arising from
> a great and pressing debt and the annual deficit in professors'
> salaries, forbid the additional burden which would result from
> the restoration of theology with its financial requirements.
>
> Under the present peculiar circumstances of general financial
> embarrassment in the various operations of the Church, requir-
> ing special economy and unity of purpose and action, one the-
> ological institution seems to be sufficient for the existing wants.
>
> The paramount needs of the western church require an institu-
> tion in which general education shall not be sacrificed to a the-
> ological specialty.
>
> The history of ten years has demonstrated that a theological
> department at Hope College has not fulfilled the promise by
> which its establishment was urged. It has not enlisted the sym-
> pathies and aid of the American churches at the west, nor in-
> creased the interest of the Holland churches, nor aided in the
> extension of the church in the West, nor called forth a larger
> supply of students for the ministry.
>
> If these reasons should seem to need more extensive setting forth,
> we beg that the Reverend C. Vander Veen, who, in the provi-

---

14 Minutes of the Classis of Holland, Sept. 1877.
15 Vander Veen Papers. Calvin College Library.

dence of God, is present at your session, may be heard as the representative of our sentiments.

Signed   P. De Pree

H. Uiterwyk

J. Vandermeulen

C. VanderVeen

A number of faculty members including Professors Kollen and Scott were also opposed to immediate restoration of Theology. In the Vander Veen collection there is the following letter from Professor Kollen:

My Dear Vander Veen:

May 18, 1878

In these days of tribulation, we who constitute the minority on the great theology question, cannot afford to stand on formality. Hence I write, though it is not my turn. I am very glad that you are to be our champion at the meeting of the General Synod next month. I think that we will find little difficulty in carrying the day in General Synod, if the members will be allowed to exercise their judgment in the matter. As one influential man mentioned the other day, "The common sense of the church is opposed to restoring theology now." The only thing that I am afraid of is that the western delegates will use such tactics that Synod will be forced to act contrary to its own judgment. There is no telling what the church East may do when they are threatened with separation by the western portion of our Zion. The best thing for us to do as it seems to me, is to make a flank movement or something like a decoy on our opponents by forcing Synod to examine into the real condition of things at Hope College. If we can get the start of them in doing this, then I have no doubt that they will learn that there are other things at Hope College that require their attention than the restoration of theology. What we need first of all is a complete reorganization at Hope. I am doing all I can to make people here see this. I have managed to get the Board of Education to incorporate such definite language in their annual report with regard to Hope College, that I think Synod will be compelled to investigate matters. Such an investigation would show that expansion would be the height of folly. I think it would be well if you should write about this to Dr. Chambers who is to be a delegate. I shall try to have a good talk with him sometime next week. Last Monday I saw our mutual friend Dr. Duryee. He is alright on the question and expects to go to Synod. As our question is not likely to come up during the first week, I

may not be present before Monday morning. Let me hear from
you soon. Any suggestions will be thankfully received.

Yours as ever,

G. J. KOLLEN

The Synod supported the minority opinion and appointed a
special committee to visit the college, examine the accounts
and the real estate holdings, receive the resignation of the President and faculty, ask the Council to amend the constitution of
1871 so as to omit Theology as a department of instruction,
and to report to the Synod of 1879. In 1879, the committee made
the following report:

> Our Holland brethren seem wedded to the idea that a college
> which does not include theology is woefully deficient. It was a
> source of regret to your committee that we could not see eye
> to eye with them on this subject. But standing upon the ground
> with the shattered wrecks of the college endowment around us,
> a theological department seemed more than ever beyond our
> reach. Our point is that while theology may be needed and will
> be supplied in due time, the welfare both of the college and
> the church demands postponement for the present. It must be
> regretted that a full and cordial agreement cannot be reached
> with our Holland brethren. We have no motive as we have no
> wish to cripple or obstruct their program. On the contrary,
> there is every inducement for us to promote their welfare and
> to draw still closer the ties that bind us together. But on the
> other hand, our Holland brethren ought to understand that
> dependence is mutual. We have rendered substantial service in
> the past and are in condition to do them good in the future.
> What we want first in the West is a college that shall be the
> peer of other colleges, commanding the respect and confidence
> of the great commonwealth of colleges. As we have already said,
> the day is coming when the church will need a seminary in
> the West no less than she needs Hope College. Your committee
> cannot but urge upon our Holland brethren the propriety of
> waiting until we can put a seminary in the West and put it
> there to stay.[16]

So ended the first experiment in Theology at Hope College,
which between 1869 and 1877 had prepared twenty-nine men for
the Christian ministry. The Professor of Theology resigned and
the constitution was amended so as to eliminate Theology as
a department of instruction.

---

16 Minutes of the General Synod 1879.

6: THE HARD YEARS

THE SUSPENSION OF THEOLOGY and the collapse of the university plan brought bitter disappointment to the founders and friends of Hope College. Although the road had been rough and steep, the story of the early beginnings is an encouraging record of the triumph of faith, hope, and determination over poverty, a hostile environment, and great indifference. The pioneer school had indeed become Holland Academy, which, with the blessing of the General Synod, had become the Western college of the Reformed Church in America; but its foundations were insecure, its financial support uncertain, and its fate was to hang in the balance for a great many years. In this respect, it was like the other early church colleges in Michigan. By 1866, six had been founded and all were in financial straits and often on the point of closing their doors. The economic climate in Michigan in the middle of the nineteenth century was not conducive to the growth of private charitable institutions. It is certain that without financial help from the East there would have been no Holland Academy and no Hope College. President Phelps in his inaugural address said, "On this school — the Pioneer School — the Board of Education expended more than $3000 before a single barleycorn of land had been secured or one brick laid upon another."[1] And in 1867, the President estimated the dollar cost of the institution to be $81,000, of which the Board of Education had contributed $28,000 for salaries and $9000 for student aid. Eastern donors gave $15,000 for buildings,

---

[1] *Remembrancer*, p. 16.

and men like elders Schieffelin and Suydam gave large sums for incidental expenses, scholarships, the payment of debts, and for capital outlay.

In spite of all this, there were growing complaints that the denomination had not fulfilled pledges made in 1850 when the Classis of Holland joined the Reformed Church in America. And the suspension of the study of Theology in 1877 caused great displeasure in the West. On the other hand, the Synod and businessmen in the East were concerned about the fact that the financial resources of the college, and the business acumen of the President and the Council, did not match their idealism. The Board of Education, R.C.A., as early as 1868 saw a financial crisis in the offing and declared,

> This Board pays a large part of the salaries at Hope. This ought not to be. The institution ought not any longer depend upon this Board. Such dependence cramps the energies, absorbs the powers, and enfeebles the capabilities of the Board. The Council must take steps to speedily relieve the Board and the Synod from such financial support.[2]

Good friends such as Schieffelin and Suydam also began to express their misgivings. In the autumn of 1869, Van Raalte wrote Phelps saying, "Suydam says that you have gone too far. You ought not to have begun the Seminary. This cannot go on forever. Nobody is going to help you and your time is wasted." Van Raalte was so disappointed that he sent Phelps this bitter letter:

> I hear synodical prayers for the school of the prophets so dear to them. They forget that they also have one in the west. It is impossible for them to look beyond New Brunswick as far as the west, which is to them some region on the moon. Such straws show the direction of the wind.

There was no question about the direction of the wind. Private donations almost ceased and income from the Board of Education was greatly reduced. To make matters worse, on the night of October 9, 1871, a disastrous fire destroyed two thirds of the city of Holland. The fires began in the timber to the south and west of Holland, and by midnight winds of hurricane force blew the ashes upon the Cappon and Bertsch Tannery

---

[2] Minutes of General Synod 1868.

A replica of Charter Hall, erected in 1876 and destroyed by fire in 1885.

sheds and the Third Reformed Church. In about two hours, the heart of the city was destroyed, two hundred dwellings were burned to the ground, and hundreds of people were homeless. While the college lost no buildings, Professor Scott lost his home and all its contents, including some of the college records. A local relief committee was organized, and the gymnasium served as a depository for the accumulation and distribution of relief supplies. One thousand dollars was donated to the college for damage done, and this money was used to convert the old Zwemer House into a suitable residence for Professor Scott. The assets of the city were greatly reduced while the liabilities of individuals and corporations were increased. The faculty suffered a great deal, because salaries remained unpaid and money had to be borrowed for living expenses at the current high interest rates. The President sought to use the occasion to increase the endowment funds on the plea that the college would be enabled to make additional mortgage loans for the rebuilding of the city, but the effort did not succeed. At the same time, gifts from individuals and churches for contingent expenses were severely reduced.

The endowment of the college was inadequate for the growing needs. Much of the money pledged for the Charter requirements was in the form of notes and promises to pay which were never honored. When the crisis came to a head in 1878, the total endowment was $52,986, of which the Council held only $28,604 in invested funds. The college held considerable real estate, which was not only unproductive but subject to annual taxes and maintenance. A few frame buildings had been erected, but in several cases the funds had been borrowed from the permanent funds. Charter Hall was erected in 1867. It was a one-story building for lecture rooms and faculty apartments. It was destroyed by fire in 1885 and only $485 insurance was collected.[3] The grammar school was a one-story building erected in 1869. In 1871, a second story was added for Council and library purposes. It served a variety of uses until 1929, when it was removed to make room for two tennis courts. In 1871, a one-story extension was added to the Oggel House for use as a student refectory. A brick printing house was erected on the present site of Graves Hall at a cost of $879, provided by subscribers to *De Hope*. All of these buildings were cheaply constructed and subject to constant repair.

The early retirement of Dr. Van Raalte from public life and his death in 1876 added to the woes of the college and the President. A sense of insecurity about the future of the college seized many, who were afraid that the President, if left

---

[3] A replica of Charter Hall is in the Netherlands Museum, Holland, Mich.

The Grammar School, erected 1869, later the Preparatory School.

to himself, was too much of an idealist to be trusted with the
fiscal management of the institution. Strangely enough, while
Van Raalte had fallen out with Taylor and Van Vleck, he remained staunchly loyal to Phelps through all his days. His bene-
factions to the academy and to the college are too numerous to
mention. He made many trips to the East and spent months
away from his family in his efforts to educate the East to the
importance of educational institutions in the West, and to collect
the necessary funds. He confessed that he hated to be a beggar,
but he never shrank from a service that was essential, though
distasteful and repugnant to him. His many letters to President
Phelps indicate almost constant physical distress and frequent
suffering. His health had never been good since his serious illness in the Netherlands. The rigors of pioneer life and the in-
cessant demands made upon him by the entire colony further
impaired his health. The situation was compounded by the
serious illness and death of his beloved wife on June 30, 1871.
A source of constant annoyance to him was the reluctance of the
community to follow him in his efforts on behalf of Christian
education. In 1862, he sought a call to South Africa. In 1867,
he gave up his pastoral duties in the First Reformed Church
of Holland feeling that it was impossible to continue his work
there by reason of dissension in the church. Over the years, both
in the Netherlands and in America, but especially since the
union of the Classis of Holland with the Reformed Church in
1850, he had been the subject of abuse and slander.

Van Raalte's experience in the matter of the Virginia lands
was an unhappy one for himself and for the college. The Classis
of Holland had appointed Van Raalte chairman of the Classical
Missionary Committee. As such, he became deeply interested in
the possibility of establishing Dutch settlements in the South.
In 1866, he made a tour of the Southern states and chose Virginia as the site for a Dutch settlement, recommending that a
settlement be made near Norfolk along the Albemarle and
Chesapeake Canal. Instead of following this advice, some eighty
persons left Michigan to settle in Amelia County southwest of
Richmond, some at Mattoax, and some at Amelia Courthouse,
ten miles away. Although Van Raalte had not chosen this site,

he accepted it and attempted to found a Dutch church and an academy, and it caused difficulties for the college. This venture was a complete failure. It appeared that the College Council had made loans to the settlers in Virginia without proper security. The Synod of 1871 censured the administration and instructed the Council to obtain bonds and mortgages on lands in Virginia to secure the payment of the loans and to place these securities in the custody of the Board of Direction, R.C.A., as part of the invested funds for the endowment of the college. This public airing of certain lax investment procedures added fuel to the fire and increased the tensions between East and West. On March 12, 1871, Van Raalte wrote Phelps as follows:

> I thank God that I have been able to do something for the people of Amelia. The capital is safe enough but it will increase your storm and hasten the crisis.

This it did; but when the crisis came, Van Raalte was gone and Phelps was left alone to weather the storm.

In 1862, Van Raalte was elected Professor of Evangelical Theology but declined the honor because of "situation and lack of strength." He received honorary degrees from Rutgers College and from New York University. He served as President of the Hope College Council until his death. On the occasion of the twenty-fifth anniversary of the founding of Holland, he delivered the historical address. On the day of his funeral the entire community paused to do him honor. One of his biographers, Dr. Henry E. Dosker, said, "He was worn out but not old. He had burned the candle at both ends and had suffered much in his last years."[4] In an article written for the first Annual to be published at Hope College (in 1905), Dosker eulogized Van Raalte as follows:

> What the pastors in New England had been, they also proved to be in Michigan. And among them the heroic figure of Van Raalte, the pioneer of pioneers, the leader of leaders, without whose dauntless courage and iron determination the unequal struggle must have ended in inglorious defeat. Great Puritan-spirited leader that he was, he saw in education the hope of the colony. It was his lodestar, it was the compass by which he steered, the anchor of hope of his storm-tossed vessel.

---

4 Dosker, *Levensschets van Rev. A. C. Van Raalte, D.D.*

The Crisis

In 1873, the Standing Committee on Professorate was convinced that help must come at once or the college would be closed. They suggested that the Board of Direction take charge of securing an endowment of $100,000 and employ an agent or agency for the purpose. The Board was authorized to borrow $5000 to pay the salaries and most pressing debts, and to repay that sum out of endowment monies collected, but it was unwilling to assume this financial responsibility. In 1877, the continuing increase in the deficits caused the suspension of Theology, a step that created much displeasure in the West. In their report to the General Synod in 1878 the Council said:

> This causes us the greatest anxiety. Our just debts remain unpaid and our professors are left without the means of meeting their expenses and are compelled to borrow and pay interest on monies due them. Is it not the duty of Synod to elect permanent professors of theology?

The General Synod replied:

> The college has received constant encouragement from the Synod. The east has given $51,000 in the last ten years. The wonder is that the enterprise has not been wrecked a long time ago. The Council is admonished to decrease expenses and to appoint a Treasurer in accordance with the terms of the Constitution, to choose a financial agent and free the President from this responsibility.[5]

The Synod further recommended that the Board of Direction audit the accounts of the President, pay what was due him out of endowment, suspend Theology, rewrite the constitution, and hold the President responsible for the actions of the Council. Pointing to the mistakes of the past, and aware of the distance between East and West, the Synod came to the conclusion that "it may be necessary to sacrifice men to save the institution." Whereupon the Synod appointed a committee consisting of the Reverend E. W. Bentley and elders Peter Danforth and G. Van Nostrand to attend the next meeting of the Council and to advise them concerning the revision of the constitution. They were authorized to ask for and to receive the resignation of the faculty and the President. At the first meeting, some complied

[5] Minutes of the General Synod 1878.

without note or comment; and Professors Beck, Crispell, and Scott sent in their resignations, accompanied by a protest about the language used by the Synod. The resignations of the President and the Professor of Theology became effective July 1, 1878, while the resignations of the others were laid on the table and never accepted. The committee visited and made their own appraisal of all the real property. They discovered some title irregularities, and, noting a great shrinkage in real values, they commented:

> It seems to your committee unfortunate that so large an amount of the permanent funds of the college have been locked up in the purchase and maintenance of real estate. Were these sums, thus appropriated, now available the college would be freed from a large part of its indebtedness.[6]

The committee insisted that the Council submit for approval by the Synod a revision of the constitution eliminating Theology as a department of instruction and include clauses safeguarding the investment of trust funds. The Council was advised to decrease the Western representation on the Council and give the General Synod five places. The Council was bitterly opposed but finally yielded with great reluctance. The actual number of Trustees was reduced from twenty-three to sixteen, each Classis to have two representatives instead of four, and the General Synod five, for terms of five years. Seats of the Secretary of the Board of Education and of the agent of the Synod of Chicago were eliminated. Provision was made for two instructional departments — the grammar school and the college — but allowed the Council to institute other departments which were in harmony with the constitution. This made the resumption of Theology possible when the right time should come. There was an important amendment with reference to the investment of trust funds which read:

> Such funds shall not be invested except in bonds and mortgages on unencumbered real estate worth double the amount of the loan; in securities of the states of Michigan and New York; in securities of the United States government. In no case shall Trust Funds be invested or used for any other purpose than that for which they were given.[7]

---

[6] Special committee report to the General Synod 1879.
[7] See constitution of 1878.

The special committee also recommended that the college place itself in line with other collegiate institutions in admitting women on the same basis as men.

All the recommendations, including the revision of the constitution, were approved by the Synod in 1879. This Synod added to the financial crisis when it resolved that:

> The Council is advised to reduce the amount of indebtedness, and, in view of the uncertainty, no pecuniary obligation should be incurred for Hope College beyond interest actually paid into the Treasury from year to year.[8]

Total liabilities amounted to $29,000, of which $17,000 was owing the President and teachers. $5300 of the President's salary remained unpaid and, in addition, $2000 was due Mrs. and Miss Phelps for loans made to the college. President Phelps' financial sacrifices for the sake of the college are memorable. In a communication sent to all the churches in 1880, he said that since April 1, 1871, he had received only $1051.67 of his salary and that he had been compelled to borrow from his friends and from the bank to pay his most pressing debts.

Phelps Refuses to Give Up the Presidency

The Executive Committee of the Council had allowed Phelps to keep his rooms in Van Vleck Hall rent-free, "provided that no other construction whatever be placed upon such occupancy."[9] This was done in consideration of his "arduous and numerous services," but it was intended to be of temporary nature. Appearing before the General Synod in 1879, he insisted that the action was illegal and unjust and demanded a full investigation, but his request was denied on the ground that the action taken in 1878 was final. He then served notice that "he reserved the right to defend his claim to the Presidency by all suitable means." He made another appeal before the Synod in 1880 and said, "I am compelled to say that the dismissal was absolutely and forever incapable of defense from any legal, moral or ecclesiastical point of view,"[10] and informed the Synod that he would not withdraw from the presidency under the present cir-

---

8 Acts of the General Synod 1879.
9 Minutes of Executive Committee, Aug. 18, 1879.
10 Minutes of the General Synod 1880.

cumstances. In an open letter addressed to all the churches in 1880, he laid his case before the entire denomination. In his letter he expressed the fear that he might be compelled to start a suit at law for the recovery of $1200, which from time to time he had loaned the Council without interest. But, said he,

> the moment that any one party has recourse to law, the entire debt will be precipitated upon the institution. And what would be the consequences? The creditors would be paid in full for the assets are more than sufficient to meet all the demands. But then what is to become of the institution? There would be great sacrifice of property and it is not likely that the college could be maintained with the balance. It is this danger which has kept me quiet this long. I cannot bear the thought that the fruit of so many years of labor and patience should have no permanency.

To save the college he suggested that each congregation raise an amount equal to one dollar per family for each of the 43,000 families in the denomination. If this were done, there would be enough to pay all the debts and leave a substantial balance. Once again he appeared before the Synod of 1881 to plead his cause, but he was forbidden to make any more appeals. In 1884, the General Synod passed a resolution asking Phelps to vacate the room in Van Vleck Hall. On November 11, 1884, he replied to the Council as follows:

> Ever since I learned this fall of the full action of the last Synod with reference to my residence in the college building, I have been endeavoring to plan how I should carry out my former expectation of leaving the premises, and at the same time keeping myself in a position for making a suitable reply to the next Synod. Though I have not yet solved the difficult problem, yet meanwhile I have withdrawn from as many rooms as I could. It is to be understood, however, that I have not formally va cated the residence, nor do I know when I shall conclude to do so before the next meeting of Synod. But as soon as providentially enabled to reach a decision on the subject, I will communicate it to the Executive Committee.

Phelps concluded his controversy with the General Synod in 1886 after he had accepted his call to two churches in New York. On June 18, 1886, he wrote:

> Ever since the appointment and acceptance of a President, I have regarded the whole relationship to Hope College as closed for it is no longer in the power of the General Synod to remedy

the matter even if there were any disposition to do so. Trusting that your labors may become increasingly fruitful and blessed, I remain your brother in Christ.

In the same year he vacated his rooms in Van Vleck Hall.

Such was the denouement in the career of a man who had been sacrificed for a cause. Certainly what happened was not due to any lack of respect for a man of integrity and intellectual ability who had given the best nineteen years of his life to an impossible task, nor to any lack of appreciation for his devoted and self-sacrificing service. Not accustomed to the hardships of frontier life, he had nevertheless brought his wife, Margaret Ann Jordan, and his infant daughter, Frances C. Phelps, to take up residence in Van Vleck Hall. He was commissioned to preach in English to the American population, and to reorganize an academy with an uncertain future. He brought together a small faculty distinguished for scholarship and devotion. In addition to the original faculty of 1866, two ought to receive special mention. One of these was William Shields of the Class of 1866. He became a Tutor in 1867 and an Assistant Professor of Rhetoric and English in 1871, serving until 1885. He was the founder of the *Excelsiora*, which was begun in 1871 on a semimonthly basis by members of the upper classes of the grammar school. Later it became a monthly, until 1893, when it was discontinued. Contributions were written in longhand with emphasis on style, content, and penmanship. It was designed to help students develop writing skills, and remains as a valuable source of information about the early history of the college. Another important addition to the original faculty was Gerrit John Kollen of the Class of 1868, who became an Assistant Professor in 1871 and President of his Alma Mater in 1893.

In the period, total enrollment grew from 64 to 104, most of the growth being in the grammar school. In 1868, President Phelps brought to the institution the first oriental students. He had made an arrangement with the Japanese Embassy which resulted in the admission of a number of Japanese students. At one time there were as many as fourteen, in two departments. The first to graduate from the college were Kumaje Kimura and Moto Oghimi, in the year 1879. It is an interesting sidelight that Kimura delivered the valedictory in the Japanese

Standing, l. to r.: T. Matsda, '83; Nanomiya. Seated, l. to r.: R. Tsugawa; K. Kimura, '79; M. Ohgimi, '79.

language. These students lived in the Zwemer House, which became known as Japanese Hall; and according to an old engraving, the southwest corner of the campus was called the Japanese Grove. In September 1896, some of these students living in Japan held a memorial service honoring President Phelps.

Sixty-five degrees were conferred upon graduates in the period, and in addition there were seven honorary degrees: three A.B.'s and four A.M.'s. Phelps developed the nucleus of a library, which was housed originally in one room in Van Vleck Hall. It received financial support from elder James Schieffelin of New York, who was often called the founder of the library. In 1871, the library was housed on the second floor of the grammar school; it remained there until 1878 when it was moved into two rooms in Van Vleck Hall. At that time the library was reported to consist of four thousand volumes.

Four of the children of Mr. and Mrs. Phelps were born in Van Vleck Hall — Philip Tertius, Eliza T., Edward J., and Theodore Seth. Frances C. Phelps was born in Albany. Edward died in infancy and Eliza drowned at Antes Fort as a result of the Johnstown flood. Frances and Philip received A.B. degrees from Hope College in 1882, Eliza in 1885. Frances C. Phelps was the first of two girls to graduate from Hope College. She married Dr. John Otte, who became a distinguished Medical Missionary in China. In the *Milestone* of 1930, Philip Tertius tells about his home in Van Vleck Hall:

> I remember, I remember
> The house where I was born
> The window in the south that looked
> Right out on the college lawn.
>
> 'Twas made of brick, three stories high
> I thought it very tall
> Trees round it reaching to the sky
> The house named Van Vleck Hall
>
> 'Twas there I got my first degree
> My M.A. spelling Ma
> 'Twas there I met the President
> For he was my own Pa Pa.

In spite of his treatment at the hands of the Synod, Phelps never lost his love for Hope College. In 1879, he gave the library a complete set of bound volumes of the Minutes of the General Synod and also of the Synod of Chicago. In 1880 he made an appeal to all the churches for financial support. In 1890 he returned to the campus at the invitation of the alumni and gave an address on "The Unity in American Education" on the occasion of the quarter-centennial celebration. He returned to the campus once again in 1894 to participate in the inauguration of President Kollen. At that time, the Council awarded him the honorary degree of Doctor of Laws, and he in turn presented President Kollen with the academic regalia which he himself had worn in 1866. In 1886 he became pastor of two small churches at North Blenheim and Breakabeen, New York. He died on September 4, 1896. Professor Henry E. Dosker wrote this tribute in the *Christian Intelligencer:*

> Though useful and honored elsewhere in the east, Hope College knew him no more until years later on the occasion of the Quarter Centennial. He came back to us, by invitation, the guest of honor of her alumni, to be thrilled through and through with love and affection of his boys. The experience of that one day must have swept away the sorrows of all the intervening years.
>
> To us he can never die. His memory is our benediction. He gave the best he had, his love, and received it back in unstinted measure. Men called him an idealist — he proved to be a prophet. ... He has bequeathed us a sacred heirloom, and gratefully we enter upon its possession. In whatever sphere he may have excelled, in whatever capacity he may have been loved, to us he will ever remain Hope's first President.

Speaking at a memorial service for the President on June 22, 1897, the Reverend Peter Moerdyke of the Class of 1866 said:

> His intellectual attainments were of the highest order. The power, culture, versatility and scope of his faculties and resources were surprising. What a wealth of equipment he brought to the task of those academy days, and later, when only a really gifted, broadly cultured and amply equipped man could meet all the growing requirements. With fascinating energy and tireless devotion, he wrought as one inexhaustible. His example diffused the spirit of industry, and his ability as a teacher awakened enthusiasm for study. It quickened the intellect and kindled aspiration of high class standing.

And President Kollen, an associate of his, said:

> Phelps was a great organizer and delighted in planning great things. His disciplinary power and influence upon the students cannot be overestimated. His zeal for the cause of Christian education and his faith were so strong that obstacles could not receive due attention.

7: THE STRUGGLE FOR SURVIVAL

WHEN PRESIDENT PHELPS RESIGNED in 1878, the Hope College Council deemed it unwise to select a successor immediately. The financial situation was precarious, and President Phelps refused to give up his claim to the office. The Council decided to choose as a provisional President the Reverend G. Henry Mandeville, pastor of the Harlem Reformed Church in New York City. He received no salary and continued his active ministry and residence in New York. He occasionally came to Holland to preside over the faculty, and the actual day-to-day administration of the institution was entrusted to the Executive Vice President, Professor Charles Scott.[1]

In the four years between 1878 and 1882, Mandeville raised about $20,000 for the college in New York City. When he resigned in 1880, Professor Scott was named provisional President of Hope College. Scott did not desire the office and did not relish his administrative duties. But he was well liked by his associates, and was highly esteemed in the East, having been President of the General Synod and honored with a D.D. degree from New York University. Together with other members of the faculty, he had on several occasions been in opposition to the more idealistic plans of President Phelps. It was generally felt that he was more practical and conservative than his predecessor, and therefore much more acceptable in the East.

Scott inherited a very difficult situation. In accordance with

---

[1] See College Catalog, 1885/86, p. 41.

the action of the General Synod of 1878, no grants were made to the college, except for the payment of interest on funds held by the boards of the church. The Synod of 1880 noted that:

> A heavy and pressing debt weighs upon the college, the weight of which cannot possibly be borne much longer. A hand-to-mouth existence like this is not worth living. Better let it die and give it a decent burial. But why must it die? Without a college in the West, it will be a vain hope that our denomination can maintain its independent existence in the West. We shall be wise, therefore, to face the emergency promptly and courageously.[2]

An illustration of the seriousness of the situation was the fact that when Scott asked the Board of Direction, R.C.A., for an appropriation of $50 to install lightning rods on Van Vleck Hall, the request was denied and referred to the Council. As a remedy, the Synod of 1880 suggested that

> the Executive Committee of the college be instructed to report to the Council at its next meeting, a plan whereby an earnest effort may be made in the Chicago Synod to secure means for the removal of the debt of the college, and for increasing the permanent fund. That a similar committee of seven be appointed for the East and report at the next meeting.[3]

The Western committee raised $1875 while the Eastern committee raised $7500 in pledges and $2384 in cash.

Why was the West doing so little? The suspension of Theology in 1877 was very unpopular. In the Western mind, a college without a Department of Theology was not a college. Another reason was the fact that the Western churches at this time were disturbed seriously by the controversy in the denomination over the Free Masonry question. The secession spirit was rampant and many congregations were lost to the denomination. And there were other churches, which, while remaining loyal to the Reformed Church, lost their property to the secessionists and were forced to build new church buildings with a smaller membership. The college itself got involved in the controversy because of certain articles appearing in *De Hope*, the official organ of the college. The editorial board undertook to curb the publication of certain abusive articles. On October 5, 1879, the

---

[2] Committee on Professorate, Minutes of the General Synod 1880.
[3] Minutes of the General Synod 1880.

Mr. Nathan F. Graves, the donor of Graves Library, 1893.

editorial board announced the adoption of certain control measures. It went on to say that while the paper was the property
of Hope College, its interests were identified with those of the
denomination. Since the paper was pledged to loyalty to the
denomination, all articles inconsistent with this were to be ex-
cluded. This did not mean that the actions of General Synod

were not subject to criticism, but that such criticism should be made in the Christian spirit. It is certain that the secession movement seriously affected the progress of the college.

In 1881, the Committee on Professorate of the General Synod reported:

> The Committee on Professorate is driven to the conclusion that the action or nonaction of the Synod and the Church in the current year is to determine whether the work at Hope is to live or die, whether the work in the West is to go on successfully or end in shameful failure. We must pay a debt of $25,000 this year to save the college from starvation.[4]

In 1881, the Council could report to the Synod that the debt had been paid with the exception of $1000 owing the Board of Benevolence, and that, in addition, $10,000 had been added to the endowment fund. One of the generous donors was an anonymous lady in New York who gave $10,000. Another donor was Garrett Kouwenhoven of Newton, Long Island, who gave $13,000. The total amount raised was $30,000, and once again Hope College was saved, not by Western donors but by benefactors in the East.[5]

Theology Restored

The Western churches were never reconciled to the suspension of Theology in 1877. They charged that "the dreadful agitations which imperiled the very existence of the church in the West were largely the outcome of the suspension of theology." They pointed to the fact that the Christian Reformed Church had established a seminary in Grand Rapids, and were on the point of incorporating a college. They pointed to the actions of Synod that had practically guaranteed that Theology in the West would be restored as soon as the college had been put on a safer financial basis. In 1884, the Council sent to the Synod a printed memorial "regarding the restoration of theological instruction in the West."[6] After reviewing the history of it, and impressing upon the Synod the urgent need, the memorial concludes as follows:

> Consider the West as the vital part of your future existence as

---

4 Minutes of the General Synod 1881.
5 College Catalog, 1885/86, p. 42.
6 See printed memorial in the College Archives.

a Church of Christ. There is success in store for us if there is
faith. Golden opportunities are slipping by. Shall we stand by
inactive and see others snatch them away from us? Do not hesi-
tate. Act promptly and decisively. A special effort in the West,
a trifling gift from every member of the church, and the coma
changes into life again, with all the possibilities and hopes. The
influence of the seminary upon the college, in a moral sense,
always was a blessed one. Return to our college boys the blessing
of the godly example of their more advanced brethren. In granting our request, we pray Synod sharply to define the boundary
line of college and seminary. Let there be no dispute in the
future. For the love of Christ and the love of Zion, and the love
of the West, beloved brethren, take this matter into serious and
prayerful consideration.

At the June meeting in 1883, the Synod recommended the
resumption of Theology, provided that the churches in the
Synod of Chicago raised sufficient funds to endow a Chair of
Didactic and Systematic Theology. By 1884, the Reverend Crispell had raised $7000 of the amount necessary. The Council me-
morial assured the Synod of 1884 that the contributions would
reach the sum of $15,000 by the time that Synod was to meet.
The Synod, meeting in Grand Rapids, resolved that "A Professor be elected at this session who shall not enter upon his
duties until the whole amount of $30,000 shall be in the hands
of the Board of Direction."[7] The Synod then elected the Reverend Nicholas N. Steffens. The Western church raised the
needed money through the efforts of the Reverends Lepeltak,
Steffens, and Dosker. Steffens was inaugurated December 4, 1884,
and the Theology Department was formally opened the next
day. The Council appointed as Lectors the Reverends Peter
Moerdyke and Henry E. Dosker. The matter of status was definitely settled by the Synod in 1885 when it took the administration away from the Council and placed it under a separate
Board of Superintendents. Now at last the West had a seminary
separate from Hope College. There were as yet no seminary
buildings, and classes were held in two rooms in the Oggel
House. Semelink Hall was erected in 1895 on the south campus
of Hope College. In 1897, the property known as Lots 5, 6, 11,
12 in Block 53 was deeded· to the Synod by the Hope College
Council for use by the seminary.

---

[7] Minutes of the General Synod 1883.

President Scott

In 1885, the Council deemed it appropriate to select a constitutional President. The financial situation looked better, and the difficulties with Phelps had been resolved. The Council nominated the Reverend John A. De Baun of Fonda, New York, for the presidency. Although confirmed by the General Synod, he declined the office. Professor Scott was then elected, and inaugurated on June 21, 1886. The inauguration sermon was preached by the Reverend William J. Taylor of Newark, New Jersey, and Professor Scott gave an inaugural address. After a lapse of eight years, Hope College again had a legally constituted President. In 1884, the Synod met in Grand Rapids and made a brief visit to Holland on Saturday afternoon. The Synod expressed pleasure with the beauty of the campus and the progress that had been made over the years. They noted, however, that there was no residence for the President. Meeting in regular session in Grand Rapids, the Synod resolved that a residence should be erected. Thirty-one hundred dollars was immediately subscribed by the delegates. In the previous year, the Executive Committee had closed the entrance to the campus on the northeast corner and instead gravelled a carriage road into the campus from 10th Street. It was decided to build the President's house west of the carriage road and fronting on 10th Street. Construction was begun and the exterior structure completed by 1887. But then funds ran out, construction stopped, and the house remained boarded up for several years. In 1889, the Council asked the Board of Domestic Missions for an appropriation to finish it. The request was referred to the Women's Executive Committee, who voted a donation of $1000. The residence was finally completed in 1892, but too late to be occupied by President Scott. It was first occupied by President Kollen. It appears that Scott had invested some of his money in the completion of it on condition that he would be repaid. After his death, his heirs asked for payment and the Council agreed to pay the estate $427.00.

New Financial Troubles

The clearing of the debt in 1883 and the resumption of Theology in 1885 did not solve the financial problems of the

*Charles Scott, D.D., professor, 1867-1878; acting president, 1878-1880;
provisional president, 1880-1885; and president, 1885-1893.*

college. In 1883/84, salaries were paid promptly and no new
debt was contracted. The Council asked the Synod to appropriate
$5000 for the following purposes: $1000 for the library, $1500
for the laboratories, $1000 for a museum collection, and $1500
for repairs. At the same time the Council suggested that $20,000

be raised for a library building and that $50,000 be raised for a new endowment. In the next year difficulties arose. There was a small deficit due to "the increase of teachers and to the lower appropriation by the Board of Education, and a very large outlay for taxes." Between 1882 and 1886, all the streets around the campus had to be graded and gravelled. In 1885/86, Charter Hall was destroyed by fire. The alumni offered to raise $15,000 to replace it, but their efforts did not match their hopes. All the buildings were frame structures in constant need of repair. In 1889, the Council overtured the General Synod for $1500 for property improvements. When the Synod did nothing the Council decided to paint the buildings, and sent the bill to the Synod. The Board of Education, R.C.A., replied,

> It is absolutely necessary to paint these buildings, but we suggest that this should not become a precedent, otherwise the Synod might be involved in liabilities for the construction of which it has given no authority. The Council should be made to understand that there are no unredeemed pledges of past years.[8]

In 1891, the Council said to the Synod,

> Hope College must be out of the race if material improvement is not made in the very near future. It appears useless to make application to the Board of Education. This Board apparently must cease to be a source of income to the college. Would that a man of God, with silver wand, might touch our beautiful campus and give it a nucleus of buildings adequate for our growing needs.

In the school year 1892/93, the Board of Education, R.C.A., gave nothing, although the Synod had voted a grant of $4000. The faculty complained that their salaries were in arrears and that promised increases were not forthcoming. On April 21, 1891, they sent a communication to the Council which said:

> It is with a feeling of regret that the faculty are under the necessity of calling your attention to the inadequacy of the present salaries. We have long hesitated to bring up the matter, hoping that some fortunate turn in the circumstances of the college might result in proper increases in salary. In this we have been disappointed. When we received our respective appointments, we were promised speedy increases.[9]

8 Minutes of the General Synod 1890.
9 Letter in the Diekema file in College Archives.

Although there were annual deficits in the operating funds, some progress was made in the endowment account. Several financial agents had been appointed on a full-time and part-time basis, without much success. In 1888, the Council appointed the Reverend James F. Zwemer as agent to raise a fund of $100,000 for three Western institutions, of which Hope College was to receive one half. He was most successful, and by 1894 reported that the entire amount had been raised. When Phelps resigned in 1878, invested funds in the hands of the Council amounted to $28,000 and those in the hands of the Board of Direction stood at $19,000. When Scott resigned, the Council held $56,000 and the Board of Direction $67,000, of which one half was for the seminary. In addition, the Board of Education held in trust for the college $5000, and the Board of Benevolence $15,000. The income of the latter fund was to be used for student aid. Although there was improvement in the endowment funds, it was still too small for the growing institution.

Academic Affairs in the Scott Period

By the end of the Scott administration the institution was still very poor, but it had weathered another financial crisis and now was in no immediate danger of extinction. On the academic front also there were some evidences of life and growth. Only Doesburg, Kollen, and Scott remained of the original faculty. In the period of the eighties, there came into the faculty a number of people who were to serve the college with loyalty and distinction until well into the twentieth century. There was Henry Boers, a Tutor in 1878, Professor of English in 1885, and Head of the Department of History from 1893 to 1913. Another was Professor John Henry Kleinheksel, a Tutor in 1878 and Head of the Department of Mathematics from 1885 to 1916. Two great classical scholars came in the persons of James G. Sutphen and John H. Gillespie. And who will ever forget John Bernard Nykerk? He began a long career as Tutor in 1885 and served as Head of the Department of English from 1895 to 1936. In 1887, Mrs. Christine Van Raalte Gilmore, daughter of the founder of the colony, became Lady Assistant and Matron.

Enrollment in the college department was very much at a standstill. The grammar school of the college grew more rapidly

The first alumnae.
Upper row, l. to r.: Sarah G. Alcott (Mrs. Erastus Whitenack), Frances
F. C. Phelps (Mrs. John A. Otte);
Lower row, l. to r.: Eliza Phelps and Mary E. Alcott (Mrs. Gerrit J.
Diekema).

and tended to absorb the time and energies of the faculty, who taught in both departments. In 1878 the total enrollment was 122, of whom only 45 were in the college. In the school year 1889/90, the total was 152, of whom only 52 were in the college. The first women were admitted to the college in the fall of

118 A Century of Hope

1878. There is no record of organized recruiting by members of the faculty until the summer of 1882. In that summer, Professor Scott visited Grand Haven, Muskegon, and places as far north as Negaunee in the Upper Peninsula. Professor Beck worked in the Classis of Michigan, and Professor Doesburg in the Classis of Muskegon. Professor Kollen visited English-speaking churches in Detroit, and in Rochester and Geneva in New York State. There is no evidence of any immediate results.

Curricular changes were few. Programs remained heavily classical in both departments with a minimum of electives. The most significant change was the introduction into the grammar school of a four-year normal course. As early as 1857, the academy circular had announced that one of the aims of the institution was "the training of teachers, and those who are fixed on teaching as a permanent profession will be allowed to take a normal course of elective subjects. If there is sufficient progress and prosperity, there will be an effort to send forth teachers for the express purpose of founding schools and academies, auxiliary to the institution." Little progress was made until the summer of 1887. At that time, Professor Patrocles Latta of Allegan was engaged to introduce a normal course "furnishing instruction for the due preparation of teachers in the public schools, and at the same time, placing no obstacles in the way of the regular and established course in the college." It was planned to begin the course in the "C" class of the grammar school and complete it in the Freshman college year. Professor Latta remained for just one semester. Arrangements were also made for a summer school of six weeks beginning July 1890. The course was intended to give teachers a review of the subjects required for First, Second, and Third Grade Certificates in Michigan. In the first summer session, which was directed by Mr. James W. Humphrey, 135 students enrolled. Members of the faculty taught the cognate subjects. The school was abandoned after five or six summers.

Student Life and Activities

As time went on, student life gradually became a little more collegiate. Students entering the institution tended to be younger than they were in the early college days. While their number was small, they began to act like the students in older institutions. In 1887, they petitioned the General Faculty for permission to publish a monthly student magazine called the *Anchor*. The first issue appeared June 1887, with John Van Westenberg as the editor. Its size was 8 x 11 inches and it consisted of twelve pages of material. There were two feature articles, one by President Scott and the other by Albertus Pieters. The *Anchor* has been published continuously since 1887, first as a monthly and now as a weekly.

The first prizes for students were introduced in 1887. In the early days, the catalogs said that "instead of the ordinary methods of prizes, incentives to progress are furnished by the positions on the honorary and classical scholarships." But in 1887, the Honorable George Birkhoff, Jr. Prizes were funded to encourage students in the study of English and Dutch History and Literature. The first English prize was won by J. M. Vandermeulen and the first Dutch prize by John Luxen.

Some new student organizations were formed in the eighties. The Meliphone Society organized by Van Vleck in 1856 continued to serve the students in the grammar school. The Fraternal Society organized by Phelps had its ups and downs until reorganized in 1890 after a suspension of several years. A Dutch literary society, called the Ulfilas Society, was organized by Professor Doesburg in 1886. Among the first officers were Samuel Zwemer and Albertus Pieters. Annual programs were given in Dutch during the commencement week and were often the highlight of the week. In 1883, a group of young women organized a literary society called the Zetalethian for the purpose of a critical study of English authors.

After several petitions, students were allowed to organize a Boarding Club. Clubs of this nature were common in Michigan colleges. The students petitioned the General Faculty in March of 1886. Permission was granted on condition that the membership be limited to fifteen. However, the club grew rapidly, and the *Anchor* reported, in January 1890, that "a new club which has been organized with sixteen members now has forty-three. The Club has spacious quarters in one of the Halls but would like the Council to erect a building for the purpose." The April issue of the *Anchor* in the year 1892 said, "The Boarding Club has disarmed ridicule, worn out prejudice, and has long passed the experimental period."

In the eighties, students began to be greatly interested in a program of physical education and in intercollegiate sports. Organized athletics began to be a normal part of activities in Michigan colleges. The University of Michigan had a well-developed program as early as 1884. The first intercollegiate football game in Michigan occurred in 1884 between the University and Albion College. The Michigan Intercollegiate Athletic Association was founded in 1888 with Michigan Agricultural College, Albion, Hillsdale, and Olivet as charter members. Spurred on by these examples, students at Hope began to manifest a greater interest in competitive athletics, and they became very restive under the restrictions imposed by the Council and faculty. Baseball was a campus sport as early as 1872. In 1887, there were reports of baseball competition with neighboring high school teams. The *Anchor* of October 1887 said:

> The common sports are entirely forgotten this year. Instead of the usual stir and excitement on the campus after four o'clock, all is quiet and the grounds present a deserted appearance. In baseball, we have never been fortunate in coping with opposing teams, and it is equally true of football, so that we had better retire from the field. We have met crushing defeats, and there is no more effective way of quitting these sports than a few defeats.

But as the enrollment increased, there were among the students some who had participated in high school athletics. Consequently, student agitation for programs in physical education and competitive sports increased. Several years were to elapse before the Council gave way and removed the restrictions.

There is also some evidence that students were becoming more sophisticated and collegiate. In 1881, they printed and distributed a Bogus Commencement Program making sport of the members of the class. This pleased the students very much, but greatly upset the faculty. In the year 1890, in connection with the quarter-centennial of the college, the Senior Class, with one exception, declined to appear at commencement and their diplomas were withheld. On May 1, 1890, the class sent the following petition:

> Whereas it has been customary to have the exercises on Wed-

The president's house. Since its erection in 1886, it is still used as the president's home. The porch was added during the tenure of President Ame Vennema.

nesday evening of the last week of the college year, and whereas the Seniors have made preparations and arrangements for said evening, and whereas, although there was an understanding that the commencement would be held at the usual time, it has been brought to our notice that some members of your honorable body are planning a change of time for the commencement this year, we, the Senior Class, kindly petition you to allow the usual evening of June 29, 1890.[10]

The class claimed that their petition had been treated with contempt and, with one exception, refused to attend. At the commencement, President Scott read an action taken by the Council relative to the conduct of the class. The Council resolved:

The presentation and delivery of a thesis at Commencement time are requisite to the completion of the work, from which a student cannot be excused except by the faculty, subject to review by the Council. That the degree recommended to be conferred on members of the class of 1890 be laid upon the table until the requirements of the former resolution be complied with.[11]

[10] See the *Anchor*, July 1890.
[11] Minutes of the Council, 1890.

The matter was not settled until 1894 when the Council modified its action of 1890 so as to dispense with the requirement of a thesis, and granted the diplomas upon receiving a written request signed by each member, and the payment of the fee required for graduation. It is a matter of interest that the professional A.M. degree was conferred upon members of the Class of 1890 in 1893, before they had received their A.B. degree.

The Quarter-Centennial Celebration

The high event in the Scott period was the celebration of the quarter-centennial of the college in June 1890. This date marked the twenty-fifth anniversary of the organization, although actual incorporation did not take place until 1866. Although the financial situation was still serious, the future of the college was more secure. There was now a considerable body of alumni, who were in a position to give moral support, though little financial assistance. The grammar school had 407 alumni of whom 90 were ministers or students preparing for the ministry. The college had 152 alumni of whom 92 were ministers or preparing for the ministry. The time was opportune for a backward look and a look into the future.

The baccalaureate sermon was preached on June 22 by the Reverend G. Henry Mandeville, now Secretary of the Board of Education. The rhetorical exercises of the grammar school were held on Monday afternoon. In the evening the Ulfilas Society pleased the audience with their Dutch program. The alumni reunion followed on Tuesday afternoon, with a public program in the evening. They sang the alumni song of 1877 and heard historical addresses by Professor Kollen and the Reverends C. Vander Veen, J. Meulendyke, G. De Jonge, and Albertus Pieters. The commencement exercises took place on Wednesday forenoon. Since the Senior Class had absented themselves, addresses were made by the Reverend C. Britt, who represented the General Synod, and the Honorable Bethune Duffield of Detroit. An article in *The Christian Intelligencer* July 3, 1890, referred to the absence of the class and said, "At first the action of the senior class cast some gloom on the program, until the audience began to see the comical side of the situation." However, it was unfortunate, because it added to the burden of the ailing Presi-

dent, who was about to retire. Some attempt was made to atone
for it when, on the occasion of Scott's last commencement in
1892, the students presented him with a costly upholstered
chair.

The quarter-centennial exercises began Wednesday evening
with a public meeting of the alumni. The main address was given
by former President Philip Phelps on "The Unity in American
Education." The alumni song composed by Phelps in 1866 was
sung. The alumni presented the college with an oil painting of
the former President. It was the work of J. Twichell of Albany
and cost $180. Former Professor William Shields wrote a long
poem for the occasion. The poem closed as follows:

> Thus may this quarter centennial year
> But show the beginning of what shall be here
> The labors, the trials, the faith of the past
> Be the seed that into the furrow is cast.
>
> That shall spring forth and burst into beautiful bloom
> As flowers arise from their last year's tomb
> The harvest abundant as year follows year
> Until the centennial birthday draws near.[12]

The convocation took place in the college grove on the morning
of June 26. The local paper reported, "In the morning, Holland
was wakened by the booming of twenty-five guns. The academic
procession formed at the First Reformed Church and proceeded
to the college grove, where seats had been prepared for 2000
people." The Reverend Peter Moerdyke of the Class of 1866
presided. Professor Nykerk directed a Glee Club of twenty voices
in the singing of a Latin song composed by Professor Henry E.
Dosker. Historical addresses were given, with John Vandermeulen speaking on the pioneer period, Ale Buursma on the
academy, and John W. Beardslee, Sr., on the college. Delegates
from various colleges brought greetings and the Reverend G.
Henry Mandeville spoke for the Board of Education, R.C.A. The
Reverend John W. Warnshuis spoke for Northwestern Classical
Academy, the Reverend W. J. R. Taylor for Rutgers College and
New Brunswick Seminary, and Governor Cyrus Luce for the
State of Michigan.

After the exercises a collation was served in the gymnasium.

---

12 *Anchor*, July 1890.

Mr. G. J. Diekema was the toastmaster, and remarks were made by Governor Luce, and the Reverends Albert Pfanstiehl and H. V. S. Peeke. There was an interesting address by Lt. Col. Cornelius Gardener of the United States Army. His subject was "Hope College and the Boys in Blue." Reminiscing about his student days at Holland Academy, he said:

> We have been pioneers in more than one sense, a real pioneer with the axe and spade, for we felled trees, fastened the timbers and built this Gymnasium, and many a square of sod did the youngsters put down of these grounds. The axe in those days was about the only plaything a boy had, and with this he was allowed, every day, to practice on the logs back of the house.[13]

At this collation, the ladies of the alumni sat in the gallery, which caused someone to remark that "man had been made to sit a little lower than the angels."

Resignation and Death of Scott

In the spring of 1893, the Council accepted the resignation of President Scott on account "of his age and conscious need for relaxation from the tensions of the ever increasing burden." He had reached the age of seventy, having given twenty-six years of his life to Hope College. Never robust, he was often in ill health. He lost his home and its contents by fire in 1871. In 1883, while on his way to Synod, he was forced to return home because he had been overtaken with a double affliction, being prostrated by sickness and called to part with a beloved daughter suddenly removed by death. In June of 1892, he had suffered a mild paralysis and was unable to preside at the commencement. Professor Beck took his place. Upon Scott's resignation, the Council nominated the Reverend Henry Du Bois Milford. When he declined the invitation, Scott consented to serve for another year. He became ill again and was unable to preside at the commencement in 1893. On October 31, 1893, Scott passed away leaving a widow and four sons. Dr. Demarest of Rutgers preached the funeral sermon in the old church at Shawangunk of which Scott had been the pastor when he came to Holland. Speaking of Scott at the seventy-fifth anniversary of the college, Demarest said:

---

13 *Ibid.*

He began his work as a professor of Chemistry and Natural Science, for he was of scientific temper, a scientist of no small stature. He had been a Lector in Theology. He taught History, Philosophy, Mathematics, Constitutional Law, Evidences of Christianity. Scholarly and untiring in his work, eloquent in speech, and the very soul of integrity, he was gentle and kind. The titles of his addresses, especially patriotic and historical, are extraordinary in number and scope.

A memorial service was held in the college chapel on June 25, 1894. The catalog pays him this tribute: "President Scott died October 31. By his death the Church sustains a great loss, the students are deprived of a true counsellor and kind leader, the faculty mourns a friend and beloved associate."

Fortunately, Scott lived long enough to see some of his hopes come to fruition. He had pleaded for funds for a chapel and a library building. He had seen the walls of the building rise on the campus. He had plans for a recitation building and a dormitory, to be followed, as soon as possible, by a Chemistry and Physics laboratory. The catalog said, "The retiring President has all of this in his hopes, sees it in a vision, not a dream, and feels that his successor will witness the accomplishment and yet more in prospect."

8: THE TIDE TURNS

THE ELECTION OF President Gerrit John Kollen in 1893 marks the beginning of a new and vital era in the history of Hope College. After the Reverend Henry Du Bois Milford had declined the presidency, the names of several possible candidates were brought to the attention of the Council at its meeting in April. Although Professor Kollen had strong support, he failed to receive enough votes to secure the nomination. However, there were seven members of the Council who held out for him and succeeded in having the election postponed until the June meeting. Kollen was inclined to withdraw his name, but his friends on the Council and on the faculty waited on him and persuaded him not to desert them. He received the required two-thirds majority at the June session and his nomination was sent to the General Synod for ratification. One of the reasons for opposition to the election of Kollen was the fact that he was a layman and not an ordained minister. It was still unusual in American colleges to give such honors to a layman. And some of the Western members of the Council had not forgotten that he had opposed the restoration of Theology after its suspension in 1877 and that he had suggested to the Synod the need of a reorganization of the college.

Gerrit John Kollen was born in the Netherlands in 1843 and came to America in 1851. In due time he entered Holland Academy, as a result of the personal solicitation of A. C. Van Raalte. The story is told of how Van Raalte visited the farm

126

Gerrit J. Kollen, president, 1893-1911.

home of Kollen's widowed mother and her sons in Overisel to urge that Gerrit be sent to Holland Academy, because he had heard that her son was a very bright boy. The mother protested on the ground that they were farmers and that children should not be brought up above their class. Van Raalte replied that she was no longer in Europe but in America, where people could rise above their class and do the kind of work for which they were best fitted. The mother was persuaded, and Gerrit Kollen enrolled in Holland Academy. Upon his graduation in 1864 he entered Hope College, and received his A.B. degree in 1868. After teaching for three years in Overisel, he became a Tutor in the grammar school of Hope College. He was elected a Professor in 1878 and in the following year married Mary Van Raalte, the daughter of the founder of Holland and of the Academy. He began his administrative duties in September of 1893, although the Synod did not approve the nomination until its session in June of 1894. The inauguration took place June 27, 1894. In addition to the inaugural, there were addresses by President Emeritus Philip Phelps and by the Reverend G. Henry Mandeville, Secretary of the Board of Education, R. C. A. Phelps presented the new President with the academic regalia he himself had worn at the first commencement. Honorary LL.D. degrees were conferred upon Phelps and Nathan F. Graves. An honorary D.D. degree was conferred upon the Reverend Peter De Pree and a Mus. D. degree upon Edward A. Bedell, who was the organist and chorister in the Madison Avenue Reformed Church of Albany. Bedell was graduated from Hope College in 1873. He was a nephew of Dr. Phelps, and was a collector of hymns. In 1891 he published *The Church Hymnary,* which was said to contain the best of Christian hymns of all nations. The General Synod of the Reformed Church adopted it and recommended its use in all churches. It was never used at Hope. There was a noticeable omission of some of the beautiful old hymns.

In 1896, President Kollen moved into the new President's home on the campus, which was to be home and office for many years. Kollen became President at a very crucial juncture. The times demanded an administrator of proven business ability and financial experience. In 1872, he had been successful in raising

$6000 for the Ebenezer Fund in connection with the twenty-fifth anniversary of the founding of Holland. The special committee which came to Holland in 1878 saw in him great promise and invited him to accept a position as financial agent for the college. When invited to do·so by the Council and the Board of Education, he accepted the challenge and was moderately successful. And in the last few years of the Scott administration, he was commissioned to raise funds for a library and chapel. His predecessors had been scholars and teachers but with little business experience. Although Kollen was successful as a teacher, his most obvious successes were in the field of finance, and such a leader was desperately needed. From 1866 to 1893, the college waged a constant battle against poverty and operating deficits. Faculty members were poorly paid and often not paid at all. There were nine buildings on the campus but only two were worthy of the name — Van Vleck Hall and the President's residence. The endowment was less that $100,000 and the income insufficient for even a small operating budget of less than $20,000. The two most immediate needs were to increase the endowment funds and to erect adequate facilities for the growing institution.

Graves Hall and Winants Chapel

From 1880 to 1894, the library collection was housed in two rooms of the first floor of Van Vleck Hall. By 1891, the library was said to contain 6000 volumes, and it became essential to have fire-resistant facilities for the growing collection. In recent years there had been several fires in Van Vleck Hall, and the librarian said, "If the hall burns down, most of Hope College is gone. It is sheer nonsense to leave a valuable library in a building constantly occupied by a score of students." In the last year of the Scott administration, the Council appointed a special committee to make provisional plans for a suitable building and the raising of the necessary funds, but insisted that it must be done without the contraction of any debt; and they commissioned Professor Kollen to raise the money. He quickly secured a few substantial gifts for a combined chapel and library building. Nathan F. Graves, President of the New York Banking Company of Syracuse, New York, donated $10,000 for a library to bear his name

An early picture of Graves Library and Winant's Chapel. Dedicated, June 26, 1894.

and made an additional gift of $700 to purchase such works as were needed in the different departments. He also promised to give the college his extensive personal library collection. Mr. Graves was a member of the Reformed Church and had been a member of the Board of Superintendents of New Brunswick Seminary. He was now nearly eighty years old and died July 21, 1896. Another donation of $10,000 came from Mrs. Gerrit Winants of Bergen Point, New Jersey, in memory of her husband. He was at one time a shipowner in New York and had moved to New Jersey in 1872. He also served on various boards of the Reformed Church as well as the board of the American Bible Society. There was also a substantial gift from Aleida Van Schaick, the daughter of an early benefactor of the college.

Plans for the structure were drawn by Mr. W. J. Johnston of Chicago, who in his later years also designed the Dimnent Memorial Chapel. The structure was built of native stone quarried at Waverly, a short distance east of the city. The chapel was 60 x 60 feet; the library had a reading room and a stack room with a capacity of 20,000 volumes. On the first floor there was a large administration room and on the second floor four large classrooms. The cornerstone was laid October 12, 1892, and the building was dedicated June 26, 1894. On this occasion, President Austin Scott of Rutgers conferred upon President Kollen an honorary degree of Doctor of Laws. Professor Henry Dosker in his address gently reminded his audience that 97 percent of the cost of the building had been contributed by Eastern donors. Upon the dedication of the building, Professor Doesburg resigned as Professor of Modern Languages and was appointed full-time Librarian. The work of cataloging began, and the reading room was opened to students in December of 1895. Elder William Brower of the Collegiate Church of New York became interested in the support of the reading room and for many years donated funds for reference books and periodicals. The old chapel now reverted to its original use as a gymnasium.

Van Raalte Hall, still serving as a classroom building as well as housing the administrative offices.

Maria Ackerman Hoyt Observatory

In 1894 a valuable addition was made to the college facilities in the form of a telescope and mountings donated by Miss Emilie S. Coles in memory of Mrs. Maria Ackerman Hoyt. The instrument was an eighteen-inch Newtonian reflector mounted on a solid concrete pier, at a high point of the campus on Columbia Avenue south of the gymnasium. It was useful in the teaching of Astronomy, but its use was limited by the fact that there was no covering dome and no rotating mechanism. It was removed when the hill was levelled in 1941.

Van Raalte Memorial Hall

The growing college was in dire need of adequate classrooms and suitable laboratories for the teaching of the sciences. In 1897, the community was to celebrate the semicentennial of the founding of the colony. President Kollen determined to use this occasion to secure funds for the erection of a campus building honoring the pioneers of 1847 and their illustrious leader, A. C. Van Raalte, and suggested the plan to the Council:

> Shall we not make this semi-centennial year memorable by erecting upon these grounds a building that shall declare to the world our love for, our appreciation of the fathers and mothers who, filled with zeal, faith and hope, laid the foundations upon which we are privileged to build?[1]

He immediately received donations in the amount of $7500 from local businessmen enthusiastic about the proposition. The rest of the community did not respond with the same alacrity, and it was not until July 1900 that the *Anchor* reported:

> It is with great pleasure that President Kollen announced just before the close of the school year that we are going to have a new building devoted to the sciences and which is to stand as a monument to the memory of the founder of Holland and of Hope College.

Another three years elapsed before the contract was awarded to Messrs. Clark and Blakeslee for $29,000.

The cornerstone was laid in June 1904 by Mr. D. B. K. Van Raalte, son of A. C. Van Raalte, assisted by Peter Semelink and H. J. Veneklasen. There were appropriate addresses by the

---

[1] Minutes of the Council, April 1897.

John B. Nykerk, the "Mr. Chips" of the campus, Professor of English Language and Literature, 1885-1936, who was also instrumental in starting the music department.

Reverends Henry E. Dosker, J. M. Conklin, Peter Lepeltak, Gerhard De Jonge, and Mr. Gerrit J. Diekema. Professor J. B. Nykerk composed a memorial hymn, sung to the tune of *America,* which read:

> God of our Fathers old,
> Thro dangers manifold,
> Safe thou hast led.
> Thy goodness we confess,—
> Thou didst in dire distress,
> On seas or wilderness
> Our table spread.

God of the Pilgrim Band,
That sought this favored land,—
When dark the hour.
God of the leaders bold,
That didst this people mold,—
The grace and Power.

God of the Pioneer,
Memorial Hall we rear
Thy name to praise,
Hope's anchor sure and fast,—
That held through storm and blast
Was in thy favor cast
With upturned gaze.

This Ebenezer now,
With prayer and solemn vow
We raise to thee.
Thy glory ever shine
Within these walls of thine,—
Our hearts, our minds refine
This is our plea.

Peace and prosperity,
Our people's portion be
Where'er they move.
May discord ne'er prevail,—
Nor doubts our Church assail
Faith, Hope and Love.[2]

Van Raalte Hall was dedicated on September 16, 1903. On the
first floor were several large classrooms and laboratories for
Chemistry and Physics. On the second floor there were some
general classrooms, laboratories for Biology and Botany, and a
small conservatory for growing plants. Two large rooms on the
third floor were set aside for the museum collection and for
choral rehearsals. Some years later a fourth floor was finished to
house the museum. The President was deeply disappointed in
the failure of the community and the entire West to support him
more generously in his plan to honor the pioneers of 1847 and
the founder of the colony. Donations fell far short of the amount
necessary and $10,000 was borrowed from the endowment funds
to complete Van Raalte Hall. He was convinced that he would
have to look to the Eastern section of the church for needed
funds for capital improvement and for permanent funds.

---

[2] *Anchor,* July 1904.

Carnegie Gymnasium, 1906.

Carnegie Gymnasium

The old gymnasium built in 1862 reverted to its original use as a gymnasium upon the completion of Winants Chapel, but was entirely inadequate to meet the growing need for facilities for physical education and athletics. In 1902, the students filed a petition for needed repairs and equipment, but the President explained that the structure was not worth repair and that he already had raised $1000 for a new gymnasium. This was in the form of an annuity purchased by Mr. Peter Semelink, a well-known benefactor of the college. Not until three years later was President Kollen able to report to the Council that "upon the kind request of the Reverend Donald Sage MacKay of the Collegiate Church of New York City, Mr. Andrew Carnegie had offered to donate $20,000 for the purpose on condition that a like amount be added to the endowment."[3] In the spring of that year, Dr. MacKay had been on the campus to speak on the occasion of the annual week of prayer for colleges, and had been

---

[3] Minutes of the Council, 1905.

deeply impressed with the progress the college was making and
the need for a combined auditorium and gymnasium.

At the turn of the century, there were in the East numerous
Reformed Church families of great wealth. The Collegiate
Church of New York had large resources and numbered among
its membership and attendants many wealthy families. Although
Andrew Carnegie was not a member, he attended the services
in St. Nicholas Collegiate Church whenever he was in New York.
Through the good offices of Dr. MacKay, President Kollen was
able to meet the steel magnate, and in the course of time they
became good friends. Kollen persuaded Carnegie to give $20,000
for a gymnasium to bear his name. Naturally, the announcement
by the President was received with great joy by the Council and
the students. The Council recommended that final approval of
the plans and specifications be left with the President and Executive Committee, but cautioned them to award no contract until
there was a reasonable certainty that there was money enough to
complete the structure. Since the original grant was insufficient,
Kollen made another appeal to Carnegie and received an additional $10,000. The new building was erected at a total cost of

Mr. and Mrs. Ralph Voorhees, donors of Voorhees Hall.

$30,688 including $1718 for equipment. The dedication took place September 16, 1906. Addresses were delivered by Dr. Mac-Kay, Governor Fred M. Warner, Senator William Alden Smith, Mr. G. J. Diekema, and President Kollen. Hope College was now the proud possessor of one of the finest gymnasiums in the State of Michigan. In connection with the dedication, Mr. Andrew Judson Kolyn of the Class of 1906 composed a song sung to the tune of "Tammany," which remained a favorite for many years. It reads as follows:

> A. C. Van Raalte in eighteen forty-seven came to town,
> And built old Hope College, of all his works the crown;
> But he chopped down trees to get his exercise, they say,—
> Now a Scotchman, Carnegie, has shown a better way.
>
> Donald Sage MacKay's a preacher in New York, N.Y.
> He's a Scotchman; he met Andy — thought he'd take a try,
> Said he, I know a school where they can use your money. So
> Andy sent to Hope just 30,000 of his dough.
>
> Doctor Kollen is the man whom all the students love;
> He's the man we honor all the other three above.
> He can get the money; he's a friend of all the boys.
> He has got our gym for us, and that's why all this noise.
>
> Chorus
>
> Carnegie, Carnegie
> He's the man who built our gym.
> We will sing this song for him.
> Carnegie, Carnegie
> Prexy we love; he got the dough from
> Carnegie

Voorhees Hall

Since coming into the presidency, Kollen had provided a library, chapel, laboratories, classrooms, auditorium, and a gymnasium. The campus had been completely transformed. The next building was a residence for women. In the year 1906/07, there were just nineteen girls in the college and sixty-six in the preparatory school; only seven of these did not live in the immediate community. Dr. Kollen was of the opinion that there were so few outside girls because there were no suitable housing or boarding facilities for them. In April 1902, he reported to the Council:

Voorhees Hall, dedicated 1907.

We have difficulty in securing boarding places for young women. We should have a dormitory of thirty or forty rooms, together with music rooms, parlors and a refectory, all under the control of a lady superintendent who would be a worthy example of Christian culture and refinement for the girls.

The Council agreed and suggested that steps be taken to raise the necessary funds.

President Kollen approached Mr. and Mrs. Ralph Voorhees of Clinton, New Jersey, who had already given the college $50,000 to endow two chairs — the Voorhees Chair of Greek and the Rodman Chair of Latin. In October of 1905, this devoted couple gave the college $100,000 on the annuity basis, of which $35,000 was to be used for the erection of a women's residence and $65,000 to be added to the permanent funds. The Council congratulated the President on his success, voted him a gratuity of $500, and suggested that he go abroad at the expiration of the year for rest and recuperation.

It seems appropriate to take special note of the careers of these donors. Ralph Voorhees was the son of an old and distinguished family. Elizabeth Rodman was the daughter of John Rodman, a well-to-do shipowner of Brooklyn, New York. Her mother was Clarabell Woodruff Nevius, who died while Elizabeth was still in her infancy. Upon Mr. Rodman's retirement, the family moved to a farm near Bedminster, New Jersey. Voorhees lived in the adjoining township, where he and Elizabeth began attending the same church and the same social affairs and soon fell in love with each other. And then Ralph suffered an eye injury which left him blind in one eye and totally blind three years later. Although Ralph had proposed marriage, John Rodman did not approve; but he did nothing to prevent the courtship. On October 12, 1887, seven months after her father had died, the marriage took place after a courtship that had lasted seventeen years. They moved to Clinton, New Jersey, where they lived until their death. They were possessed of moderate means until the death of Elizabeth's uncle, Robert Woodruff Rodman, who left Elizabeth a large fortune. Thereupon the couple decided that all the increments would be used for charitable and mission projects. Large gifts were made to many institutions at home and abroad, to Voorhees College in India, to the School for the Blind in Bombay, to colleges such as Rutgers, Coe, Huron, Maryville, Lafayette, Carroll, Hope, and others. Ralph Voorhees died April 1, 1927, but his widow lived until September 21, 1934. In her lifetime, Mrs. Voorhees returned to the college a total of $30,000 in interest payments on the annuity.

Voorhees Hall was dedicated in June 1907. There were addresses by the Reverend Oscar M. Voorhees of Highbridge, New Jersey, the Reverend Ame Vennema of Passaic, New Jersey, and by Mr. Edwin W. Booth of the Grand Rapids *Press*. There was a solo by Miss Estelle Kollen, daughter of the President, a vocal quartette composed of the Misses Kollen, Browning, Yates, and Larkin, and music by a girls' chorus. The building was formally opened with a dinner on September 18, 1907. The cost was $40,183 including $2886 for equipment and furniture. Mrs. Gilmore, daughter of the founder of the college, A. C. Van Raalte, was appointed Dean of Women and took up her residence in the Hall. The business affairs of the residence were managed by Professor Edward D. Dimnent. Since the building had a refectory for men and women, it filled a large and immediate need. It became the social center of the campus and was a great asset in the promotion of the cultural life of the college. As the number of girls increased, the basement rooms were furnished and became the meeting places of the various societies for women. In the first year of operation, there were just thirteen girls in Voorhees Hall, but in succeeding years the number quickly increased.

President Kollen and the Endowment Funds

Between 1894 and 1907, the campus took on a new look. Some of the ancient buildings had been replaced by more adequate and modern facilities, and the college had a physical plant quite the equal of most of the church colleges in Michigan. Nor was the President neglecting the financial needs of the institution. His election in 1894 had been attributed to "his efficient services both in the securing of funds and in the wise and prudent management of the funds." Disappointed in the response of the West, he turned chiefly to the East and spent a great deal of time away from the campus contacting men and women of means, particularly in the New York and New Jersey areas. The present writer was a student in the Kollen era and has distinct recollections of Kollen's frequent absences, the fact that he never left on one of his missions without informing the students of some of his plans, and how they soon became accustomed to his success stories. Dignified in appearance, cultured in manner, fittingly attired with top hat, frock coat, and cane, he was able to get introductions to families of great wealth in the East, and made many friends for the college. Upon assuming the presidency, he quickly launched a campaign to add $100,000 to the endowment. The catalog for the year 1897/98 indicates that this was more than successful and records large donations totaling $122,000. By 1902, the endowment fund amounted to $273,000, of which $25,000 came from the sale of the Point Superior lands. After his retirement in 1911, he undertook as President Emeritus to raise an additional $100,000. This venture was a complete success; among

The faculty of Hope College, 1910.

Seated, l. to r.: D. B. Yntema, James G. Sulphen, President Kollen, John H. Kleinheksel, Henry Boers, Frank N. Patterson.

Second row, l. to r.: Edward D. Dimnent, John B. Nykerk, Mrs. Hackley Durfee, Alma G. Martin, Elva N. Forncrook, John E. Kuizenga, Edwin Brown, and Dr. Almon T. Godfrey.

Upper row, l. to r.: John W. Beardslee, Jr., Albert Raap, Wynand Wichers, and Peter T. Schlosser.

the larger gifts were donations of $25,000 from Andrew Carnegie, and one of $25,000 from the Collegiate Church. By 1913, the total endowment rose to $451,000 including $74,000 in trust and annuity funds.

The President was less successful in getting contributions to the contingent or operating fund. The emphasis upon large individual gifts had much merit and was absolutely essential, but also resulted in decreased church support. The impression grew in the churches that the President was attempting to secure a large endowment in order to make the college quite independent of annual appropriations by the Board of Education and by the local congregations. But no matter how the endowment grew, it was never large enough to meet the current needs, and consequently there were steadily increasing deficits in the current fund. In the year 1910, total church contributions amounted to a mere $151. When a special attempt was made in 1911 to liquidate a debt of more than $10,000 on Van Raalte Hall and $5000 on Voorhees Hall, only a hundred churches responded, with total contributions of $2004.

Since the campus and buildings were legally the property of the General Synod, Kollen began to put pressure on the Synod and the Board of Direction for extra funds to maintain the buildings and grounds. In 1895/96, the Board of Direction of the Synod gave an extra $500, and similar amounts were reluctantly granted for a few years. In the preceding year the Board of Education had contributed nothing. In 1907, the General Synod appointed a committee of five members to meet the immediate needs at Holland and to take steps toward the establishment of an endowment fund, the income of which was to be applied to the maintenance of the property. In 1909, the committee reported that no money had been received from the Committee on Properties. In 1910, President Kollen expressed his disappointment and complained that "the Reformed Church Forward Movement has not yet resolved the educational work of the church. It would seem rather that a Forward Movement in Missions means a backward movement in education."[4]

For some time, the President had urged the Board of Direction to invest that part of college funds held by the Board in Western securities where higher rates of interest were prevalent. And in 1896, he asked the Board to transfer to the college all the funds held by the Board in trust for the college. The Board replied that this was illegal since the Charter of the Board obligated the Board to invest all of its funds in New York. A minority report favoring the action failed of passage.

An Academy at Cedar Grove, Wisconsin

In April 1900, the President told the Council that he deemed it desirable to establish academies in different places in the Chicago Synod, both for the sake of increasing interest in higher

---

[4] Minutes of the Council, April 1902.

education in the West, and also in order that the academies might serve as feeders for the college. He pointed to the success of the Northwestern Classical Academy established in 1882 at Orange City, Iowa, which had already sent to the college many promising students. With the approval of the Council, the President took steps to open an academy in Cedar Grove, Wisconsin. In his annual report in April 1902, President Kollen said that the success of the Wisconsin Memorial Academy warranted thinking of establishing other academies. Instruction began in the academy on November 13, 1901. Fifty-six students enrolled. A delegation from Hope was invited to attend the dedication on June 26, 1902. Someone said that it seemed to be providential that the community and the State in which Van Raalte might have settled in 1846, in later years was to be signally blessed.

The burdens of the presidency were heavy, and in time they began to make inroads upon the health of President and Mrs. Kollen. He was disappointed in the lack of support from the Western section of the church. This was increased when the community seemed to lack enthusiasm for a memorial to the pioneers and failed to contribute the necessary funds. At the April 1902 meeting of the Council, he resigned his office. He said that it was not a hasty action but that it had been considered for some months.

> The plain fact is that I am tired and worn out. But this is not surprising when it is remembered that it will be thirty-one years next September that I became officially connected with Hope. And during those years, there were always so many things outside of my regular profession that needed the attention of some one, such as the Ebenezer Endowment work, visiting the churches to secure students and repeated endeavor to bring relief to our paper *De Hope* and in later years to seek funds for new buildings and endowment that the so-called vacations were nothing but a chance for harder work, with always the same object weighing heavily upon my mind.[5]

He said that he did not complain because the work was assumed voluntarily and that he was not disappointed with his work, "but the fact remains that the bow has not been unstrung for thirty-one years."

---

5 *Ibid.*

The Council had been apprehensive for some time. In 1897 it had resolved, "We respectfully suggest to our President the conviction that cessation from some of his numerous public engagements and rest for a time would be conducive to his health and the welfare of the institution."[6] The resignation was referred to a committee. After meeting with Dr. Kollen, this committee reported that "in view of the earnest and unanimous desire of the Council and the vital interests of the college, the President consented to withdraw his resignation." The Council offered him a year's leave of absence with continuation of his salary. The President, however, decided not to accept the leave of absence and continued his labors until 1911. Significant contributions were made in the period between 1902 and 1911, but the burdens did not become lighter. On March 16, 1905, his beloved wife, Mary Van Raalte, passed away; but he continued to throw himself with vigor into the work of promoting the interests of the college, which still needed more buildings and more money. He again resigned in April 1911, effective September 1, 1911. After eighteen years in the office he was named President Emeritus. Even then he continued his activities and proceeded to raise an additional endowment of $100,000.

Some well-deserved honors had come to him. In 1905, he was made a Knight in the Order of Orange-Nassau by her Majesty Queen Wilhelmina of the Netherlands, "in recognition of his service in behalf of the descendants of Hollanders in America, the Queen's former subjects." After his retirement, President Theodore Roosevelt gave him an appointment as a delegate to the Opium Congress at the Hague and to attend the dedication of the Peace Palace.

He passed away on September 5, 1915, on the eve of the semicentennial of the college. The faculty passed the following resolution:

> While Dr. Phelps was the inspirer of Hope's high ideals and her unbounded faith in her glorious future, it remained the special mission of our late lamented President to realize those ideals and that future, and to make our institution what it is today. . . . As a man, Kollen inspired our deep respect by virtue of his sterling character, his puritanic principles, his lofty ideals,

6 Minutes of the Council, 1897.

his high sense of honor, his unwavering opposition to injustice and wrong, his genuine sympathy with the weak, the erring and the unfortunate.

The Council likewise expressed its tribute, and remarked, "He had anticipated with enthusiasm and great pleasure of sharing in the approaching semi-centennial of the college, and we all desired him to be a prominent figure and participant in such joy, but the will of the Lord was otherwise." The semicentennial *Milestone* in 1916 was dedicated to his memory by the students, who said that he, "by virtue of his uprightness of character and conduct, his uncompromising attitude towards injustice, and his large-hearted sympathy in time of trouble and trial, exercised an influence that will be an inspiration to studentry for years to come. Though dead, yet speaking in 'thoughts that breathe and words that burn.' "

9: FRUITFUL YEARS

WHEN PRESIDENT KOLLEN ANNOUNCED his intention to resign, the Council appointed a special committee to recommend a candidate for the office. The committee drew up certain specifications of qualities requisite in the presidency. On May 18, 1911, it recommended the appointment of the Reverend Ame Vennema of Passaic, New Jersey, and he was unanimously chosen by the Council. He was an alumnus of the Class of 1879 and had been a member of the Council since 1905. He had done some financial work for the college and had established a $2500 scholarship in honor of his mother. He was a man of distinguished bearing, a pulpit orator of note, and highly esteemed both East and West. He was the personal choice of President Kollen, who saw in him the man for the hour. The new President arrived on the campus in August and was inaugurated February 19, 1912.

Finances were his immediate concern. He began his administration with a deficit of $28,000 in the contingent fund. To rectify this situation he began immediately to cultivate the churches and to urge upon them the need of regular and annual contributions. This had been neglected to some extent in the previous administration. Although Dr. Kollen had secured large gifts for buildings and endowment, he had been less successful in winning regular and constant support. From 1901–1911, direct contributions from churches had amounted to a total of only $1300. President Vennema was determined to change this situation. By preaching in the churches, by correspondence, by meet-

146

Ame Vennema, president, 1911-1918.

ing with consistories, he was able to make some immediate progress. In 1908/09, only eighty-five churches made any contributions to the operating budget. Seven years later, there were more
than two hundred churches, with total contributions in the

amount of $8562. By 1918, the annual contributions were more than $4000 a year. With frugal management and increased help from the churches and the Board of Education, R.C.A., he began to show small balances in the annual budgets. The operating budget in 1918 had risen to more than $40,000 with no deficiency.

The tide in the financial affairs of Hope College had definitely turned. President Kollen's skill in securing substantial gifts for buildings and endowment from individuals of large means, was matched by President Vennema's success in the improvement of congregational benevolences for the operating needs. This does not mean that President Vennema neglected the endowment funds. In the first few years, he worked closely with President Emeritus Kollen. Later he used with some success financial agents such as Professor Raap and the Reverend G. De Jonge. In 1913, he proposed to the Council that a jubilee fund in the amount of $40,000 be raised in advance of the semicentennial year. This plan was endorsed by the General Synods of 1914 and 1915. Actually the amount raised was $56,000 including a legacy of $15,000 from the Jesup estate and $2500 from Mrs. Ralph Voorhees. By 1916, the permanent fund amounted to $518,000 including annuities in the amount of $107,000 and trust funds in the amount of $27,000. In the year 1916/17, the constitution of the college was amended to make possible the investment of funds in securities that were legal for savings banks in Michigan.

Athletics

In 1911, when President Vennema took over the presidency of Hope College, intercollegiate athletics were still under the ban. The Council had not given permission for playing games outside of the city. There had been frequent petitions to lift the ban, but favorable action had not yet been taken. Students complained that since the Council was composed of clergymen, for the most part, the members favored no programs except the theological. When the Michigan Intercollegiate Athletic Association made basketball an official sport in 1911, the situation at Hope became more exasperating, since the college developed superior teams but was not allowed to join the M.I.A.A. In the fall of 1913, the basketball team defied the rules and was suspended. The Student Council requested permission to hold a mass meeting on the campus. When their request was denied, they were invited by the mayor of the city to hold their meeting in the city hall. The situation was further complicated by the fact that there was a feeling that the students had been abetted by some members of the faculty as well as by the city authorities. A resolution was adopted by the faculty as follows:

> The President was entirely within his rights in suspending the basketball team for violating the out-of-town rule. It was only the lawless interference and flagrant violation of their own wise and law-abiding constitution that the Student Council headed the student strike. The revolt of the student body was without justification, and the strike for recognition, so called, is only to be condemned.[1]

The strike was soon settled, but it gave the students another opportunity to put some pressure upon the administration. At the Council meeting, the President read the following statement:

> There is a matter of considerable importance to the Council upon which we would like a deliverance. There is an unwritten rule of the college, of long standing, which prohibits any of our athletic teams from leaving the city, during term time, in order to enter into a contest with outside teams. This rule is supposed to be in accordance with the wish of the Council as reflecting the sentiment of the churches, particularly in the Particular Synod of Chicago, from which we draw most of our students. So strong is the desire on the part of the students that they are constantly tempted to violate the rule out and out, or to evade it by not going as regular organization teams, but by forming a different combination known as a Pickup Team, and then going. This is a somewhat involved matter and a many-sided question, having a bearing upon the finances, the scholarship, the morals and college spirit of our student Body. The rule is more difficult to enforce because some of our students come from other of our church academies, having enjoyed the freedom before they came to Hope. What especially the writer of this report is desirous, is whether the Council would have us maintain this position or whether, according to the wish of the students, we may feel at liberty to recede from it, and if so, to what extent? Personally we have no disposition to deny to any student any pleasure, if it is thought that they may engage in it without working harm to themselves or to the good name of the college.[2]

---

[1] Preparatory school minutes, 1913.
[2] Minutes of the Council, April 1914.

No definite action seems to have been taken. In June 1914, the students presented another petition. This resulted in a motion to abolish athletics altogether. Wiser counsels prevailed and the matter was referred to a committee, which recommended that the petition be allowed subject to the appointment of a Board of Control, consisting of Professors Milton J. Hoffman and Wynand Wichers, representing the faculty, L. Hekhuis representing the alumni, and Messrs. M. Stegenga and G. Steininger the Athletic Association. There were the following restrictions: a three-year trial, parental consent, proper chaperons, and all games to be played after the close of recitations on Friday and in such time that the teams could be home by midnight of Saturday. There was to be no intercollegiate football. Another petition on April 25, 1916, asked for a coach. The Council approved this petition and promised that it would endeavor diligently to find someone qualified. The proper person was not found until John L. Schouten was chosen in 1920.

In June 1917, the Council received another petition with reference to intercollegiate football. This time the students pointed to the fact "that the only other college [Central College] under the care of the Reformed Church fosters this deservedly popular game with the apparent sanction of its constituency." In 1917/18 the Council granted the request by the narrow margin of nine votes to eight.

The Semicentennial

The high point in the Vennema administration was the celebration of the fiftieth anniversary of the incorporation of the college. Two men who had been expected to take leading parts in the celebration were missing, which took away some of the joy of the occasion. President Emeritus Kollen passed away on September 5, 1915, and Professor John Henry Kleinheksel died just a few days before the celebration. It was fortunate that the latter lived long enough to complete a brief history of the institution, which was published in the 1916 catalog. Both had married daughters of Albertus C. Van Raalte and were among the last links between the academy and the college. In the last five years three other professors had gone to their reward, who together had given more than 150 years of service, and "who thought it worthwhile to give their whole lives to the cause of Christian Education."[3]

For the first time in history, the General Synod honored the college by holding its official sessions in Holland. The Synods of 1884, 1895, and 1904 had made brief visits while holding their sessions in Grand Rapids. The Synod of 1916 was housed in the spacious Ottawa Beach Hotel on Lake Michigan, but held its official sessions in Hope Church, Holland. The Reverend Peter Moerdyke, Class of 1866, was honored and elected President of the General Synod. He was still in good health, meticulous in dress and appearance. For some time he had been a Lector in Theology at the college, and served on the Council for many years. He had received honorary degrees from Hope, Alma, and Heidelberg Colleges.

The celebration began on Friday, June 16, 1916. An academic procession began at Carnegie Gymnasium and moved west on 12th Street to River Avenue, where the procession was reviewed by the mayor and city officials. Teachers and pupils of the public schools formed ranks on three sides of Centennial Park to greet the procession. The procession returned to Carnegie Gymnasium by way of 10th Street. The program began at 10 o'clock with President Vennema presiding and welcoming the Synod to Holland. In his address of welcome he said:

> You find yourself in Holland,
> Not the land across the sea
> of windmills, dikes and gallantry;
> Its western namesake, the retreat
> Of the oppressed, the chosen seat
> Where enterprise and piety are happily combined,
> Free exercise and scope and fair reward, have
> Sought to find.[4]

He pointed to the successes of the college in the fields of scholarship and oratory, to the 248 graduates who had entered the ministry, and to 52 men and women who had gone into foreign mission fields.

The President of the Synod responded and said that he was proud that his lot had been cast in the early pioneer days and

---

[3] Hope College Bulletin, Nov. 1916.
[4] Hope College Bulletin, Nov. 1916.

in the struggle for the development of the college. Professor
Henry E. Dosker of the Class of 1876 read a long historical
poem, and the Reverend G. De Jonge of the Class of 1882 told
the story of the preceding years. The alumni address was delivered by the Reverend John M. Vandermeulen in his own
characteristic style. The address for the Council was given by
the Honorable Gerrit J. Diekema, Secretary of the Council since
1893. The Reverend Gerrit Dangremond of the Class of 1868
was present and pronounced the benediction. At three o'clock,
there was an excursion on Lake Michigan, and in the evening
the alumni dinner was held at the Ottawa Beach Hotel with
members of the Synod as guests. The officers of the Alumni
Association in 1916 were the Reverend W. J. Van Kersen, President, the Reverend Henry J. Veldman, Vice President, Wynand
Wichers, Secretary, and Edward D. Dimnent, Treasurer. The
gathering sang the alumni song composed by the Reverend
Henry Dosker of the Class of 1887 and arranged by Harris Meyer
of the Class of 1916. In 1916, the college alumni numbered 561,
of whom 310 were ministers, 40 doctors, 18 lawyers, and 107
teachers. The alumni song remained the official college song for
many years. The words are:

> Old Hope, thy sons around thee standing,
> Now raise their banner high above.
> To thee a song we sing,
> To thee their tribute bring
> A tribute of praise and of Love.
>
> Ye hosts of ancient classic worthies,
> Whom we loved or hated with a will,
> Your lore is half forgot
> But your memory is not,
> For your ghosts are haunting us still.
>
> As boys we dreamed of days before us
> Of a distant longed-for by and by,
> But now amidst the strife
> Of a busy carping life
> We look at the past and we sigh.
>
> Many a one is silent at the roll call;
> Never more they will cheer us on the way,
> But our love for them will last
> With the memories of the past,
> Of our careless and bright college days.

> In the past we loved our Alma Mater,
> In the present we will love her still,
> And we make this solemn vow,
> As we sing this ditty now,
> That our boys our places will fill.

Chorus

> Shout a shout, sons of Hope,
> Like a bugle blast.
> Alma Mater, sempiterna sit,
> Sing in jolly college lays
> Of our golden college days
> And the merry, merry life of the past.

On Saturday night, the Class of 1916 sponsored the Pageant of Hope. It was a historical pageant tracing the history of the college from the time that Van Raalte left the Netherlands to the present. Miss Anna Kolyn was the author of the words. Mr. Harris Meyer composed and directed the music, and Miss Christine C. Van Raalte, a great-granddaughter of Albertus C. Van Raalte, was a member of the cast, which was directed by Arthur Cloetingh. The Prologue read:

> 'Tis wondrous good when on the present day
> We count the miles we have covered one by one.
> And now a little nearer we have come
> To whom the goal is met thru Hope's day.
> Her golden milestone passed, with pleasure may
> Look back upon the goodly journey now
> And witness what the fifty years have done
> In this the Pageant of our Hope.

The commencement exercises were held on June 21. Five orations, and the valedictory by Miss Christine C. Van Raalte, marked the close of the semicentennial year. Honorary D.D. degrees were awarded to eight men who had distinguished themselves in the ministry and in law. Among them were Henry Hospers and John E. Kuizenga of the Western Theological Seminary, and A. Livingstone Warnshuis, a celebrated missionary in China.

World War I

The most serious threat to the continued progress of the college at the beginning of the second fifty years of corporate history was World War I. Although Europe had been a battlefield since 1914, American colleges were not deeply affected until the

United States declared war upon Germany and her allies in April 1917. In his annual report to the Council, Vennema expressed grave concern and solicitude as he viewed the prospects for the coming school year. In May, the enactment of the Selective Service Act brought the war nearer home, and it became clear that student enrollment and financial income would suffer. The Secretary of War and the college administration made every effort to counsel students to stay in college until called into service. The official bulletins announced that "for the time being, the government was most in need of munition, food, and educated men," and predicted that these would soon be in short supply unless the colleges, universities, and technical schools maintained their normal enrollment. The slogan for the hour was "Enlist for college and serve your country best." In the summer of 1917, the Michigan church colleges joined in a cooperative effort to spread this gospel among high school seniors and undergraduate students. But they were not easily persuaded, because they were young and patriotic and were deeply moved by the prospect of a war that they felt would make the world safe for democracy. Moreover, they preferred voluntary enlistments, which gave them the opportunity to choose the type of military service for which they seemed best fitted. By November of 1917, thirty-nine Hope men were already in service, and the college President declared,

Armistice Day Parade, 1918.

A dinner, in The Hague, given in honor of Gerrit J. Diekema, United States Envoy Extra-ordinary and Minister Plenipotentiary to the Netherlands, 1929-30. Mr. Diekema, of the Class of 1881, is seated third from the right.

> The regret and disappointment felt because we do not have as large an enrollment as last year are more than offset by the satisfaction and pride of knowing that Hope College is as ready to serve the nation in its need as she is to serve the church.

In his annual report in April 1918, the President said:

> For more than a year the somber cloud of war has hung over our land and has cast its shadow upon our institution. The call to the colors has been answered by no less than sixty-four of our young men and they are busy in all lines of service. Our students have felt it difficult to concentrate on their studies, yet they have applied themselves with commendable fidelity and have made creditable progress.

A month later, he reported that eighty-one men had left the college since the opening of the school year. War extension courses were introduced into the curriculum and servicemen were encouraged to take these courses by correspondence. In announcing the program, the President said:

> The emergency calls for vision, fortitude and energy. For the better days to come, Hope College is preparing, and as a step

in that direction, it proposes to inject its spirit into the Camp
and into the Barracks.

The President Resigns

Early in 1917/18 the President informed the Executive Committee of his intention to retire at the end of the school year.
He said: "I have now concluded seven years of service. I have
occupied the position one year longer than the average term
of American College Presidents." The Council pleaded with
him to withdraw his resignation, pledging their unanimous
support. The President, however, asked the Council, "in view of
all the circumstances affecting the situation, to accept his resignation." He was not in good health, and felt that a younger
person should be elected to meet the pressing problems that
would arise. Accordingly, he was made President Emeritus. He
passed away in 1925.

The Council passed resolutions praising the President for his
accomplishments in maintaining the standards of high scholarship, and for his efficiency in adding $100,000 to the permanent
funds and for the large increase in enrollment. The writer of
a historical sketch in the 1926 catalog eulogized him as follows:

> The President's financial sagacity was proved most by the fact
> that he kept the capital outlay at the lowest possible figure
> while he sought to pay the operating costs as they accrued.
> This too was the period of war strain and stress, and the burdens
> of oversight were greatly increased. But never did the Presi-
> dent waver from the clear and certain values which he laid down
> for himself. Finance was important, but scholarship remained
> the principal product of the college, a scholarship which was to
> guide the spiritual and moral welfare of the denomination to a
> large extent, and to go out beyond the denomination into so-
> ciety and into the civic and intellectual life. A new era was
> about to dawn. President Vennema in the last days of his ad-
> ministration had a sure message to give. He pointed the way
> for workers of the coming day. (p. 17)

In 1918, the official yearbook of the college, the *Milestone*, was
dedicated to President Vennema. It read:

> A gentleman of the old school, embodying all the virtues of
> Christian manhood, and possessing the grace of godliness, the
> charm of personality, and the power of eloquence — qualities that
> made him a peer on the platform and in the pulpit.

10: HOPE COLLEGE IN TRANSITION

SINCE ALL INSTITUTIONS are constantly changing, it is difficult to pinpoint transitions that deserve special mention. Change is inherent in education, because education is a process and not a static condition, and is always affected by the cultural and economic climate in which it operates. However, we can say with assurance that the twenty-five years beginning with 1890 were significant years in the history of the college. We are reminded of the words of John Harvard, who, when asked by the King what he was doing in the New World, replied, "I have planted an acorn, which, when it grows into a sturdy oak, God only knows what the fruit there of will be." In the forests of Michigan, Van Raalte had planted a tree which in 1890 was beginning to bear fruit.

In 1890, there were on the campus a few decrepit buildings, and the President's house, still unfinished and unoccupied. Eighty-five students were enrolled in the preparatory department, and a mere forty-seven in the college. Among the older professors were Scott, Kollen, and Doesburg. The younger men just coming to the staff were Henry Boers, John H. Kleinheksel, James G. Sutphen, and John H. Gillespie. Life on the campus was provincial, since most of the students were local boys of Dutch descent. There was no School of Music, there were no intercollegiate athletics, and no public dramatic exhibitions. There was little feminine influence since there were only six alumnae. By 1890, Hope College had not reached the stature of most of the church colleges in Michigan.

157

By 1916, the picture had materially changed. Under President Kollen, new buildings had been erected. A total of 232 students, in 12 distinct departments, were taught by 22 instructors. The alumni had formed an association which met once a year, to renew friendships and to pledge their loyalty and support. The college was now an appreciable factor in the cultural life of Holland and in the religious life of the Middle West. Alumni were bringing honor to their professions, and were fulfilling the prayers of the founders that their sons and daughters might become light-bearers in the dark places of the earth.

In this chapter, I would like to mention some significant changes. By 1916, Hope College was an institution accredited by the North Central Association of Colleges and Secondary Schools, a status which the college has enjoyed to the present time. The University of Michigan began to include Hope College in the list of colleges whose graduates were eligible to receive State College Fellowships for graduate work in the University. Another unusual honor came to two alumni, Milton J. Hoffman and Hessel Yntema, when they were chosen as Rhodes Scholars. Hoffman became a Latin Professor at Hope College in 1913, and in 1917 was elected President of Central College (Iowa). Later, he became Professor of Church History at New Brunswick Theological Seminary. Hessel Yntema was a distinguished son of illustrious parents, and became a Law Professor at the University of Michigan.

Students in the period began to insist upon a change in the manner of conducting the commencement exercises. Up to 1890, each graduate was required to prepare and deliver an oration at the annual commencement. The Class of 1889 had petitioned the faculty to omit the usual student orations and provide an outside speaker, and the request was granted. The Class of 1891 returned to the old style with an oration by every member of the class. On November 3, 1891, the Class of 1892 sent the following petition to the faculty:

> Whereas the Council has left the appointment of the Salutatory and Valedictory honors to the faculty, we, the Columbia Class of 1892 ask the faculty to appoint such honors.

The request was granted upon condition that each member prepare a thesis on a subject previously submitted by the faculty.

The delivery of the usual orations was omitted, and the Reverend G. Henry Mandeville, now Secretary of the Board of Education, R.C.A., delivered the address. Members of the Class of 1896 also petitioned the faculty to be excused from the delivery of an oration, giving as reasons that it was impossible to do justice to the treatment of any subject in the time allowed. The Council did not grant this request. But in 1897, the class was so large that it was impossible to continue the former practice. In 1904, the Council took no action when the class requested that one Senior be chosen to deliver the valedictory and that an outside speaker be chosen to deliver the main address. By 1916, some representatives were chosen by the class and some by the faculty, including the valedictorian. The Class of 1945 was the last to follow this custom.

In 1890, students began to insist upon written examinations rather than oral. Originally all examinations were oral and conducted by committees of the Particular Synod of Chicago. Upon the incorporation of the college, these duties were assumed by the Council. The chief objection was the fact that at the end of each quarter, students had to remain until the Council had finished its other business. In 1890 the students petitioned for a change, saying:

> Examinations as here conducted can hardly be satisfactory to either students or teachers. How can a half-hour examination, in which each student gets four or five questions, begin to show his knowledge. Let us hope that the college may soon adopt the plan of other colleges.[1]

In January 1905, the *Anchor* announced that "at the close of the year we witnessed the first trial of a new examination system. We welcome the change as a step in advance."

Changes in the Curriculum

The most significant change was in the field of science education. As time changed and the number of students increased, there were obvious reasons for a diversified curriculum. Slowly the faculty began to yield to these pressures. After it had been announced that courses in Science would be introduced as soon as proper facilities were available, some elective courses were

---

[1] Minutes of the Council, 1890.

introduced; but courses in Science were taught for their disciplinary value and not as a preparation for a profession. As late as 1890, most of the faculty still felt that courses in Science had no place in an undergraduate curriculum. As a result, Hope graduates found themselves at a great disadvantage when they entered professional schools. One of the early critics was Dr. John Vanderlaan of Muskegon, who said that Hope students did very well in one or two professional schools, but that they compared unfavorably in the field of science education. He said that the teaching methods were rudimentary and that the equipment was inadequate and often not worthy of the name. He upbraided the Council and faculty for their neglect of this field, and reminded the President that it was just as easy to raise $25,000 for a science laboratory as it was for a library.

President Kollen was not unaware of the need and took steps in 1893 to establish a Chair of Chemistry and Physics. To head the Chair, he brought D. B. Yntema, Hope 1876, from St. Johns, Michigan, where he was Superintendent of Schools. He had a Master's degree from Michigan State Normal College. In 1904, President Kollen added Dr. Almon T. Godfrey, Hope 1900, to the staff. In 1909, two departments were created, with Dr. Godfrey as Head of the Chemistry Department, and Professor Yntema Head of Physics. Professor Yntema retired in 1918, and died in 1920. All of his children were educated at Hope. His sons all earned the Doctor's degree, and his daughter a Master's degree. One of the sons, Dwight Yntema, Ph.D., taught at Hope for twenty years and retired in 1967. Mrs. D. B. Yntema was still living in 1967 at the age of 100 years.

While Dr. Godfrey was a Medical Doctor and not a professional chemist, he must be given credit for laying the foundation of a strong Chemistry Department. He began to use his top students as laboratory assistants and prepared them for graduate work. One of the first graduates was G. J. Van Zoeren, Hope 1912, who went to the University of Illinois as a graduate student. The first Hope alumni to earn the Ph.D. in Chemistry were Harry Kremers, Gebhard Stegeman, and Edward Wichers, all of the Class of 1913. Kremers went into Industrial Chemistry. Gebhard Stegeman taught at the University of Pittsburgh for more than thirty years. Edward Wichers went to the Bureau of

Standards, Washington, D.C. He became Head of the Chemistry Division and later was appointed Associate Director of the Bureau. Soon Hope College began to be a leader in the preparation of chemists for higher degrees. Dr. Godfrey died after a brief illness in 1923 and was succeeded by Dr. Gerrit Van Zyl, one of his pupils.

In 1899, the President took the second step and established a Chair of Biological Science under the care of Samuel O. Mast. Mast resigned in 1908 to earn a Ph.D. degree, and rose to distinction in his field at Johns Hopkins University. In the fall of 1909 Frank W. Patterson came to head this department. He had earned a Ph.D. degree at Harvard, and was an able and successful teacher, although somewhat eccentric in his teaching methods. But his students loved him, and after his death established the Frank W. Patterson Prize in Biology.

Similar progress was made in teacher education. There was no attempt to establish a formal curriculum in Education until 1899, when a four-year course was set up, beginning in the preparatory school. A distinct Department of Education was established under Adoniram J. Ladd in 1898. The first Seniors to receive Provisional Certificates were seven members of the Class of 1900. These Provisional Certificates could be converted into Life Certificates by giving evidence of three years of successful teaching. The number of students interested in teaching increased greatly, and by 1916, sixty-eight alumni were teaching in the public schools of Michigan.

By 1916 all the departments had increased their offerings, which were arranged in five groups. Classical, Philosophical, Natural Science, Modern Language Mathematics, and Modern Language English. In addition to the required courses in each group, a sufficient number of electives might be chosen to make thirty units of one hour of daily work for twelve weeks.

Extracurricular Oratory

There was great interest in speech and oratory in the period. Oratory had never been a lost art, since most of the students were preparing for the ministry. Formal courses in public speaking, called Elocution, became a requirement. But the fame of Hope College in oratory really began when John B. Nykerk be-

A group of students ready to board a train for the oratorical contest at Albion College, 1905.

gan the teaching of Elocution. He had unusual gifts in the interpretation of the English classics. In 1897, he was instrumental in organizing some of the Michigan colleges into the Michigan Oratorical League. The contests between representatives of the various schools began in 1899. The first contestants were John W. Beardslee, Jr., Albertus T. Broek, and Cornelius Vander Meulen. There is an amusing account of one of these contests when a large number of students accompanied the orator.

> One hundred students and friends boarded a special train for Kalamazoo. Away they sped along the Allegan line, toward their destination. All were in a flutter of expectancy and confidence in the ability of their representative. "Nothing but first place is good enough for Hope," they shouted as they passed through village after village. Evil forebodings were present as soon as Kalamazoo was reached. Save for the former Hope students, not a soul came to meet them. Not even the mighty college yell with

the Indian war whoop could waken the sleepy Kalamazooites. — — — Eight orators competed. Kalamazoo was announced for first place and Hope was put at the foot of the ladder. Is it any wonder that the boys and girls were disappointed. If sermonettes and pedagogical, historical summaries are to gain place in these contests, and no allowance is made for originality of style, manner of presenting a subject, if gestureless rehearsals, barren of all enthusiasm and spirit is to count for more than fire of soul and body, Hope certainly was utterly lost. But as long as oratory is the outward expression of deep convictions, the judgement of the judges is inexplicable. Hope, nor her friends, wish to kick against a righteous judgment. Evidently something was wrong. One thing is certain, that unless the League makes laws according to which the standards of oratory may be judged, then the contests will be less than useless. However, the boys did not lose their spirit. The first rays of dawn began to glimmer when Holland was reached, and soon all noise was laid aside, and Morpheus gently clasped the weary heads and minds to his bosom and all cares were soon forgot.[2]

In 1903, A. J. Muste took first prize in the state contest with his oration on John Sobieski. Muste won second place in the interstate contest held at Cleveland, Ohio.[3] In 1912, the Women's Division of the Michigan Oratorical League was organized and Irene Staplekamp (Dykstra) took the honors. In 1913, Cornelius Wierenga took first place in the Men's Division. In 1916, Hope contestants took first place in both contests, Anna Kolyn (Elferdink) winning the honors for the women, and George Steininger for the men with his oration, "The Military Uniform and the Christmas Tree." In the interstate contest, and again in the national contest, Steininger won first honors. In five successive years, beginning in 1916, Hope's orators were victors in five contests, with three dual victories in the period.

Two prizes were established which greatly stimulated competition in oratory. The J. Ackerman Coles Debating Prize was founded in 1906. The award was a bronze bust of George Washington. The first contest was held in 1907 and was won by Peter H. Pleune. The second was in 1910 and was won by Clarence P. Dame. The third, held in 1913, went to Jacob Heemstra,

---

[2] Ottawa County *Times*, May 11, 1900.

[3] A. J. Muste went on to become a leading pacifist and advocate of nonviolent action; upon his death in 1967, tribute was paid him throughout the world.

and the fourth, held in 1916, was won by George Steininger. The
A. A. Raven Prize in oratory was established in 1908. The
winner of this award was also the representative of the college
in the Michigan Oratorical League.

Drama, Music, and Literary Societies

As in nearly all other church colleges, drama was late in
coming. This was due to the prevailing religious hostility to
the theater. No public exhibitions were allowed until 1904,
when the Class of 1904 presented *Antigone* by the Greek drama-
tist Sophocles. Translated by Professor Dimnent, it was shown
privately to the faculty, and when approved by them, was pub-
licly presented. Five years elapsed before another play was
presented. This was a Temperance Play, given by the Class of
1909 under the coaching of Professor Vandermeulen. There
were several performances and it was financially successful. The

*Sophocles' "Antigone," presented by the Class of 1904. Played by an all-
male cast. It was the first play produced at Hope College.*

The orchestra at Hope College before the turn of the century. The first orchestra was organized in 1893 through the efforts of Professor John B. Nykerk.

class left as a memorial the stone steps from the gymnasium level to the lower campus. Once again, seven years elapsed, until another play was presented by the Senior Class of 1916. The next year a Hope Dramatic Club was organized by James Muilenburg, and public exhibitions became popular.

Great progress was made in music education between 1890 and 1916. In 1890, the *Anchor* noted:

> A Glee Club is at last a reality. The child is not yet well matured but it already has some color. With Nykerk as a nurse it will soon make its influence felt in the social world.

In 1893, the name of John Bernard Nykerk first appears in the college faculty list as Professor of Music and Assistant Professor of English. In 1895, a Glee Club of thirty voices was giving public concerts. In 1900 the Glee Club became the Choral Union and gave yearly concerts. By 1916 there was a Men's Glee Club and a Ladies' Glee Club. Upon the completion of Voorhees Hall, studios and practice rooms were available and enrollment in the School of Music increased rapidly. Music in 1916 was still extracurricular.

National Greek Letter societies have always been discouraged at Hope. In the semicentennial year the catalog said:

> We have no Greek Letter fraternities, which are often expensive and are apt to divide the students into discordant classes. As the student's life is largely the formative period of the professional man's character, and since man's usefulness depends much upon his sympathy with men, irrespective of classes, it is, therefore, desired that a democratic spirit should characterize the Christian college. Moreover, plain economical living is encouraged in order that the young, not favored with an abundance of the world's goods, may be able to acquire a liberal education. In our opinion, fraternities and chapter houses do not lend to such mode of living as we desire for our students.

The Fraternal Society had its ups and downs until reorganized in 1890, after a suspension of a few years. In December 1890, the *Anchor* said, "The Fraternal Society has awakened from its deep sleep with a new vigor." The Cosmopolitan Society was organized in 1890, and the Ladies' Literary Society came into ex-

The Anchor *staff, 1895. Edward D. Dimnent is seated in the front row, second from the right.*

istence during the same year. In 1902, it was reorganized and called the Minerva Society. In 1905, the college girls organized the Sorosis Society and left the Minerva Society, which continued for the girls of the preparatory school. A Dutch literary society called the Ulfilas Society was organized by Professor Doesburg. Among the first officers were Samuel Zwemer and Albertus Pieters. By 1916 it had been disbanded, only to be revived by Professor Thomas E. Welmers in 1925. In the semicentennial year, the following societies were in the college: Fraternal, Ulfilas, Sorosis, Cosmopolitan, Knickerbocker, Delphi, and Philadelphian. The Pleids, organized in 1916, were a group of women studying French Drama, and the Phi Beta Epsilon in 1896 were studying Belles Lettres.

Public Lecture Course

A public lecture series was organized by Professor J. B. Nykerk soon after he began to teach. At that time, the college owned only one small musical instrument, which was in the chapel and closely guarded against student use. Professor Nykerk began a public lecture series in order to provide funds for the purchase of musical instruments. It was very successful for a while, as talent of superior quality was brought to the campus for the students and other patrons. The first instrument purchased was a Steinway grand piano for Winants Chapel. In 1918, Dr. Nykerk became discouraged and abandoned the program, saying:

> I assumed charge of the lecture course because of my desire to start a School of Music. Kollen said "go ahead and I will stand by you" in case of loss. I never consented to this. Now comes the World War and I am forced to relinquish the job.[4]

He also found that the opening of the Knickerbocker Theater in Holland was cutting into the sale of season tickets. Nykerk incurred some losses, for which he gave the bank his personal notes. When he concluded this work, he sent the cancelled notes to the Council and also delivered a savings book showing a balance of $558, which he had set aside to use for the erection of a Y.M.C.A. in Holland. Over the period he purchased musical instruments and other necessities, and gave more than a thousand reference books for the library.

---

4 Council file, in College Archives.

The football team in 1895.
Upper row, l. to r.: E. Kelder, Wm. Van der Haart, M. Hyink, John Banninga.
Seated, l. to r.: J. De Bey, H. Schipper, H. Sluiter, H. J. Wiersum, A. L. Warnshuis.
Reclining, l. to r.: J. Kuizenga, F. C. Warnshuis.

Physical Education

Over the years, there had been sporadic attempts to organize baseball and football teams. In 1893, Professor Erastus Whitenack came to the campus. He received permission to train a football squad made up of college and academy boys. Henry Sluyter was the captain, and at least one game was played, with the Holland City Newsboys, which the varsity team won. In 1895 there was a good team, of which A. L. Warnshuis was the captain. Suits were provided and many challenges were received — and declined — from out-of-town teams. Since the rules did not allow out-of-town games, interest in sports decreased. In 1892, the old gym reverted to its original use and interest in a program of physical education got a fresh start. A running track was installed and some physical apparatus was purchased. Girls were given permission to use the gym one afternoon a week, and a basketball team called the Basquettes was organized.

Samuel O. Mast came to the college in 1899 to teach Biology. He had had some training in Physical Education, and volunteered his assistance. The catalog for 1899/1900 announced:

> Classes in dumb bells, Indian clubs, chest weights, etc. are held daily at such hours as best to accommodate the students. By proper use of the advantages offered in this direction, they acquire physical strength needed to endure the mental strain incident to student life. While physical culture is valued highly, it is not encouraged at the expense of education and morality.

In 1900 the Council made three hours of work in Physical Education compulsory for Freshmen. The Ottawa County *Times* on March 20, 1900, said:

> In this respect Hope College is falling in line with other institutions. The students may consider themselves fortunate in having for an instructor a man as well qualified for the work as S. O. Mast.

An item in the same paper reports:

> The baseball team is in readiness for the season's work. Hope athletes now have brand new blue shirts, through the kindness of the ladies.

The first girls' basketball team, 1905.
Lower row, l. to r.: Theodora Thurber, Mina Coggeshall, Lilla Thurber, Hannah Hoekje, and Jennie Veneklasen.
Upper row, l. to r.: Ada Lahuis, Alyda De Pree, Edith Hodge, Maude Turnbull.

The erection of Carnegie Hall not only provided excellent facilities for a well-rounded program in Physical Education, but it also furnished a playing floor for basketball which was among the finest in the state.

Intercollegiate Athletics

In the eighties, organized athletics began to be a normal part of college activities in most of the Michigan colleges. The University of Michigan had a well-organized sports program as early as 1884. The first football game between two Michigan colleges was played in 1884 between Albion and Michigan. In 1887, the Michigan Agricultural College, Hillsdale College, and Olivet College competed in a field day. The Michigan Intercollegiate Athletic Association was founded in 1888 with Albion, Michigan Agricultural College, Hillsdale, and Olivet as charter members. This association sponsored a field day in May 1888. Spurred on by these examples, Hope students began to manifest a greater interest in athletics and became more restive under the restrictions imposed by the Council. Although Hope College was not a member of the M.I.A.A., its teams began to receive challenges from other institutions. In June 1891, the *Anchor* says:

> To the unspeakable relief and joy of many college presidents and professors, the baseball and football craze is gradually subsiding. There is much less interest shown this year than three or four years ago. But whether this is a cause for congratulations or of grave concern is not yet plain. There is a disposition which leads to an undue fostering of the mental qualities -at the expense of physical sports or enjoyment.

In the *Anchor* for October 1899 appeared an article signed "Signatos," which caused a flurry in the faculty. The title of the article was, "The Student Partner in College Administration." It was essentially a protest against the ban on intercollegiate athletics. The writer posed the question why students should have no voice in decisions of this kind. But the President and the faculty interpreted the article to favor student government. "Signatos" replied in the November issue. He asserted that the article was misunderstood, that the students did not advocate anarchy and that they were not asking for the right to choose their instructors as had been alleged, but that the article was intended to voice student grievances in the matter of athletics.

In the same year, the college catalog said:

> Believing that intercollegiate athletics have a strong tendency to interfere with regular work, and they generally are not helpful to the development of Christian Character, it is held that a denominational college like ours cannot afford to support it.

By that time the most progress had been made in basketball. The Annual in 1905 could say:

> In one department at least, Hope College need yield the palm to no one. Her success in baseball and football may ebb and flow, but when she turns out a basketball team, definite results can be expected. Last year Hope had a basketball team that could easily lay claim to state intercollegiate honors. That such a banner cannot be landed at Hope this year is due only to the fact that intercollegiate athletics are under the ban.

This team was composed of Abraham Muste, Peter Pleune, Henry Vruwink, Judson Kolyn, George De Kruif, John C. Hoekje, and

The first basketball team to win a championship, 1907.
Upper row, l. to r.: A. J. Van Houten, manager, J. A. Roggen, H. Oltmans, H. Rottschaefer, J. Vruink.
Middle row, l. to r.: H. Vruwink, P. Pleune, M. Stegeman.
Bottom row, l. to r.: Geo. De Kruif, A. Veenker.

August Veenker. The manager was R. H. Nichols and the student coach was George De Kruif. The team was organized by Peter Pleune, who came to the preparatory school in 1901. There were no eligibility rules, except that members of the team had to maintain an average of 85 percent. Peter Pleune played through his entire course of eight years, and Veenker played for six years. By the fall of 1905, the team joined the Interurban League, and in 1906/07 won the championship of the league. Finding it difficult to find competition in this league, the team began to play Michigan Agricultural College, Notre Dame, Hull House, Davenport, and Iowa College. By the time of the semicentennial, the college was in position to make an application for admission to the M.I.A.A. and compete in all sports except football. However, it was still without a full-time athletic director. A petition from students, dated April 25, 1916, was presented to the Council at its April meeting. Part of the petition reads as follows:

> Whereas the inability of Hope to perform successfully and to gain a place of honor and supremacy along athletic lines, has been largely due to the lack of able leadership and coaching, we the undersigned students and friends of the college request that in engaging professors and teachers for the ensuing year, the Council engage a person, part of whose duty it shall be to coach and supervise all branches of athletics in said college.

The Council approved the request and promised that they would endeavor diligently to find a person who could qualify in these two capacities.

There were many other evidences of the changing college. The first college Annual was produced in 1905 and dedicated

> To the Pilgrim Fathers of the west, those brave heroic souls who toiled that we might triumph, sowed in tears that we might reap with joy; who in their vast unfaltering faith, saw through the distant darkling vista of the future trail, arise the sure fulfillment of their glorious hopes. . . .

In March 1916, an official college yell was chosen after a contest among the students. It read:

> H-O-P-E Zip Rah Bang
> Liliukalani and a Li Hung Chang
> Boom Zah, Ta Rah, Calliope
> Bow Wow, Yum, Yum, Rah, Rah, Hope

Dedication

To the "Pilgrim Fathers of the West," the brave, heroic souls, who toiled that we might triumph, "sowed in tears," that we might "reap in joy;" who, in their vast, unwavering faith, saw through the distant darkling vista of the forest trail, arise the sure fulfilment of their glorious hope,—do we, their children, in loving and respectful memory, dedicate this book . . . . .

The dedication of the first annual, 1905.

And for the pageant in 1916, Harris Meyer and Arthur Cloetingh published a Hope College Song Book. It contained all the old alumni songs and some new ones such as "The Orange and Blue," and a song composed by Henry Pasma and set to music by A. J. Kolyn. Only the chorus is familiar:

> In that dear old town, Holland, Michigan,
> By the inland sea,
> Stands Hope College. O how I wish again ever there to be.
> Alma Mater loyal, true, we will ever be to you,
> When we're old, our song this still will be, H-O-P-E

About the only thing that had not changed was the cost of going to college. There were no tuition charges, and incidental fees were eight dollars per term. Board at Voorhees Hall was three dollars per week, and if that was too much there were at least two cooperative boarding clubs.

11: SPIRITUAL CLIMATE

IN HIS ADDRESS in 1866, the Reverend Isaac N. Wyckoff said, "It is intended that the college shall be a seminary of evangelical religion as well as of secular education." This surely was the intention of the founders, who labored under the conviction that a well-rounded education included the study of religion. It was for that reason that formal Bible study and required chapel attendance were asked of all students. The practice of required chapel began with the Reverend John Van Vleck, who met all the students for prayers at eight o'clock in the morning, and all those who lived in Van Vleck Hall at 9:30 in the evening. The whole student body might on occasion absent themselves, not so much because chapel was unpopular, but in the spirit of fun. The faculty conducted the services in rotation except when city clergymen were invited to conduct the service. Alumni sometimes came back to regale the students with amusing stories of the pranks they played when they were in school. Immediately after such addresses, there was a rash of pranks to divert the regular routine. Sometimes visiting dignitaries came to speak. In that case, the first-hour classes would be much shorter than usual. But there was very little criticism of required chapel until recently.

And so it was with required Bible courses. In the early days, most of the students were preparing for the ministry. By 1916, 63 percent of all the male alumni had entered the Christian ministry. By 1926, there were about a thousand alumni of whom four hundred were ministers, missionaries, or theological pro-

174

fessors and students. A Department of Sacred Literature was established by Principal Phelps, even before the college was incorporated. The early curriculum included Harmony of the Gospels, Moral Science, and two terms of Evidences of Christianity. The last-mentioned course was the capstone of all the work in Bible until thirty or forty years ago. The courses were taught by such worthies as Professors Oggel, Crispell, John J. Anderson, and John H. Gillespie. No formal department was established until the Kollen period, when a Department of Bible and Ethics was organized and placed in charge of the Reverend J. Talmadge Bergen, the pastor of Hope Church. Later these courses were taught by full-time faculty members such as Professors J. M. Vandermeulen, John W. Beardslee, Jr., and John E. Kuizenga. Professor Paul E. Hinkamp came from Cedar Grove Academy in 1918 to occupy a Chair of Bible and Philosophy. In 1922 two separate departments were created, with Professor Hinkamp taking the Philosophy Chair and Professor Albertus Pieters taking the Chair of Bible. Since 1945 courses in Bible have multiplied, and the staff is now composed of a number of outstanding men in the field.

A YWCA group, 1931.
Upper row, l. to r.: E. Steketee, A. Koeman, B. Olgers.
Second row, l. to r.: J. Van Oss, M. Klooster, B. Siebers, H. Paalman, F. Hinkamp.
Seated, l. to r.: A. Brunson, M. Lordahl, R. Haldane, L. De Wolfe.

The Student Volunteers, 1923.
Top row, l. to r.: Blaauw, Korver, T. Vander Ploeg, Schermer, J. Vander Ploeg, Veneklasen, Timmer, M. De Young, Dykstra.
Third row, l. to r.: Hoeksema, Harsevoort, Klow, Iben, Kruyf, Broekema, Keizer, Kleinheksel, Everse.
Second row, l. to r.: Decker, Veldman, Top, Karsten, Kuyper, Van Kersen, D. Schermer, Buikema, Bonner.
Bottom row, l. to r.: Rynbrandt, Rottschafer, Van't Hof, Hogenboom, De Yong, S. De Young, Vander Spek, Temple, Van Zanten.

The Christian Organizations

In 1878, the college was invited to send delegates to the state Young Men's Christian Association convention held in Ann Arbor. Messrs. J. P. De Jong and Sybrant Wesselius attended as delegates and were much impressed. Upon their return they made a report to the students, with the result that a Y.M.C.A. was organized with J. P. De Jong as the first president. The Young Women's Christian Association was not organized until 1901, although for five years previous to this the young women had held weekly prayer meetings. The first president was Grace Hoekje, who later became Mrs. Gerrit Hondelink. Joining in an association Union, these two organizations became responsible for most of the social and religious activities of the college. They conducted Bible and mission study classes, and began to conduct Sunday school classes in outlying places. In 1912, the report of the college to the 'General Synod indicated that the Union was conducting six Sunday schools with thirty teachers. They conducted the yearly receptions for new students, and many of the social activities of the day. Important arms of the association were the Student Volunteers and the Home Volunteers, later known as Alpha Chi. Professor Paul E. Hinkamp was largely responsible for the activities of the group.

The Minutes of the General Synod indictate that in 1917, under the direction of the Student Volunteer Band, students and faculty assumed the salary of John D. Muyskens, Principal of the Madanapelle High School in India. During the school year 1927/28, students and faculty had built up an endowment of $10,000 for the support of a Hope alumnus in India. No one can overestimate the importance of the Union in the religious life of the campus, and nearly every student was a member of it. But there came a time when the students thought that the Union had outlived its usefulness, and the two associations were replaced by the National Student Christian Association, which worked with smaller groups. National leaders addressed the annual retreats.

In 1907, Margaret Sangster came to the campus to address the students. Impressed by the religious character of the college, upon her return to her home she composed a processional hymn to be sung to the tune of "The Son of God Goes Forth to War." This processional was sung at every commencement until 1946. The words are as follows:

The Home Volunteers, 1923, later called Alpha Chi.
Top row, l. to r.: Minnema, P. DeGraff, De Boom, Parsons, H. Mentink, De Maagd, C. W. Lubbers.
Second row, l. to r.: Scherpenisse, Ten Hoeve, Borst, Bruinix, Van Farowe, Prins, Poole, De Moor, Kots.
Bottom row, l. to r.: Vruwink, Nyboer, Roughgarden, Dykhuizen, B. Wierenga, Van Lare, R. Lubbers, Kinkema, Roos.

For Alma Mater fair and true,
The steadfast and the strong,
With ardor ever flaming new
We lift a loyal song.
Of stainless name, of spotless fame
Before her vistas ope;
Thy sons and daughters loud proclaim
The radiant name of Hope.

Her children bear her lessons forth
To many lands and far
And east and west, and south and north
Her pride those children are.
Here burns the torch that lights the way
To learning's hoary steeps:
Here with her students day by day
New stores of wisdom deep.

For God and native land and man
In every clime and zone
We pledge our strength for what we can
Before Jehovah's throne.
Oh cherished mother, here we stand
Thy band of students true
And heart to heart, and hand to hand
Our ardor flames anew.

Prayer Days

In the early days, there was a Day of Prayer for Colleges. Students looked forward to this day because classes were dismissed and the meetings in Winants Chapel were addressed by notable ministers. The writer recalls one of these. The speaker was the Reverend James I. Vance of Nashville, Tennessee. Shortly after his departure, each student received a free copy of his book *The Altar Stairs,* a book which I still cherish. In the spring of the year there was an annual week of prayer, more recently called Religious Emphasis Week. A report to the General Synod in 1887 said that fifty-two students made confession of their faith as a result of the week of prayer.

Home Missions

On June 15, 1847, Judge John R. Kellogg, of the executive committee of the Allegan County Bible Society, addressed a letter to the secretary of the American Bible Society in New

York informing the Society about the needs of the Hollanders who had just arrived. He wrote as follows:

> They were of course wholly ignorant of our language, but being nearly all of them Protestant Christians (no Romanizers among them) they were well versed in the Scriptures, and it was soon discovered that the most ready, easy and instructive way for them to acquire our language, was to put into their hands the Bible in English, for by comparing it with their own, they soon got a knowledge of our language which is very necessary and which they are anxious for — and every man, woman and child among them seems anxious to possess an English Bible — but there are many who cannot pay without taking it from a scanty portion of their daily food — and these my dear sir are the groups for whom we seek aid from the Parent Society. — I could in truth add more, but is it necessary? Give to this people a Carte Blanche for what they want, and God will supply the vacuum.

In answer to this letter, the American Bible Society sent one hundred Bibles and two hundred New Testaments. The early Dutch settlements were considered home mission fields to be cared for by the Eastern section of the Reformed Church in America. When they became more prosperous, they gave first thought to the establishment of new churches in the Middle West. Only after they had done this did they begin to turn their attention to missions among the Indians, the Mexicans, and the Negroes. At one time, Van Raalte himself was seeking a call to do missionary work among the Dutch in South Africa. To catalog the home missionaries, it would be necessary to catalog all the ministers in the Middle West.

In the college, a Domestic Mission Prize was established in September of 1910 by the Reverend and Mrs. S. F. Riepma of Oklahoma City, and the first award on this foundation was made in 1911. It was given to a student writing the best essay upon a topic concerned with domestic missions. In 1915, Mrs. Walter Roe established a prize to be given to a student writing the best essay on "The American Indian." We must name as pioneers in domestic missions the Reverend G. Watermulder for a long career among the Indians in Winnebago, Nebraska, the Reverend and Mrs. William A. Worthington at Annville, Kentucky, and the Reverend and Mrs. John Kempers for a pioneer effort of long standing in Mexico.

The Hope and Wilhelmina Hospitals in Amoy, China, built by Dr. John
A. Otte in 1898. He was the first medical missionary of the Reformed
Church to China.

Foreign Missions

Interest in foreign missions began with the laying of the
keel of the missionary ship in 1864. Hope College soon achieved
a reputation for preparing men and women for the foreign
field. The first alumnus to go was the Reverend Enne Heeren,
who went to India in 1872 and returned for reasons of health
in 1877. The next was the Reverend Lambertus Hekhuis, who
also went to India and who died there in 1888. They were the
first of a great company of heroic souls who spent their lives
in foreign fields at a time when it was very difficult. Dr. John
Otte and his wife, Frances C. Phelps, went to China in 1887,
where they built a hospital at Siokhe, and the Hope and
Wilhelmina hospitals in 1898. Dr. Otte caught the pneu-
monic plague from one of his patients and died in China in
April of 1910. One of the most notable of all the foreign missionaries was Samuel Zwemer, Hope 1887, who has been called
the "Flaming Apostle to Islam." He was born in Vriesland,
Michigan, on April 12, 1867, the thirteenth of fifteen children.
After graduating from New Brunswick Theological Seminary,
he went to the most difficult of all mission fields, going to
Arabia while the Turks were still in control. He became the
forerunner of many who later went to Arabia. One of his first
books was Arabia, the Cradle of Islam. With John R. Mott and
Robert E. Speer, he organized the Student Volunteer Movement,

which has been credited with sending 14,000 men and women into the missionary field. Dr. Kenneth Scott Latourette ranks Zwemer among the great heralds of Christ in this country. In 1918 he established the Nile Mission Press, and was its editor for thirty years. In 1922, he was called to the Chair of Missions in Princeton Theological Seminary. He retired at the age of seventy and died in 1952. No one who has ever heard him speak can forget his flaming passion for missions. He was proud of Hope College, and several of his children became alumni.

The Reverend and Mrs. Albertus Pieters graduated in the same class with Zwemer in 1887, and went to Japan in 1891, where he originated "newspaper evangelism." They returned to America in 1925 and he taught Bible at Hope. Later, he was called to a chair in Western Theological Seminary. He was a great and inspiring teacher. His logical and scintillating mind was a great source of delight to his students. He became the author of several books.

The Reverend and Mrs. Harry Boot spent many years in China, and their children followed in their footsteps. The Reverend James Moerdyke went to Arabia in 1900 and remained there the rest of his life. He was a quiet, retiring person but thoroughly devoted to the cause.

In the Class of 1897 was the Reverend Abbe Livingston Warnshuis, who went to China in 1900, when the Boxer Rebellion was at its height and the siege of Peking was in process. In 1911, Warnshuis and the Reverend Henry De Pree were co-authors of *Lessons in the Amoy Dialect*. In 1914, Warnshuis moved to Shanghai, and in 1921 began his work as National Evangelistic Secretary; after a few years he became a leader in the International Missionary Conference. After living in London and New York he gave up the task and became interested in the World Council of Churches. In 1943 he was elected Treasurer of the Board of Direction, R.C.A., and was instrumental in transferring $250,000 from the Rutgers University endowment fund to Synod's Board of Direction. The income from these funds is used to assist students preparing for the ministry at Rutgers. He retired in 1953 and died suddenly on March 16, 1958.

Other missionaries of international fame were the Reverend and Mrs. Henry A. Poppen. They went to China in 1909 and remained until the Communists took over the country. He became subject to house arrest and was given a public trial and sent out of China. His later service was in Singapore, and now he is associate pastor of the Garden Grove Community Church, California.

The Reverend and Mrs. Bernard Rottschaefer went to India in 1900. Taking charge of the Katpadi Industrial Institute, he supervised the making of all the pulpit furniture and basement chairs for the new Dimnent Chapel. Mrs. Rottschaefer is now living in Holland, Michigan, following the death of her husband in 1967. Their children were all educated at Hope.

One other missionary needs to be mentioned. He is John Van Ess, Hope 1899, who went to Arabia in 1909 and founded a school for Arab boys at Basrah. This school was an important factor in the life and culture of Arabia. Boys were trained here who came to Hope College to complete their education. Many of them found places in the government and industry in Arabia. Because of his knowledge of Arabian life and culture, he was often asked for counsel by the United States government.

I wish it were possible to name all the Hope alumni who

The first commencement processio

heard the call to the foreign field. There were doctors such as Albert Oltmans, Edward Strick, Clarence Holleman, William Moerdyke, Lewis Scudder, Gerald Nykerk, and Bernardine Siebers. We hold them all in high honor — doctors, evangelists, teachers, nurses, and ministers. In 1941, the Women's Board of Foreign Mission published a list of 140 missionaries, all alumni of Hope College. Dr. Edgar Franklin Romig, President of the General Synod in that year, said:

> Hope's claim to fame is not alone in having an avowedly Christian institution, or again in having a notable record, but in the fusing of the two features. Within its walls, from the beginning, earnest devotion to the faith of the Bible and disciplined intellectual endeavor have flourished apace. The fruits have been a royal succession of graduates in the arts and sciences whose service to the world has been without measure.[1]

If the percentage of missionaries in each class is not as large as it once was, it is because of the great difficulties in the foreign fields and because graduating classes are much larger than before. This reduces the percentage of ministers and missionaries who devote their lives to the building of the church, in and outside their native country.

---

[1] See A Tribute to Hope College, 1941, in College Archives.

newly-erected college chapel, 1929.

12: THE DIMNENT ERA

ON JUNE 8, 1918, the Trustees elected Edward Daniel Dimnent to succeed President Vennema. For the second time in Hope's history the Trustees had elected a layman to guide the affairs at Hope College. The election surprised no one, because Dimnent had been with the college for a long time, and had been chosen Vice President in 1916. He carried a full teaching load, and in addition had been Registrar, manager of Voorhees Hall since its dedication in 1907, and Treasurer since 1915. Edward Daniel Dimnent was born in Chicago on August 14, 1876, and came to the preparatory school of the college, graduating in 1892. He received his A.B. degree from Hope College in 1896 as the valedictorian of his class of eight young men, all of whom, except Dimnent and John VanderVries, went into the ministry of the Reformed Church. Dimnent became a Tutor in 1897 and was elected Voorhees Professor of Greek in 1898, succeeding another brilliant classical scholar, the Reverend John H. Gillespie, who became Professor of Greek at New Brunswick Theological Seminary.

The present writer was a pupil of Dimnent for six years, and bears testimony to his keen scholarship and to his skill and success as a teacher. He was formally inaugurated on May 14, 1919. He was installed by President Emeritus Vennema, and the inaugural address was by Dr. William Liggett. The main theme of Dimnent's inaugural was the role of the state, the church and the individual in the educational process. In 1919 he was awarded three honorary degrees: an honorary L.H.D.

184

from Hope College, an LL.D. from Central College (Iowa), and a Litt.D. from Rutgers University. Since he was a bachelor, his sister, Mrs. Nellie Dykhuizen, and her family came to live with him in the President's house, and to assist him in his social obligations.

Students in Khaki

A revolutionary change took place in the program and curriculum in October 1918. On May 3, 1918, the Secretary of War addressed a circular letter to all institutions of collegiate grade, announcing plans for the provision of military service for college students during the emergency caused by World War I.

> The purpose was twofold — first to develop as a military asset the large body of young men in the colleges and, second, to prevent the unnecessary depletion of the colleges through indiscriminate volunteering by offering students a definite military status.[1]

Military instruction was to be provided in each institution of collegiate grade that would enroll, for this instruction, one hundred or more able-bodied students over the age of eighteen. Enlistees were to be inducted into the United States Army, liable to active service at the call of the President, but with the assurance that they would not be called into service until they reached the age of twenty-one, unless urgent military necessity made an order essential.

After much discussion and with a great deal of reluctance, the Council authorized the college President to make an application for the establishment of such a unit on the campus. The application was approved, and a unit of the Student Army Training Corps, familiarly known as the S.A.T.C., was organized on the campus. The unit was under the command of Lt. Jacobsen of the United States Army. He was assisted by Lts. Dabney and Friedlung and Sergeant Major Danforth, all of the regular army. Dr. H. H. Nichols was named Chief Surgeon and Cadet Hospers was named Acting First Sergeant. Carnegie Gymnasium served as barracks, canteen, and officers' quarters, while Van Vleck Hall was set aside as a dispensary and infirmary. Kitchen facilities were prepared on the third floor of Van Raalte Hall,

---

[1] Minutes of the Executive Committee, May 1918.

Edward D. Dimnent, president, 1918-1931.

which served as the mess hall. The members of the Corps were in uniform, under military discipline, and marched to Chapel and to their classes. Academic subjects were taught by regular members of the faculty, while military subjects were taught by army officers. The present writer taught the course in War Aims.

For the first time in the history of the college, men in khaki went to college with civilian men and women. Among the civilian students there was frequent resentment of the fact that the military tended to dominate the campus, while on the other hand, men in S.A.T.C. were often critical of men not in uniform. The S.A.T.C. was of value to the college only as it kept a large number of men in school and was a source of revenue. However, the situation was not a happy one. Conflicts of authority arose between the President of the college and the commanding officer. The signing of the Armistice brought the war to an end, and in December 1918, the S.A.T.C. was disbanded with proper ceremony.

An epidemic of influenza claimed the lives of two cadets, William Janssen and George Roosenraad. When the second semester of the year 1918/19 rolled around, the situation became normal and most of the 150 men who had seen service returned to complete their studies. The enrollment doubled and new standards of excellence were achieved.

General Education

Great changes were taking place in all areas of life, including education. The growing pressures of economic interests and the increasing dominance of science posed problems that were bound to be reflected in the changing purposes and standards in the field of education. All colleges were taking a look at their traditional·programs. In many cases, the humanistic studies began to suffer before the onslaught of technology, vocationalism, and specialization. As a classical scholar, it was natural that President Dimnent should continue to favor the classical tradition. Early in his career as Registrar, he had devised a system of requirements for graduation and arranged them in several groups. In his annual report to the Council in 1922, he expressed himself in his own characteristic style:

> What becomes of the student who browses without guidance in the fields of the intellect, and thrusts aside the ancient classics, those original sources of the thought upon which our western civilization is founded? He has heard so much sport made of Latin and Greek by his intellectual forbears, that he is convinced that they contain nothing worthy of his budding powers. He has taken with avidity to the modern social sciences, and finds himself at sea, because they have in a self-styled scientific spirit, started with nothing as a base, and have found their terminus in the same satisfying locus. It was characteristic of an age brought about by the intellectual chaos, and an unsound educational policy. But that kind cannot be the saviors of the world or of their own soul. But Hope College is in an enviable position to cope with the situation. It has held firmly to a conserva-

tive policy during all previous administrations. The elective
system has never dominated it, and the College was almost a
pioneer in the group system.[2]

In the same report, President Dimnent suggested that the
man of liberal training must be a man of universal knowledge,
and of its practical application. He proposed that the Trustees
consider

> whether the time is not ripe to modify all courses, that each
> student shall be required to cover a minimum amount of his
> work in the culture systems of the ancient world, either through
> the medium of the ancient languages, or through an adequate
> portrayal of the ancient civilizations in the English language.[3]

While he was unable to achieve this goal, he did succeed,
through the medium of the group system, in placing a new
emphasis on general education, with a minimum of free electives. Like his predecessors, he would have all of his students
strive for a broader knowledge, high ideals, and the possibility
of the Good Life, while at the same time relating their plans
and purposes to the realities of practical experience. He made
it clear that education was not for the intellect alone, and that
learning was not merely for learning's sake, but a preparation
for useful service in all areas of life. He had the conviction that
the highest service lay in responsible citizenship, and in a dedicated devotion to the Christian cause. To teach his pupils the
former, he composed a ten-point pledge of allegiance which his
students memorized and recited on all patriotic occasions. To
teach them devotion to the Christian cause, he suggested as
a motto "A purposeful Christianity."

This kind of thinking was reflected in the chapel service and
in the classroom, and in the administration of the academic
affairs of the college. In the early twenties, he divided the Chair
of Bible and Philosophy into two distinct departments. Paul
E. Hinkamp became Alumni Professor of Philosophy in 1922.
In 1923, the Reverend Albertus Pieters was named to the Chair
of Bible. The churches in the Classis of Holland developed a
strong interest in it, and for many years supported it in the
amount of $3000 a year. A similar attempt was made to have

2 Minutes of the Council, April 1922.
3 Ibid.

the alumni support the Philosophy Chair. A total of $7000 was raised for its support. The alumni had not as yet been conditioned to annual donations, and after a few years the plan was abandoned.

In June 1928, a Chair of Religious Education was established and Paul E. McLean was chosen as the head. He was given a year's leave of absence and assumed his duties in the fall of 1929. President Dimnent also established a Chair of Political Science with a legacy from the estate of Arend Visscher, the lone graduate of the Class of 1872. The following tribute to Mr. Arend Visscher appeared in the Holland *Evening Sentinel,* January 23, 1921:

> Mr. Arend Visscher died January 23, 1921. He was born in Holland of pioneer parents 71 years ago. He was a child of sturdy stock, a product of Christian training and the stern discipline of colonial life. Upon graduation from Hope College, he went to the University of Michigan to study law. He practiced his profession in Holland. From that day until the day of his death, Mr. Visscher was taken into the counsels of every important organization. He was part and parcel of Holland's business life and made a deep impression upon the social and religious life of the city. He was a charter member of the Third Reformed Church and of the Century Club. He became a member of the College Council in 1885 and was the Treasurer of the college from 1902-1915. He gave his time and ability to the cause as a member of the Executive Committee. He was one of the Alumni who was always present at the business meetings of the association, and every banquet was graced by his presence.

His college account book is found in the College Archives.

Beginning in 1919/20, the traditional three-term system was replaced by the two-semester plan. In the same year, the faculty adopted a proposal to award the A.B. degree with honors, and the first such degrees were awarded in June 1921. Christian De Jonge, Tena Holkeboer, and Evelyn Zwemer won the degree Summa Cum Laude, and Helen Bell and Emma Reeverts received the degree Magna Cum Laude. The traditional A.M., awarded to graduates completing three years of professional study, was abandoned after 1927. In 1928, the college enrollment passed the five-hundred mark, while the preparatory school enrollment reached a low of forty-three.

Because of the President's great interest in music, the faculty approved his proposal for a music curriculum leading to the Bachelor of Music degree. The first degree of this nature went to Cornelia Nettinga. In 1919/20, the President brought to the campus Mrs. Grace Dudley Fenton to teach voice and singing. He suggested to her that she organize a "B Natural Chorus" of girls chosen from the different literary societies. Meeting twice a week, this group soon became an accomplished group of singers, which in 1923 became the Girls' Glee Club. In 1924 it began to make concert tours in the Midwest, and in 1926 into the Eastern states. In 1925, the club entered a musical contest in Kalamazoo and won first place. In 1927, the club repeated this accomplishment at Hillsdale College, and in 1928 at Albion. The latter contest was judged by Professor Howard Hanson of the Eastman School of Music, who remarked, "I have given first place to the club, which performed the most extraordinary ensemble singing I have ever heard." Mrs. Fenton also organized a permanent Men's Glee Club, which made its first Eastern tour in 1930. In 1929, President Dimnent brought to the campus Mr. and Mrs. Curtis W. Snow. Mr. Snow was the college organist and director of music. He laid the foundation of music education, which has proved to be enduring. An unusual organization known as The Hope Trumpeters was organized by President Dimnent after he came back from New York City, where he had heard the Gloria Trumpeters.

Two large-scale pageants were produced. The pageant of 1926 was produced by the Senior Class, commemorating the sixtieth anniversary of the college. The words were written by Lois Brockmeir. Fred Olert was the director, and Paul Gebhard was the business manager. In charge of the music was John L. Kollen. The pageant was given before large audiences on May 31, June 2 and 3. In 1928 the alumni produced a pageant to mark the 300th anniversary of the Reformed Church in America. The words were written by a committee headed by Miss Hannah Hoekje. The production manager was Fred Olert, and the business manager was Simon Heemstra. The pageant in five episodes was shown in Holland on June 15, 16, and 19. It was also shown in Grand Rapids and Kalamazoo, supported by local groups.

In oratory and forensics, Hope students continued to take

superior ratings. Professor Nykerk, who had founded the Michigan Oratorical League, was now the dean of the league and its most successful coach. In the Men's Division, his students took five first places between 1917 and 1922 — Irwin J. Lubbers in 1917, Walter A. Scholten in 1918, Roscoe M. Giles in 1919, Harry Hager in 1920, and Simon Heemstra in 1922. In the Women's Division Gertrude Schuurmans took first place in 1918, Tena Holkeboer in 1920, Nella Cole in 1920, Marian Van Vessem in 1925, and Harriet Heneveld in 1926. There were dual victories in 1918, 1920, and 1922.

Changes in the Preparatory School

Until the year 1913/14, the preparatory school enrollment was larger than that of the college. After 1912 this began to decrease, due to the development of public education, and the establishment of the Christian High School in Holland by members of the Christian Reformed Church. President Dimnent gave great importance to this department, and in his annual report to the Council in 1919, he said:

> Strong efforts are being initiated for the increase of the Preparatory School numbers in as much as national statistics show that the Church must depend on these schools as their recruiting agencies for the work of the ministry and other religious factors. The strongest support of all the churches and of the General Synod should be given to this aspect of the work.[4]

In the year 1918/19, only seventy-five were enrolled. The next year the enrollment rose to ninety-seven, and the President said, "The increase is gratifying as it is an evidence of the success of the work which was done to enlarge this field of work." In the year 1920/21, the number of students increased to 134. The annual report said:

> Your attention is called to the steady growth of the Preparatory School, a fact which is in line with our desire, in as much as the aims of the institution receive strong recruits from secondary schools who will be adequately trained for collegiate and graduate work.[5]

But in 1926/27 there was a sharp drop and the enrollment

---

[4] Minutes of the Council, April 1919.
[5] Minutes of the Council, April 1921.

reached a low of forty-three. Until the year 1924/25, the faculty of the college taught classes in both departments. The North Central Association took note of the matter and the college was warned that a continued arrangement of this sort might jeopardize the accreditation of the college. As a consequence, efforts were made to bring about a complete separation of the two departments. Professor Thomas Welmers was named principal, and a separate staff appointed for the secondary school. A more radical change took place in the fall of 1928. The State Board of Education had increased its requirements in formal education courses. Fifteen hours of practice teaching and classroom observation were now required. With this in mind, the President suggested that the preparatory school become a free school with its own faculty, but under the supervision of the Council. College students would do their practice teaching and observation work in this high school. The plan was approved and the printing house on Columbia Avenue was rebuilt to provide classrooms and assembly rooms. Garrett Vanderborgh was named principal. Other members of the staff included Mildred De Pree, Adelaide Dykhuizen, Clarence De Graaf, and Edward Wolters. The school was named Hope High School and began operations in the fall of 1928. There was an immediate increase in enrollment, which reached a peak of 103 in the year 1931/32 and then began to decline again.

The razing of the old grammar school building left the Meliphone and Fraternal Societies without a home of their own. The Fraternal Alumni sought permission to erect or lease a fraternity house off the campus, and to conduct a financial campaign for funds. A special committee of the Board of Trustees suggested that they would not attempt to resist the efforts of so large an alumni group, but cautioned the alumni to consider the effect that this campaign might have on the solicitation of funds for the operation of the college, and also to consider what the moral effect might be upon students living in a chapter house. The idea of erecting a chapter house was abandoned and the Fraternal Society leased the Wheeler home on the corner of Columbia Avenue and 10th Street. Other societies soon followed suit. The Knickerbockers leased the house on the corner of Central Avenue and 12th Street now occupied by the Netherlands Museum.

The Emersonians leased the Beach house on the corner of Columbia Avenue and 12th Street where Kollen Hall now is located. Chapter houses, so long frowned on, now became the rule.

Changes in the Constitution

In 1922, the General Synod approved certain changes in the constitution of the college. This became necessary to correct certain practices in the composition of the Council that were in violation of its provisions. For example, the constitution provided for six members to be elected by the Synod, while nine had been elected and were serving. The constitution also provided for two members from each Classis in the Synod of Iowa. But since that time, the Particular Synod of Iowa had been organized and the Classes, within the Synod, began electing representatives. As amended, the constitution provided for nine members from the General Synod and two from each of the Classes in the Synods of Chicago and Iowa. The total membership was increased to forty. The original charter was renewed for a period of thirty years, and the corporate name now was changed to The Board of Trustees of Hope College. This cumbersome title created difficulty in later years when new buildings were being built with federal funds, and the corporate name was again changed to Hope College.

Business and Finance

The President made great efforts to improve the appearance of the campus. To secure the necessary funds, he sought the help of a committee of businessmen in the Classes of Holland, Grand Rapids, Muskegon, and Kalamazoo. Sufficient funds were raised for the complete remodeling of Van Vleck Hall, for the improvement of the athletic field, and for the completion of the fourth floor of Van Raalte Hall. The catalog announced that the athletic field was to be named Phelps Field and that the museum was to be designated as Scott Museum. Van Vleck Hall was converted into a dormitory for women. The old grammar school was razed to make room for two tennis courts made possible by the generosity of Mr. Cornelius Dosker of Grand Rapids, a frequent benefactor of the college.

Like his predecessor, President Dimnent adopted a conserva-
tive policy in the management of the business affairs of the institution. He, too, tried to keep capital outlay at the lowest
possible figure while seeking larger individual gifts and church
support for the growing needs of the college. But even then, income did not keep pace with the growing needs and there were
almost yearly deficits in the operating funds, until they totalled
$24,000 by 1924. The operating budget rose from $45,000 in 1918,
to $72,000 in 1921, to $92,000 in 1923, and to $133,000 in 1930.
Professor Albert Raap, who had been on the faculty since 1903,
gave valuable assistance as Financial Secretary from 1918–1924.
For the Eastern section of the church, President Dimnent employed the Reverend C. Muste of Brooklyn, New York. In 1922,
the President set a ten-year goal expecting to add $2 million to
the endowment funds. The rising prosperity of the twenties
promised some hope for the achievement of this goal, but it
became impossible when the gay prosperity of the early twenties
ended in the greatest financial disaster in our history.

Gradually, the denomination began to wake up to the needs
of the college. In 1921, the Reformed Church in America
launched a Five-Year Progress campaign to lift the sights of the
denomination along different lines and to increase the benevolent
giving. Although the campaign was not without value in raising
levels of benevolence, it had little effect on the immediate
financial needs of the college. In 1921, the General Synod also
authorized the Board of Education, R.C.A., to make a special
appeal to the churches to erase the deficits at Hope and Central
Colleges. In 1922, this Board was authorized to raise a centennial
fund of $100,000 for additional endowment of the two colleges.
Although not supported enthusiastically by most of the congregations, there were sufficiently large donations to make the
effort a successful one. Among these were donations of $25,000
from the Collegiate Church of New York City, $5000 from the
Harlem Reformed Church of New York City and $5000 from the
Ocean Grove Reformed Church of New Jersey. When the
General Synod met in Holland in 1929 in connection with the
dedication of the chapel, the fund was still $14,000 short of its
goal. $6000 was raised on the floor of the Synod, and before long
the first major effort of the denomination in behalf of the

John L. Schouten, first coach and athletic director, 1920-1962.

colleges became a success. Some hopes had been aroused by the Interchurch World Movement, in which the Reformed Church and the college were included, for large sums of money, but the movement was of short duration and failed to reach any of its goals.

To meet the growing budgets of the college, the President was forced to resort to tuition charges for the first time in the history

The
Memorial
Chapel

of the college. In 1920, the practice of collecting contingent fees was discontinued, and a tuition fee of $35 per year was substituted. Four years later, the fee was raised to $50. In 1925 it was increased to $60, to $100 in 1929, and to $135 in 1931.

Athletics

In 1920, John L. Schouten became Director of Athletics. Hope College was admitted to membership in the Michigan Intercollegiate Athletic Association in 1926 and the athletic fortunes of the college began to improve.

The Memorial Chapel

The crowning achievement was the erection of the Memorial Chapel. It was the culmination of many years of dreaming that some day Hope might have a chapel large enough to contain the student body, a chapel whose size and beauty might typify the place of religion on the campus. It was the fourth chapel for student worship since 1857. The first was a single room in Van Vleck Hall, the second was a drab frame building literally carved out of the forest by the students themselves. The third was Winants Chapel, more beautiful and larger than the others. The noblest of them all was the Memorial Chapel, built of steel and Bedford stone, in modern Gothic style, and impressive in both size and form. It was designed by W. K. Johnston of Chicago, who in earlier years had designed Graves Hall and Winants Chapel. The matchless stained-glass windows of the Memorial Chapel, executed by Zucchi, an Austrian from Venice, were replicas of famous European windows and bore representative symbols of medieval church history. These, together with its tower, 120 feet in height, made it the dominant structure on the campus. With its large auditorium for assembly and chapel purposes, adequate facilities for the religious organizations, its great organ and tower chimes, and its pulpit furniture, made of solid rosewood in Rev. Bernard Rottschaefer's Mission School in Madanapelle, India, it surpassed in beauty any college chapel in Michigan.

The main four-manual Skinner organ was the gift of the sons of Mr. Bernard Arendshorst, a pioneer baker in Holland. Other contributions to music in the chapel were the echo organ, by Mr. and Mrs. R. E. Vander Veen and Mr. and Mrs. Arthur Le Roy Dwight; the chimes, by the family of Mr. C. M. McLean; the harp and celeste, by Mr. and Mrs. Edward W. Freyling; and the grand piano, by Mr. and Mrs. Albert H. Meyer. The chancel window, depicting Christ blessing the children, was the gift of the sons of Professor J. H. Kleinheksel, a member of the faculty from 1885 to 1916; the rose window was the gift of the Class of 1916, and other memorial windows were made possible by the alumni, by the Women of Hope, and by the classes of 1901, 1907, 1925, and 1926.

The chapel was in keeping with the conviction that religion and education were two sides of the same shield, and with the personal conviction of the President that religious worship was part of general education. Planning, consequently, was started early in the President's administration, and he made substantial personal gifts to start the financial campaign in 1921. When the General Synod met in Holland in 1926, he announced that donations in the amount of $100,000 were in hand and that one half of this amount had been given by the Reverend and Mrs. William Bancroft Hill of Poughkeepsie, New York.

The cornerstone was laid on October 12, 1927, by Mr. C. M. McLean, Vice President of the Board of Trustees, and the principal address was by the Reverend H. J. Veldman, who spoke on "The Preeminence of the Christian Religion in the Life of a Denominational College." He remarked, "I lay no claim to the prophetic gift, but I venture the assertion that what we are doing here today, as friends of the institution, will prove to be the entering upon a new epoch in the history of Hope College." The dedication took place on June 7, 1929, in the presence of the General Synod. Addresses were made by the Reverend William Bancroft Hill on the subject, "Religion and Higher Education," and by the Reverend Malcolm McLeod of the Collegiate Church of New York on the subject, "What Does the Church of God Stand For?" The dedication reads as follows:

> In Memoriam
>
> In memory of all those who have given of their goods, meager or plentiful, for the maintenance and growth of Hope College,
>
> Who have shared freely with their wisdom, born of rich talent and courageous travail;
>
> Who as teachers have given long hours of consecrated toil in abundance of faith, yet with scant remuneration;
>
> Who as officers and trustees have taken added responsibilities upon themselves for no personal gain, and have, from almost nothing, builded nobly for the glory of God, for peace on earth, and for good will among men:—
>
> Hope College pays sacred tribute to all, the living and the dead, from whose valiant shield she has taken title to her own creed.[6]

The Commencement of 1929

The baccalaureate sermon was preached in the new chapel on June 15, 1929, by the Reverend William I. Chamberlain, Secretary of the Board of Foreign Missions. The organ and chimes were dedicated on June 17 by Walter Blodgett, organist at the University of Chicago; the first commencement in the chapel took place June 19. On June 27, there was an organ recital by Palmer Christian of the University of Michigan School of Music, concluding the dedicatory ceremonies.

---

6 See dedicatory booklet in College Archives.

The Depression

Just a few months after the dedication, the prosperity of the twenties came to a sudden halt, and the severest financial depression in the history of the country rocked the economy of all financial and educational institutions. The immediate causes were overproduction in industry, and in credit, and the prevailing optimism which pushed the price of securities far beyond their earning value. The stock market crash occurred in October 1929. Michigan was especially hard hit, because her economy rested to a large extent upon the automotive industry. Public and private educational institutions suffered heavy losses. The private institutions felt the blow most keenly because they were wholly dependent upon benevolent contributions and tuition, and also because their assets were invested to a large extent in mortgages and real estate securities, which were the first to suffer.

President Dimnent Resigns

At the spring meeting of the Board of Trustees, President Dimnent announced his resignation, to take effect September 1, 1930. Earnest efforts were made to have him withdraw his resignation, but the Board was reluctantly compelled to accept it. Although he had planned to retire in 1930, by mutual agreement with his elected successor he continued to serve until July 1, 1931. Before his successor took office, two stalwart members of the Board of Trustees passed away. One was the Hon. Gerrit J. Diekema, who had been a member of the Board and of the Executive Committee for thirty-seven years. Mr. Diekema was the leading lawyer in the town, president of the First State Bank, served a term in Congress, and had been a candidate for the governorship of the state. Currently he was Minister Plenipotentiary in the Netherlands. He died at his post on December 20, 1930. The other was C. M. McLean, who died on April 29, 1931. He came to Holland as Superintendent of Schools and remained as a citizen whose success as an industrialist and financier was matched by his generosity. He was elected a member of the Board in 1920. The President-elect had expected to lean heavily for counsel on these two men. Both of them seemed to be indispensable.

The Trustees wished to honor Dimnent by naming the chapel the Dimnent Memorial Chapel, but this honor was respectfully declined. He was, however, invited to remain as a member of the faculty as Professor of Economics. In this way, he continued to serve with distinction until his retirement in 1946. Students took his courses not merely to study economics, but especially to listen to his rich fund of knowledge. He also endeared himself to the students by his chapel talks and by taking them on chapel visits to explain the symbolism in the windows.

Dr. Dimnent was no mean poet, and among the best of his literary contributions was his translation of the Book of Job. He also authored "The Pilgrim" in 1941 in connection with the pageant arranged for the seventy-fifth anniversary of the college.

President Dimnent was named President Emeritus in 1947 and died July 4, 1959. His portrait hangs in the President's room in Graves Hall. On August 14, 1959, the Board of Trustees named the chapel The Dimnent Memorial Chapel in his honor. Paraphrasing the words of the 1945 *Milestone*:

> For over half a century he gave of the riches of mind and heart to Hope College. Beloved by many generations of students, this scholar, teacher and businessman gave of himself to the cause of Christian education with noble devotion, and with scant financial reward, won the affection of countless students and citizens. It is men like Edward Daniel Dimnent that have made Hope College special and distinctive.

13: THE DEPRESSION AND WORLD WAR II*

WYNAND WICHERS was born of Dutch parents, February 15, 1886. Mr. Wichers was the product of the Hope Preparatory School, from which he was graduated in 1905. He continued his career as a student in Hope College, and received his Bachelor of Arts degree in 1909 as the valedictorian of his class. President Kollen kept him on the campus by appointing him to a teaching position in the preparatory school. This established a connection with Hope College which, beginning in 1901, continued for an unbroken span of sixty-two years until he was elected President Emeritus and an honorary member of the Board of Trustees in 1963.

After serving as an instructor in the preparatory school for four years, he was appointed Professor of History in the college. He took a year's leave of absence for teaching and graduate study at the University of Michigan in 1917/18, where he held the rank of Instructor. During the ensuing summer he was granted a Master's degree by the University. Upon his return to the campus he resumed his duties as Professor of History and was appointed Registrar, an office vacated by Edward D. Dimnent when he assumed the presidency.

Dr. Wichers' direct association with the college as a member of the faculty was interrupted when he resigned in 1925 to accept the position of cashier of the First State Bank of Holland. However, in the same year he was elected a Trustee by the Classis of Holland. Four years later he was named a member of the

---

* This chapter was written by President Emeritus Irwin J. Lubbers.

Executive Committee of the Board, and in 1930 was elected President of the Trustees.

The qualities of leadership and loyalty which endeared him to his Alma Mater were no less appreciated in wider circles. He served two terms on the city Board of Education and two terms as president of the Holland Chamber of Commerce. He held memberships in the city's Library Board and Planning Commission and was the first chairman of the Holland Zoning Board. In 1931 the General Synod of the Reformed Church elected him to membership in two denominational bodies, the Board of Education, R.C.A., and the Board of Pensions. In 1937 he was elected President of the General Synod, the first and thus far only layman to be elected to that high office.

It was in his chosen profession as an educator that he received his greatest recognition. In 1936 he was nominated on the Republican ticket as a candidate for membership on the Michigan State Board of Education. He was elected for a term of six years, and reelected in 1941. Beginning in 1944, he served two terms as a member of the Commission on Higher Education of the North Central Association of Colleges and Secondary Schools. He served as president of the Michigan College Association in 1944/45 and was chosen chairman of the Department of Christian Education of the Michigan Council of Churches in 1946/47. In addition to honorary degrees from Hope College he received the degrees of L.H.D. from Central College (Iowa) and Litt.D. from Rutgers University in 1940.

The Netherlands influence in American life, dating back to the days of New Amsterdam, has been pervasive and persistent though not widely heralded. Occasionally it takes the center of the stage through the achievements of outstanding personages such as the two Roosevelts, Edward Bok, Gerrit John Diekema, Arthur Vandenberg, Everett Dirksen, and others. Hope College's involvement in the Dutch tradition is attested to by the fact that all of the afore-mentioned with the exception of Franklin D. Roosevelt hold honorary degrees from this institution. Wynand Wichers was the outstanding spokesman of this tradition. In August 1933 he was the principal speaker on Netherlands Day at the Century of Progress Exposition in Chicago. The Netherlands Society of Philadelphia invited him to be the orator at its

Wynand Wichers, president, 1931-1945.

formal meeting on January 23, 1942. He was honored at a testimonial dinner on May 30, 1936, and made a Knight in The Netherlands Order of Orange-Nassau. In 1947 his rank was raised to that of Officer in the Order.

Critical Years

Hope College was indeed fortunate that a man of Wynand Wichers' stature and background assumed the presidency in the critical year 1931. Beginning his duties in July of that year, he was inaugurated on October 12, 1931, with President Grant Ruthven of the University of Michigan giving the principal address, on a topic which thirty-five years later seems prophetic, "Some Reflections on Student Government."

When Wichers began his administration, the country was rapidly sinking into the worst economic depression in its history. In 1931, a considerable portion of the college endowment was already in default. In February 1933, all the banks in the city were closed, and a month later, a presidential edict closed all the banks in the country. The new President's first concern was the maintenance of a reasonably adequate budget. This was no time for "dreaming dreams" of expanding Hope. The overriding question was whether the college could survive the crisis.

In an appeal to the churches in 1933, the President said:

> We must call your attention to the fact that we have no means of support except as it comes from the churches. I am at a loss to know how to continue to pay salaries and other necessary operating costs unless every church will come to the rescue with its proper and just share of support.

But this cry for help was not the only recourse. Hope College possessed sources of strength that were equal to the emergency. There was complete cooperation between administration, faculty, and students in "tightening the belt." The Board of Trustees omitted its April 1933 meeting to save expense. Large student parties were eliminated. In 1932 all the literary societies voted to forego their annual spring banquets — a highly cherished tradition. The faculty voluntarily accepted a 10 percent reduction in salary and in 1933 agreed to accept 10 percent of their salaries in script in lieu of cash.

Fortunately there was no substantial loss in enrollment during the depression years. After a slight momentary reversal, the trend of enrollment continued upward and passed the five-hundred mark in 1939. Contributing to this growth was the Federal Emergency Relief Act, which enabled the college to employ some needy students on various campus projects. In 1939 the National

Youth Administration took the place of the Federal Emergency Relief Act, and in that year a hundred students were employed. The program continued to 1940 and was a source of great financial assistance. Students worked as laboratory assistants and on special projects such as renovating the college museum and building a regulation-size football field and cinder track. The total earnings amounted to thousands of dollars, all of which came into the treasury by way of tuition and fees. As early as 1935 the new turn of events enabled the Treasurer to report, "The receipts are larger than last year due entirely to increased tuition payments. We are confident that the college will weather the storm."

One of the major problems was the recovery of losses in the endowment fund. In the early years of the crisis, the college was handicapped by restrictions in the by-laws, which limited investments to federal and state bonds and to real estate securities legal for savings banks in Michigan. Since the depression had greatly depreciated real estate values these real estate securities were particularly vulnerable. In 1935 the Executive Committee resolved that "in order to secure diversification and also to provide for the possible recovery of losses, the Committee is authorized until the next regular meeting of the Trustees, to reinvest funds secured from the sale of defaulted real estate issues in other securities listed on the New York Stock Exchange, provided that in the judgment of the Committee such securities are suitable for the investment of college funds." The change in the by-laws made it possible to sell defaulted securities at the market, and with the proceeds, purchase other securities of corporations that had been refinanced and showed promise of increasing in value. The committee received valuable assistance from Mr. Omar P. Stelle of Muskegon, a dealer in reorganized securities. The method proved to be successful. By 1938 the endowment assets had increased to $789,000. The sale of a large apartment house in Detroit netted a profit of $50,000. In this period the college received a legacy from the C. M. McLean estate of Holland in the amount of $18,135. Of this amount, $10,000 was added to the endowment fund and the balance put into a scholarship trust fund. A legacy of $20,000 was received from the Bussing estate of New York City.

The Science Building, dedicated 1941.

The Science Building

In the depths of the depression the President had announced to the churches that it would be necessary to postpone needed expansion of physical facilities. However, by careful management it was possible to make needed improvements as the finances of the college improved. The large and impressive classrooms on the ground floor of the stately Memorial Chapel were made effectively usable by installing acoustic ceilings; the campus heating service was improved by installation of automatic stokers in Carnegie Gymnasium and a central heating plant to serve Graves Hall, Voorhees Hall, and the President's home. Provisions for improving student social life were made through the addition of a complete kitchen in Carnegie Gym, a student commons in the old high school building, and the installation of a stage and equipment for play production.

However, the crowning achievement of the Wichers administration in the area of facilities was the construction of the

Science Building. Increased enrollments were crowding all facilities, and particularly the science laboratories. The Trustees could not see their way clear to embark upon a building program in view of the stringent financial situation. This was further complicated by the numerous campaigns for funds either in progress or in the planning stage by various boards and institutions of the church. In the late thirties the country was gradually emerging from the depths of the depression, and after intradenominational negotiating Hope College graciously agreed to postpone its campaign for an additional year, to be assured two full years for its campaign without conflict with other agencies.

In the fall of 1939, with the approval of the General Synod, Hope College set out to make its appeal to all congregations in the denomination. The goal was set at $250,000. The whole denomination was well organized. The campaign began in Holland under the leadership of Professor Clarence Kleis. The Reverend Anthony Luidens organized the work in the Eastern Synods and the Reverend J. William Pyle in the West. The largest gift came through the efforts of Dr. Samuel M. Zwemer, one of Hope's most illustrious alumni. It was a donation of $35,000 from Miss Margaret Hopeman and her two brothers, Bertram and Albert Hopeman of New York, in memory of their mother, Grada Aleida Hopeman.

The campaign was generously supported by the alumni of the college, who were especially cognizant of the service rendered by the Science departments. The Alumni Bulletin of January 1939 said:

> Ever since William Van Putten M.D. was graduated in 1869, a steadily increasing number of alumni have been trained for scientific work of some kind — medicine, dentistry, industrial chemistry, research, nursing, science teaching, etc. Since Van Putten's day the number of graduates with science majors has grown to 12 percent of all alumni.

The Holland alumni accepted a goal of $50,000. Muskegon alumni followed with a goal of $15,000. On March 19, 1941, Hope students pledged $800. The following June 3rd, ground was broken, and on September 16, 1942, the building was dedicated free of indebtedness. The fund-raising had been a complete success.

Milton L. Hinga, athletic coach and teacher 1931-1960.

The dedication ceremony was combined with the fall convocation. The speakers were the Reverend C. P. Dame, Vice President of the General Synod, and Dr. L. Hopkins of the University of Michigan, who spoke on "The Weigh House."

With the removal of the science laboratories from Van Raalte Hall much additional space was made available for classrooms and offices. Hope College now faced the future with adequate facilities for an expanding program in all departments, and with one of the finest science buildings in the state. These fine facilities and equipment, adequate for an expanding program in science education, placed Hope College among those liberal arts colleges of the country who were in the forefront of the movement for the training of scientists that developed as an aftermath of World War II.

Time Marches On

No less significant than the addition and improvement of physical facilities was the President's concern with personnel problems. Mrs. Gilmore, who was the daughter of the founder of Hope College and was its first Dean of Women, died in April 1933. With her passing, the last direct link between the pioneers of 1847 and the present was broken. From the day the father first set foot on the virgin soil of western Michigan to the day the daughter was buried in its Pilgrim resting place was a span of eighty-six years. In this period three generations of dedicated and scholarly men and women devoted their talents to the building of Hope College. The closing phase of the third era coincided with the Wichers administration. Among both Trustees and faculty were those whose passing served to emphasize the necessity of finding worthy successors to carry on their well-wrought but never finished work.

President Wichers was guided and aided by a stalwart group of the Board of Trustees from the local and nearby communities, who were alike in their devotion to the college and their willingness to contribute time and talent and money for her welfare.

Among them were Mr. C. J. Den Herder, a Zeeland banker whose services were invaluable during the financial crisis. The Honorable Judge John Vanderwerp of Muskegon provided the legal talent and experience of which the Executive Committee and the Board of Trustees stood constantly in need. Dr. C. D. Mulder from Spring Lake did not find the exacting demands of the practice of medicine too great to devote time and energy to the college he loved. The Reverend Nicholas Boer of Grand Rapids carried the responsibilities of the presidency of the Board for many years with the same passion that characterized his highly successful ministry. This remarkable galaxy of men of diverse talents — banker, jurist, doctor, and minister — all died in the decade of the thirties. Fortunately others of equal talent and ability were elected to the Board. For example, there was Mr. Titus T. Hager, a lumberman from Grand Rapids, helper and co-worker for the cause of Hope. He served on the Board until the sixties when he retired in favor of his son. And the Reverend John A. Dykstra, pastor of Central Reformed Church, Grand Rapids, followed Dr. Boer in the presidency of the Board until the early sixties.

In this period death took its toll of faculty members. Chief among these was John B. Nykerk, Professor of English Language and Literature and Dean of Men. An innate refinement further developed by a year's study at Oxford enabled him to bring to the pioneer campus a cultural influence that played a large part in developing a unique college image. Besides outstanding work in his own field he laid the basis for the development of the library, the Music Department and the Department of Speech. At a testimonial dinner in Lansing in September 1930, the Michigan Oratorical League paid tribute to his success as oratorical coach by giving him a medal. He died months after becoming Professor Emeritus, in June 1936. On a bronze tablet in the narthex of the chapel the immortal words of his beloved Tennyson announce to passing generations the admonition which his life and teaching embodied.

> Let knowledge grow from more to more
> But more of reverence in us dwell
> That mind and soul, according well
> May make one music as before
> But vaster.

Closely associated with Dr. Nykerk in these high accomplishments was the Dean of Women, Mrs. Winifred H. Durfee, who came to Hope from Keuka College in New York. Though she lived a few years after retirement, she also left the campus in 1936. The naming of Durfee Hall, a women's residence, is a tribute to her memory. The college also suffered severe losses in the death of two faculty men in the prime of their lives. Curtis W. Snow, who in six short years had built up the Music Department to a position of prominence in the state, died in December 1935. The following February the Music faculty of the University of Michigan came to the college to present a memorial concert. Three years later a similar development in the Department of Speech was suddenly interrupted by the untimely death of an equally competent young man, Professor Roland Shackson. Miss Magdalene De Pree, secretary to President Dimnent and college librarian, played a quiet and inconspicuous but vital part in inculcating upon the lives of students the subtle spirit of Hope. Her passing severed another tie with the colonial tradition.

But time marches on, and new runners took up the torch. Miss Margaret Jane Gibbs came from Knox College to become the college's first professional librarian in 1931. She established a Department of Librarianship which was approved by the State Board of Education in 1941/42. Dr. Elizabeth Lichty of the University of Wisconsin became the successor to Mrs. Durfee.

Dr. William Schrier, Associate Professor of Speech at the University of North Dakota, took up the unfinished work of Mr. Shackson in 1939 and followed in the footsteps of Dr. Nykerk in the field of oratory. Mr. Milton Hinga was appointed Instructor in History and Varsity Coach in 1931. He was destined to become the much-beloved successor to Dr. Nykerk as Dean of Men. Mrs. Curtis W. Snow took up the work her husband had so auspiciously begun. These and many others were brought to the campus by President Wichers to provide the new faculty for the years ahead.

Another link with the past was severed with the closing of the preparatory school. The enrollment having reached a low ebb of forty in 1926/27, the tide was turned by changing it to a tuition-free high school with its own staff and physical facilities. After an immediate increase in enrollment which crested at 103 in 1931/32, a steady decline again set in. Without tuition income the operation of the school was a drain on the college's resources. As a facility for practice teaching it was not adequate. The matter came to a head when Hope College applied for accreditation by the American Association of Universities. To accomplish this it was necessary either to abandon the high school or to seek a separate endowment for its maintenance. In 1934, President Wichers recommended the discontinuance of the school, and by action of the Board of Trustees this historic institution was closed.

A similar fate befell another appendage of the early days. The Dutch publication *De Hope* had already succumbed to the Americanization of the college's clientele, but an English paper, *The Leader,* was published under college auspices as a church weekly. In June 1933 the Trustees received an overture from the *Christian Intelligencer,* an Eastern paper belonging to the Board of Publications of the Reformed Church, looking to a merger of the two weeklies. The merger was consummated the following year. General Synod requested the college to assume responsibility for the publication of the new paper, making provision for the formation of an editorial council representing all areas of the church. On January 1, 1937, Rev. Bernard J. Mulder became editor and manager in response to a call from the editorial council. The subscription list grew from 7000 to 11,000 in the next four months. The Synod voted a subsidy and in 1939 asked the college to relinquish its ownership, in order that *The Leader* might be incorporated as an organ of the denomination. The Trustees acquiesced on condition that the President of the college be named a permanent member of the editorial council. Thus President Wichers was again called on to bring to a fitting close another facet of the college's life that had outlived its usefulness.

Looking Forward

Hope College was again in a position for all-out progress. It placed itself squarely on the side of the single-purpose undergraduate College of Arts and Sciences. The degree of Bachelor of Music and the earned degree of Master of Arts were discontinued. In 1939 the college was accredited by the Association of American Universities. This was the fruit of a ten-year effort. Though the Association has now discontinued its accreditation policy, the distinction is a cherished one.

Hope College's traditional isolation was now abandoned. In 1938/40 the college participated with twenty-one colleges and universities in a study of general education at the junior college level. In conjunction with the Michigan Cooperative Study of 1941/42, Hope College joined in a study of teacher education in the liberal arts colleges holding membership in the North Central Association of Colleges and Secondary Schools.

Internally the ferment was also at work. In 1930 the first honors assembly was held to pay tribute to students who had excelled during the school year. The following year an archaic system of symbols for grading was replaced by the modern honor-point system of 4-3-2-1 on a descending scale for grades A, B, C, and D. Commencement exercises too were changed in 1939 from the traditional student program to a valedictorian's address and a commencement address by a visiting orator. In 1938 students and faculty adopted an honor code, a revival of and improvement on the first code which was adopted in 1915. A summer session was inaugurated in 1942, and in September of the same year the faculty held its first presemester workshop, a two-day conference in the delightful Castle Park Hotel. This is a practice that has continued ever since, with profit to all concerned.

New Student Activities

A further evidence of the progressive spirit that permeated the campus in the decade of the thirties is the number and type of student organizations and activities that had their origin in that period. The first all-college banquets were held in 1930/31. An Inter-Society Council for cooperation among women's literary societies was established in 1932. This soon developed into the present Pan Hellenic Society. The Blue Key, a national Senior men's society for the promotion of constructive cooperation, was established on the campus in 1932. Their most noteworthy achievement was the opening of a small bookstore in Graves Hall in 1936. During the ensuing years it has grown into the Blue Key College Store of the present day, which under the efficient management of a full-time experienced businessman annually grosses tens of thousands of dollars in serving the college community. The same year marked the beginning of the annual Nykerk Cup contest between Sophomore and Freshmen women in the field of dramatic and literary endeavor. This too has flourished during the thirty years of its history and has become an elevating tradition in interclass rivalry. The following year, under the leadership of the new Dean of Women, Miss Elizabeth Lichty, Alcor, a Senior women's society, was formed and the May-Day festival was founded. At long last, women's rightful place in a coeducational college was given due recognition in a charming and beautiful rite. More than twenty years later it was to be the privilege of another Dean of Women, Miss Emma Reeverts, to preside at the ceremony that transformed Alcor into the Hope College chapter of Mortarboard, the college women's national honor society.

Of a slightly different type is an organization that came into being with the opening of the first "little theater" in the Commons Room of the old high school building. In 1939 Miss Metta Ross organized Palette and Masque, a student club for the production and appreciation of drama. Since then a succession of directors of drama in the Speech Department have developed the program of dramatics to a significant place in the college curriculum, and greatly enhanced the prestige of Palette and Masque to an honored place in the traditions of student co-curricular activity.

The most dramatic of these new developments in student activities occurred in 1940 with the advent of the first "all-college sing." For a quarter of a century it has continued as the event that involves more persons in a single worthy student activity than any other similar event. From three to four hundred students, under student directors, representing all the campus fraternities, sororities, and other groups, practice for weeks the singing of two musical selections for competition. On the appointed evening, before overflow audiences, the coveted prizes are awarded by three professionally competent judges.

It is a tribute to the life values held by the students, faculty, and administration of Hope College that in one brief decade they could set in motion these wholesome student activities that have stood the test of the years.

Stronger Stakes and Longer Cords

Not as conspicuous as the activities of students and faculty, but perhaps even more basic to the growth and development of a college, is the behind-the-scenes performance of administrators and Trustees. One of the most significant indications that Hope was reaching maturity as a responsible college organization was an action by the Board of Trustees in June 1944 providing for retirement of faculty members. After long discussion it was agreed that all faculty members might enroll in the R.C.A. Contributory Annuity Fund, with the college paying a share of the contribution. The plan was made compulsory for all new faculty members. Though the plan was modified in subsequent years, this action firmly established the college's policy of making adequate provision for faculty retirement.

A series of measures was also taken to firm the organization by revising the by-laws. In 1932 authority was given to certain officers to sign necessary legal documents. Another revision determined the succession in case of the death of the President and Vice President of the Board of Trustees. A complete revision of the by-laws in 1936 created a number of standing committees of the Board and defined their respective duties. In 1944 a significant departure from the old constitution was the provision that empowered the Trustees to elect five members-at-large.

Besides strengthening the stakes, the administration also proceeded to lengthen the cords of the college's habitation. Except for a few sporadic issues of an alumni bulletin, in past years there had been no organized attempt to keep in touch with alumni. In October 1937 was published a mimeographed edition of the Alumni Bulletin containing a tribute to Dr. J. B. Nykerk by the Reverend Benjamin J. Bush, D.D. Beginning in October of the following year regular semiannual bulletins were published until interrupted by World War II. This effort was supplemented in 1940 by the organization of an alumni chapter in Grand Rapids and three chapters in New York State: Rochester, Albany, and New York City. The alumni responded to their Alma Mater's gestures of concern by a vigorous expression of interest. There was considerable agitation for alumni representation on the Board of Trustees. This reached its climax in an appeal from the president of the Alumni Association, Mr. George Pelgrim, in the alumni bulletin. When the change in the constitution empowered the Board to elect five members-at-large, they utilized this prerogative to elect alumni irrespective of geographic location. This served to create a closer bond between the institution and its alumni.

Other pioneering steps were taken to cultivate closer relations with the community and the church. Interest was created by entertaining 300 high school students from Grand Rapids in 1934. The following year there were 368. When this approach was repeated in 1940 there were 600 students from Grand Rapids, Kalamazoo, and Muskegon. These were the experimental beginnings of a recruitment program that has subsequently grown to a major administrative function. The Home Furnace Company sponsored a Saturday evening radio program, originating in the college chapel, over Station WOOD in Grand Rapids. The program was under the direction of Paul E. Hinkamp and continued through the first six months of 1940. In May of the same year, 400 members of Consistories of Grand Rapids churches were dinner guests on the campus and visited evening laboratory classes.

In this same period direct efforts were made to emphasize the relationship that exists between Holland in America and Holland in Europe. Special convocations were held to pay tribute to and confer honorary degrees upon Henry A. Van

President Wichers conferring an honorary Doctor of Laws degree upon Her Royal Highness, Juliana, Princess of the Netherlands.

Coenen Torchiana, Netherlands Consul in San Francisco, Jonkheer H. M. Van Haersma De Witt and Alexander Loudon, Netherlands Ambassadors to the United States, and Her Royal Highness the then Princess Juliana, who with her husband Prince Bernhard visited the college in 1941.

Seventy-Fifth Anniversary

The dynamic decade of the thirties culminated in 1941 with the celebration of the seventy-fifth anniversary of the conferring of the first Bachelor of Arts degrees. The general theme was: "The Place of the Christian College in the World Today." The General Synod, R.C.A., held its annual meeting on the campus in honor of the occasion. The visit of Princess Juliana and Prince Bernhard referred to above, also coincided with this auspicious event.

The first major convocation on June 10 was held in conjunction with the meeting of General Synod honoring the Royal Princess, at which time President Wichers conferred upon her the honorary degree of Doctor of Laws.

Academic procession before conferring the degree on Princess Juliana, June 10, 1941.

The visit extended over a period of three days in which the royal visitors were feted at a dinner given by the Governor of Michigan, a luncheon given by the mayor of Holland, and a reception given by President and Mrs. Wichers of Hope College. And so it was that less than a century after Dr. A. C. Van Raalte and his intrepid followers left their native land, the Princess of the House of Orange graciously accepted the plaudits of their descendants on the occasion of a significant event in the history of the college which through the years had been their anchor of hope.

The second major convocation was on June 17. Scores of delegates resplendent in academic garb marched down the aisle of the stately chapel to hear an address by Dr. W. H. S. Demarest, President of Rutgers University, on "The Men Who Built Hope." At the luncheon for delegates the greetings brought by selected guests revealed how well the college had fulfilled the dream of its founder that his people should some day take their place in the mainstream of American life. Speaking on behalf of their

respective organizations were Gould Wickey of the National
Council of Church-Related Colleges; Eugene Elliot, Superinten-
dent of Public Instruction for the State of Michigan; E. E. Fell,
Superintendent of Holland Public Schools; John L. Seaton,
President of Albion College and of the North Central Association
of Colleges; and Edward R. Krauss, Dean of the University of
Michigan.

The afternoon conference was perhaps the high point of the
seventy-fifth birthday celebration. Dr. Leonard Yntema, Professor of Chemistry at the University of Illinois, delivered the
lecture and led the discussion on "The Place of Science in the
Christian College." It is a tribute to President Wichers' sound
judgment that, though he was himself a historian, he focused
the symposium not on the college's deserving past, but on its
destined future in the ever broadening field of Science. Moreover, his perception of the meaning that lies hidden in the
subtle unfolding of human events, led him to choose for this
assignment a brilliant scientist who was not only an alumnus
of Hope College but the son of the first Professor of Science
at Hope College, who was in turn a product of those early days
of struggle and vision that produced this unique Christian
college.

The three candidates who were given honorary degrees at
this historic commencement were aptly chosen. The Doctor of
Divinity degree was conferred on Henry Poppen (Hope 1914)
of China, who within a few years was to be singled out by the
Chinese Communists as the arch foe of Atheism and made to
stand the mockery of a public trial for his acts against the people as a Christian missionary. The Doctor of Science degree was
given to Edward Wichers (Hope 1913) of the Bureau of Standards in Washington, D.C., and the Doctor of Laws degree to
Adriaan J. Barnouw, Professor of Dutch Language and Literature in Columbia University.

The keynote speakers also caught the deeper meanings of
the anniversary. Dr. John S. Badeau, Dean of the American
University in Cairo, redefined the spiritual goals of the Christian college in his baccalaureate address on "The Ultimate Discipline"; and Dr. Joseph Sizoo (Hope 1907) of the New York
Avenue Presbyterian Church of Washington, D.C., brought the

program to a fitting close, recounting history without apology and looking forward without fear, in his ringing commencement address entitled, "Unashamed and Unafraid."

A unique feature of the seventy-fifth anniversary was a pageant written and directed by Edward D. Dimnent entitled, "The Pilgrim." This was a combination of fact and allegory portraying the history and the spirit of Hope College. It was the third in the series that included pageants presented in 1916 and 1926, the fiftieth and sixtieth anniversaries of the college. Though the presentation of pageants by amateur performers seems to have run its course, "The Pilgrim," which had four showings, and its predecessors form a valuable record for historical scholars intent on searching out the meaning behind the facts in the life of Hope College.

The seventy-fifth anniversary celebration did more than bring to a close three quarters of a century of history. It marked the end of a significant college year. At the close of the year 1940/41, the Secretary of the Board of Trustees in his annual report to General Synod said, "We rejoice in the fact that the year has been one of the best in the history of Hope College." He pointed to an enrollment of 549, to honors won by students in debate and oratory, to a successful tour by the Glee Club, and to a strong spiritual life on the campus. Dr. Wichers had good reason to point with pride to the accomplishments of his first decade as President and to look forward with confidence to the new decade of the forties.

The Specter of War

Before the calendar year of 1941 drew to a close, the idyllic prospect suddenly vanished. The specter of war once again began to shake college life. After Hitler's invasion of Poland in 1939, the European continent had become involved in World War II. Although the United States passed a Selective Service Act in 1940, conditions at the college remained fairly normal. But this condition changed when the United States declared war on December 8, 1941. The year 1941/42 opened with an enrollment of 555, but the situation began to deteriorate as the school year went on. In April of 1942 the Secretary reported to the General Synod:

Like all other colleges, Hope College has been greatly affected by the war. A great many boys who were with us in September are now in the Armed Forces of the country. The college has adopted an accelerated program by which a student can complete his college work in one year less than the normal length of time. This is made possible by the elimination of vacations and by introducing a summer school, which will open June 19. Continuation of the war will drastically affect the life and work of all educational institutions, and the small church college will suffer in proportion. In the face of a situation which seems almost inevitable, we ask for the special concern of the churches, and appeal to their generosity.

In the year 1942/43, the situation became even more serious. The year opened with an enrollment of 529. By the end of the year, the number had been reduced by 150 students. The Trustees asked the Synod to authorize an emergency fund, "in order that the work may be sustained and the college kept strong not only for the immediate opportunity but also for the great responsibilities that lie ahead." The low point in enrollment was 288 in the year 1943. Hope College followed very much the

Trainees of the Army Specialized Training Program taking a test under the eagle eye of Capt. Homer L. Morgan, 1944.

Some of the Hope men who made the supreme sacrifice in World War II.

First Row: John Ayers, '45; Eugene Baker, '44; E. Raymond Boot, '38; Edward De Pree, '42; John P. Eisenberger, '42; Leroy W. Ellerbrook, '41. Second Row: Lewis J. Geerlings, '28; Lester Lampen, '43; John Palmer, '42; Leonard Pape, '45; Clark Poling, '33; Ralph Wallace, '42. Third Row: Willis Smallegan, '43; G. Steinenger, '16; Edwin Tellman, '31; Louis Van Dyke, '44; W. Van Faasen, '45; Roger Van Oss, '38. Fourth Row: Milton J. Verburg, '44; Benjamin VerMeer, '31; Leonard Vos, '46; Wallace Riemersma, '43; J. Whitworth, '44. A complete list of all Hope men who have lost their lives in wars through the Korean conflict is found in the Appendix.

pattern of all Michigan institutions as to enrollment. In all the Michigan colleges and universities enrollment dropped from 60,000 in 1939/40 to 40,000 in 1943/44. Decreased enrollments resulted in the suspension of many normal college activities. The fraternity houses were closed due to the lack of civilian students. Intercollegiate athletic programs were suspended. A most unusual situation was the organization of Tri Alpha Men's Union. Instead of meeting in individual fraternities, all men met together under one organization. Meetings were held each Friday evening. The *Milestone,* 1944, reports:

> These meetings were interesting and helpful to the fellows, culturally, intellectually and socially. Besides enjoying themselves, they discussed such subjects as "Post War Peace", "The Japanese Army", "Harlem's Divine Being", and many others. . . . The organization is now drawing its first year to a close with huge success. True, the members of the inactive Frats still hold fast to the ties that bind them to their Frats but by pulling and working together they have been able to provide the new students at Hope with the brotherhood and spirit that goes with the campus life of the college.

Two Colleges on One Campus

From September 16, 1942, to March 21, 1944, there were two colleges on the campus — a civilian college and a war college. The federal government established a Civilian Pilot program on July 22, 1942. This was an extracurricular program for regular students. On September 16, 1942, an Elementary Glider School was established. This program consisted of eight-week courses for men sent to Hope by the Service Department. These men were housed and boarded on the campus and received flight training at the Municipal Airport. A more extensive program became available when the War Training Service was set up on January 23, 1943. A much larger contingent of men, these trainees were members of the Army to be trained as pilots. The equipment and instructional expenses, as well as housing and messing, were provided by the government. These men were housed in the Park Township Community Hall and did their flying at the Municipal Airport. This service was of short duration and was discontinued during the second semester of 1943.

In the fall of 1943 the college contracted with the Army for the establishment on the campus of a unit of the Army Specialized Training Program. The first men arrived on October 11, 1943. The complete unit consisted of a battalion of 258 men in two companies, from thirty-six states in the union. They were between the ages of eighteen and twenty-two, and all were graduates of high schools. The men were housed in the seminary dormitory. Carnegie Gymnasium became the mess hall and drill hall. A sick bay and dispensary operated in Van Vleck Hall. The commanding officer was Captain Homer L. Morgan, assisted by First Lieutenant Lawrence A. Read and Second Lieutenant John E. Moore. The curriculum was one in basic engineering, taught by members of the college staff. Army officers taught military science. Professor Bruce Raymond directed the academic training, Professor Paul McLean directed the housing and messing program, and Mr. John L. Schouten directed the physical education program. The men were allowed to participate in all normal college activities but not in intercollegiate athletics. They attended Chapel, and had required study hours in the evening in the college library. To introduce them to Hope College, the administration published an illustrated booklet in November 1943, entitled, "You're in the Army Now." The A.S.T.P. was of short duration. It came to an end in 1944 with a farewell chapel service on March 21. The speaker was Lt. Mayo Hadden of the Naval Air Force. The program was of great financial help to the college. The final settlement with the Army showed a substantial profit, which was added to the endowment fund by resolution of the Board of Trustees.

The Denomination Begins to Take Notice of the Needs

It is certain that without the financial assistance given by the federal government, the college would have been in dire need. The Reformed Church in America had not yet responded to the cause of higher education as it was to do in the future. In the year 1940/41 the churches contributed a mere $26,000 out of the total budget of $120,000. Attempts to obtain more denominational support proceeded very slowly; receipts from the churches in 1941 were $31,000. Total receipts from all sources were $140,000. In the year 1942/43 church receipts were $28,000 out of a total budget of $148,000. In June 1943, the General Synod resolved to raise an emergency fund of $140,000 in the year 1943/44 for all the benevolent causes of the denomination. Included in this amount was an item of $53,000 to be raised for the three colleges. In 1943/44 Hope College received from this source $17,200 in addition to $20,000 from churches and

church boards. The emergency fund was continued into the
year 1944/45, when it produced $22,000 for Hope College.

Return to Normalcy

By autumn of 1944 the Army units had left the campus and
academic conditions became more normal. During the war
years the college had been able to maintain a strong educational program and at the same time had made a patriotic
effort to serve the nation. The college had survived one of the
severest crises in her history. It was not done without sacrifice
of precious lives. The *Milestone* of 1945 contains the photographs
of twenty-three Hope men, out of a total of forty-one, who gave the
"Last Full Measure of Devotion." It was time to look ahead and
lay plans for a greater Hope College. Among the plans was a campaign for $300,000 to build a new women's dormitory. Planning
was begun as early as 1942 for a dormitory to house 150 women.
The plan had to be held in abeyance while the local community
was involved in another major campaign for funds. In June 1945,
the Trustees authorized the employment of Victor Thebaud,
the architect of the Science Building, to prepare plans and
specifications. In 1945, the Trustees reported to the General
Synod:

> Plans have been drawn for a new residence for women. When
> completed, Voorhees Hall will be refitted and converted into
> a residence for men. These facilities are badly needed as we
> have no residence for men at present. The Board of Education
> has approved a joint campaign for $300,000 by Hope and Cen-
> tral Colleges for dormitory purposes.

At the time, $40,000 had already been set aside at Hope for
this purpose. The architect's drawing of the proposed dormitory
appears in the *Milestone* for 1945.

To the very end of his administration President Wichers was
planning for the future. Though changing situations forced
alterations in the details he had projected for men's and women's
housing, his foresight provided the impetus for a vastly larger
development than even he had anticipated.

Well Done

Early in 1945 President Wichers informed the Executive Committee of the Board of his intention to resign at the close of the

school year. The burdens of the depression years and the war years had taken their toll, and the President felt it necessary to seek relief and to leave to his successor the responsibility of leading the college in the days to come. His resignation was accepted by the Trustees in June, and simultaneously he announced that he had accepted a position as Vice President of Western Michigan University in Kalamazoo.

Letters from alumni and friends, far and near, pouring in from all sides were preserved in a bound volume and presented to him as a memorial of appreciation. Tokens of esteem were presented by Trustees and faculty. The college officially pronounced its "Well Done" by conferring upon him at the commencement exercises the honorary degree of Doctor of Education.

In fourteen action-packed years Wynand Wichers placed his stamp indelibly upon the record of Hope College. The impact was doubly impressive because they were years fraught with great danger, beginning in the worst depression of all time and ending in the most devastating of all wars. Seldom have the life of an individual and the life of an institution shown more clearly the awesome reality of an overruling Providence. In its hundred years of history, Hope College faced its severest crisis in the period from 1931 to 1945. In the sixty-two years of Wynand Wichers' direct association with Hope College these same years were the years of his greatest strength and vigor. Here was the right man in the right place, at the right time, for the right purpose.

14: A COLLEGE OF DISTINCTION

THE BOARD OF TRUSTEES of Hope College met in special session in May of 1945, and unanimously elected as President Irwin Jacob Lubbers, who currently was President of Central College (Iowa). Accepting the presidency, he came to the campus in the summer of 1945. Dr. Lubbers was born in Cedar Grove, Wisconsin, November 15, 1895. His early schooling was in the public schools of Cedar Grove. His secondary work was done in the Cedar Grove, Wisconsin, Memorial Academy, graduating in June 1913. This was an academy of the Reformed Church in America, founded in the days of President Kollen of Hope College, which had sent many promising students to Hope College. Dr. Lubbers received his A.B. degree from Hope in June 1917. After a year of service in the United States Army as an Air Cadet, he spent the next three years as a lecturer in Voorhees College in Vellore, India. Upon his return he became an Instructor in English at Hope for a period of six years. He was a popular teacher and an efficient coach of debate. He took his A.M. degree at Columbia University in 1927, and then spent a year at Northwestern University. In the year 1929 he was at Carroll College (Wisconsin) as an assistant to the President and an Instructor in Psychology and Education. In 1931, Northwestern University conferred on him the Ph.D. degree, his dissertation being "College Organization and Administration."

He was the author of several articles, among them, "Are College Endowments Safe?" and "Who Controls the Liberal Arts College?" Dr. Lubbers married Margaret Van Donselaar of the

226

Irwin J. Lubbers, president, 1945-1963.

Class of 1922, and they are the parents of two sons, Irwin J. Lubbers, Jr., and Arend Don Lubbers, who is now President of Central College (Iowa). In 1945, Lubbers received three honorary degrees — an LL.D. from Central College, a Litt.D. from Rutgers University, and a Litt.D. from Hope College. As President of Central College from 1934 to 1945, he served during the depths of the depression and World War II, meeting the same problems that his predecessor had met at Hope College. By virtue of his training and actual experience, he was ready for the task at Hope. He had qualities of imagination and organization that were necessary in the difficult years ahead, and he had the courage to meet the challenging problems of a church college in 1945.

A New Administrative Structure

Arriving on the campus in the summer of 1945, he quickly began to assess the changes necessary in the postwar period. Without the formality of an official inauguration, he decided that the most urgent immediate need was an administrative structure that would give him time to evaluate what needed to be done. He retained the services of Milton L. Hinga, who had been named Dean of Men in 1944. The first new office to be created was that of Dean of the College, and he appointed to this office Dr. C. E. Wimmer, who also was Professor of Chemistry. Dean Wimmer held this office for one year and was followed by Dr. John W. Hollenbach of the English Department. In 1955, Hollenbach was given a two-year leave of absence to teach in the University of Cairo. After he returned, he was named Vice President of the college. Another leave of absence was given him in 1965/66 to represent the Great Lakes College Association on the faculty of the University of Beirut, Lebanon.

The second office to be created was that of Business Manager, and Professor Paul E. McLean was assigned to that position. After one year, he was followed by Dr. Bruce Raymond, who returned to the college after a term of service with the Veterans Bureau in Detroit. When Dr. Raymond became Secretary of the Michigan College Foundation, Mr. Rein Visscher was chosen to assist in the renovation of the old buildings and the erection of the new. Until he retired in 1965, he worked closely with Henry Steffens, who was named Treasurer in 1947, succeeding Henry Winter. Mr. Steffens was a Hope graduate in the Class of 1930, and had earned a Master's degree in Business Administration at Northwestern University.

A new and much-needed venture was the establishment of a student Health Center in charge of Dr. Abraham Leenhouts, a grandson of Jannes van de Luyster, the founder of Zeeland, Michigan. Although he had been hired on a part-time basis, he became so intrigued with his work that he gave up his private practice to give full time to his new job. In 1957, the Executive Committee of the Board of Trustees gave up the idea of a resident physician and appointed Dr. Otto VanderVelde as the physician in charge until his retirement in 1965.

President Lubbers named Willard C. Wichers Director of Alumni Relations. In 1947, he began the publication of a quarterly alumni magazine. Before this time there had been efforts to produce an alumni magazine of high quality, but all the efforts resulted in failure. In 1949, Mr. Clyde Geerlings became Director of Alumni Relations and Mrs. Marian Stryker was appointed editor of the alumni magazine. Professor Albert Timmer was named Director of Admissions. Dr. William Vander Lugt became Dean of the College, and E. Duffield Wade became manager of the college bookstore. Janet Mulder became Archivist in 1952. All of these were housed in Van Raalte Hall, where offices had been carved out of classrooms.

War's Aftermath

In 1945, war veterans began to return to college and many problems waited on the decision of the President. The teaching staff was constantly enlarged. Problems in housing and boarding had to be met, and these had to be settled rather quickly. The federal government encouraged veterans to go back to colleges of their choice by paying each single veteran $60 a month and each married veteran $90 a month, and in addition paid the college tuition, fees, and book costs. And so the stampede of students returning to college began. In the fall of 1945, the Registrar reported about 400 students. In the year 1947/48, there were more than 1200 enrolled, of whom 533 were veterans.

The big problem was how to house and feed this large number of students. The Federal Housing Authority came to the rescue and gave the college a men's dormitory and four smaller units for veterans. For married veterans, six buildings were provided, each composed of four apartments. For a while the Housing Authority retained the title, but after a few years the title was given to the college. Soon the east end of the campus and the public park adjoining began to look like an army camp.

But this was not enough. Zwemer Hall was leased from Western Theological Seminary, and the East Junior High School was leased from the Board of Education and converted into a dormi-

Winifred H. Durfee Hall, 1950.

tory for women. The first floor of the Masonic Temple was
leased for dining purposes. The residence of Walter Walsh was
purchased and converted for the use of the Music Department.
Some private houses were purchased for new members of the
faculty. And then the number of students began to decline. The
enrollment reached a low of 700, and in 1950 the President said
that the income of the college had been reduced by $140,000.
Fortunately an appeal to the churches erased a year-end deficit
of $85,000.

In 1947, Mr. William B. Eerdmans, Sr., of the Eerdmans Publishing Company of Grand Rapids, gave the college title to the
A. C. Van Raalte homestead. Mr. Eerdmans was honored at a
dinner given by Mr. Titus Hager, a member of the Board of
Trustees and of the Executive Committee of the Board. Some
years later, additional land was purchased and the property
was named the Van Raalte Campus, to be used by the Physical
Education Department. All the facilities for college sports are
being developed there.

The Population Explosion

In the late fifties and early sixties, another rush to the colleges began as economic conditions improved and high schools graduated increasing numbers of "war babies." Hope College was no exception, and the number of registrations began to increase until it reached 1571 in 1963. The President carefully weighed the alternatives. A choice had to be made between restricting the registration and building adequate buildings. The President wisely decided that high enrollments were here to stay and that adequate new facilities must be erected. The first necessity was to build a new central heating plant and a dormitory for women. Since there were no available funds, it became necessary to borrow $400,000 from the Penn Mutual Life Insurance Company. The Board of Trustees and the General Synod mortgaged the original campus to the insurance company for the repayment of the loan. Since the General Synod had title to the property, permission was secured from the Board of Direction, R.C.A. This was the first time in

J. B. Nykerk Music Hall and Snow Auditorium, 1956.

Kollen Hall, 1956.

the history of the college that the property had been mortgaged. Both heating plant and dormitory were erected. The dormitory was named the Winifred Durfee Hall for Women in memory of the long-time Dean of Women and Professor of French. Following the erection of these new facilities came the complete revamping of Carnegie Gymnasium for the Department of Physical Education. The galleries were removed, greatly changing the interior. In 1956, another new building was added for the Department of Music, which was named the John B. Nykerk Music Hall in honor of one who had given his life to the teaching of music and to the interpretation of literature. And now the federal government passed legislation for the erection of dormitories. The first building to be erected with public funds was Kollen Hall for Men. The next was Phelps Hall for Women, completed in 1960. When President Lubbers retired in 1963, Gilmore Hall for Women was in process of completion as well as a large complex for the social fraternities. All the federal loans were to be liquidated in forty years.

The Van Zoeren Library

Gerrit John Van Zoeren, born in 1884, spent eight years on Hope's campus as a student in both preparatory school and the college. He graduated in 1912. With the help of his chemistry teacher, Dr. Almon T. Godfrey, Van Zoeren was the first Hope graduate to be awarded an assistantship in Chemistry. Upon receiving his doctorate at the University of Illinois, he was for a time associated with MacDonald College, in St. Anne de Bellevue, Quebec, Canada. He then ventured into the business of making arsenicals. After years of hardship and self-denial, he sold his business to Miles Laboratories for a small fortune. In 1958, Van Zoeren and his wife, Elizabeth, informed Hope College that all of their property had been willed to Hope. However, when Mrs. Van Zoeren passed away, her husband decided to honor her by making the substantial gift to the college at once rather than after his own death. The college had in 1959 launched the "Looking ahead with Hope" financial campaign in which a new library was the big item. On July 3, 1959, Van Zoeren turned over to

Gilmore Hall, 1963.

The donor, John G. Van Zoeren, viewing the interior of the new library, October 8, 1961.

President Lubbers securities valued at more than a half million dollars. This was the largest gift the college had ever received. Supplemented by additional donations, it made the new library possible as it sparked enthusiasm among the supporters of Hope College. A site was purchased from the First Reformed Church, a site that Dr. A. C. Van Raalte had once donated for the erection of a public school. Ralph Calder and Associates designed the three-level building in contemporary style. The ground floor houses the Carley Room, which offers facilities for film projection and viewing. The library was completed and dedicated with a public ceremony on October 8, 1961.

Remodeling Graves Hall

Graves Hall had served the college very well when the student enrollment was small. When the Van Zoeren Library was completed and all the books had been brought to the new library, it became possible to remodel the interior of Graves Hall for other uses. The cost of the renovation was $125,000, three times the cost of the original building. It now is a general-purpose building with offices, recitation rooms and an assembly hall. In the building is a beautiful presidents' room made possible through the generosity of the Misses Adelaide and Geraldine Dykhuizen, nieces of President Dimnent, and by Dr. and Mrs. Harold Dykhuizen of Muskegon, a nephew of the late President. The room is tastefully furnished and on the walls hang the portraits of all the presidents of Hope College. Another interesting room is a small meditation chapel, which is a gift contributed by the family and student friends of the Reverend Henry Schoon, who died April 23, 1954.

The Village Square

Since 1925, a Women's League had been in existence under the leadership of Mrs. George Huizinga and Mrs. C. J. Dregman, wife of the college's Treasurer. Concerned about the barren and unattractive lounge in Voorhees Hall, this Women's League appealed to the Reformed Churches and received enough support to buy drapes, lamps, and furniture. On May 8 of each

Exterior of the Van Zoeren Library.

*A scene of the chicken barbecue supper held annually as a part of the
Village Square festivities since 1957.*

year in celebration of the birthday of Mrs. Voorhees after whom
the Hall was named, the League would meet on campus in
order to be of further assistance to the college. Although the
League raised initially but a small amount of money, its very
existence was a step in the right direction. More and more
Reformed Church women began to take an active interest in
the college. A tribute must be paid to Mrs. Irwin J. Lubbers,
who provided much of the inspiration for the development of
the League's program by personally promoting and founding
chapters of the League in Illinois, Indiana, Wisconsin, and
New York.

When Durfee Hall was under construction, the League undertook the important step of furnishing the building. Mrs. Eva Leenhouts Pelgrim chaired the steering committee for this venture. To raise the money, the League adopted as a method the Village Square, a festival to be held at Hope College early in August, 1957. Many chapters of the League participated, making the Village Square an immediate success.

As additional buildings were constructed, the League pledged the amount of money necessary to buy the furnishings. Over the past ten years, 1957 to 1967, the League has raised more than a quarter of a million dollars. Other institutions were so impressed by this amazing success that they copied the Village Square. An additional benefit accrued to Hope in the form of goodwill toward the college in congregations where chapters of the Women's League were established.

New Associations

On August 8, 1948, the presidents of five of the small colleges in the state met in Lansing for the purpose of incorporating the Michigan College Foundation. The incorporators were Presidents Lubbers of Hope, Samuel Harrison of Adrian, Harvey E. Turner of Hillsdale, Alvin Johnston of Emmanuel Missionary College, and Dale Welsh of Alma. President Lubbers was the prime mover in organizing the foundation. In January 1948, Mr. Frank Abrams, Chairman of the Board of Standard Oil Company of New Jersey, addressed the National Association of College Presidents. In his address, he presented the idea of a joint solicitation of funds from industry for the non-tax-supported institutions. President Lubbers felt that here was something for the private colleges of Michigan, and persuaded four other presidents to join him in the enterprise. The other colleges were invited to join the organization. Some were reluctant supporters of the plan but in the end there were sixteen private colleges in the group. Since that time other colleges in most of the states have organized similar associations. The Foundation was incorporated and Dr. Bruce Raymond of Hope became the first secretary. Four years later the colleges began to get returns on the investment they had made. It was felt that business leaders ought to be among the incorporators to make the project even more successful. In 1961, Mr. Den Uyl, of Bohn Aluminum and

Participants in the Vienna Summer School, 1954.

Brass Company of Detroit, and a former Hope student, became president of the Foundation; and in 1965, Mr. James Vermeulen, a graduate of Hope and now president of the American Seating Company, became president. The Foundation is increasingly successful. In the year 1956/57 fifty industries contributed $232,-000 to the Foundation. Hope College now gets about $50,000 a year from this source.

The Vienna Summer School

The Vienna Summer School has been conducted by Professor Paul Fried of Hope College since 1956. Professor Fried is a graduate of Hope College, of the Class of 1946. He holds a Master's degree from Harvard and a Doctor's degree from Erlangen, Germany. As the Director of International Relations he began the Vienna Summer School as a part of the regular college program. During the last ten years 276 students from Hope and 195 students from other colleges have participated. European teachers in the summer school are appointed to the Hope faculty to complement the work done by members of the Hope staff, who are selected ·for the summer. About six weeks are allowed for study and six weeks for travel. At the end of the summer they meet again for a reevaluation of the project.

The Great Lakes Colleges Association

The Great Lakes Colleges Association in recent years has played a very important role in the development of the educational and cultural program of Hope College. In March 1960, the Executive Committee of the Board of Trustees agreed to a proposal by the President to participate in the development of an interstate association of twelve liberal arts colleges in Indiana, Michigan, and Ohio. The colleges that combined to form this new Great Lakes Colleges Association were Albion, Antioch, Denison, De Pauw, Earlham, Hope, Kalamazoo, Kenyon, Oberlin, Ohio Wesleyan, Wabash, and Wooster. The association is incorporated in Michigan and has an executive office in Detroit.

The GLCA is in no sense a money-raising organization. Its purpose is to provide an effective instrument whereby the member colleges can engage cooperatively in educational activities that no individual college would have the human or financial resources to carry independently. It is in essence a program designed for mutual self-help. Through the administrative channels of the association, proposals for experimentation and research are presented to foundations. Through these channels meaningful exchange of ideas at all levels of the college structure — administrative, faculty, and students — is facilitated. Thus, while still maintaining institutional autonomy, member colleges have been able to provide for their students some of the opportunities formerly available only in the larger universities. During the years of its operation, Hope College has been actively involved in all the various phases of the activities of the association. Perhaps the most significant area has been that of international education.

Besides the international program of the GLCA, Hope has participated in many other cooperative projects. Under the Kettering Foundation Internship Program, each year for the past several years a well-trained chemist or biologist has come to the college for a year of teaching and research. Under the terms of the foundation grant he is able to explore under most favorable conditions the profession of college teaching. Through such involvement and through the many meetings of professors from twelve colleges to discuss issues and programs in the respective disciplines, Hope has profited significantly in its continuing effort to improve the quality of its instruction and the richness of its program. Hope's own international program, the Vienna Summer School, has been greatly strengthened by student and faculty participation in several GLCA overseas ventures.

National Affiliations

Hope College has long been accredited by the North Central Association of Colleges and Secondary Schools. But during the Lubbers era, the college earned accreditation by the National Association for the Accreditation of Teacher Education, the American Association of University Women, the American Chemical Society, and the National Association of Schools of Music. It maintains membership in the American Council on Education, the Association of American Colleges, the Michigan Association of Colleges and Universities, and the Mathematical Society of America. As a result many local organizations have become chapters of national honor societies.

Academic Ratings

How does the quality of work done in liberal arts colleges compare with that in the universities? It was not until 1947 that certain scholars set themselves to find out. In that year Dr. J. R. Steelman, chairman of the President's Scientific Research Board, applied himself to this task. He reported that some of the small colleges in the country had produced more candidates for the Ph.D. degree in Chemistry than many of the larger institutions. In 1949, Dr. R. L. Zwemer reported that in this respect Hope College stood eighth in the nation. In February of 1951, the *Journal of Industrial and Engineering Chemistry* listed seven authorities in the field of rare metals, and of the seven, three were Hope alumni. In 1955 Drs. Joseph Greenbaum and Robert Knapp checked fifty colleges and ranked Hope among the leaders in the production of candidates for the Ph.D. degree in Chemistry for the period 1948–1951. And in the April 16, 1959, edition of the Chicago *Tribune,* Hope was placed among the ten best liberal arts colleges in the nation, which led President Lubbers to temper college and community enthusiasm by posing the question, "Are we on a pedestal or on the spot?"

Now that the college was 'rated as superior in the scientific fields, financial grants from industry began to come. The President was always ready to encourage any faculty member who wished to seek a grant for his department. It was inevitable that most of the grants were in Chemistry, but other departments soon began to receive their share. The largest grant to be received was one of $237,000 given by the Ford Foundation for faculty salaries. President Lubbers proposed that this sum be matched by a similar amount from the church or from alumni. The grant was matched by the Reformed Church in America. The Chemistry Department received grants in varying amounts for experimentation by Dr. Gerrit Van Zyl. Dr. Van Zyl was highly rated in Chemistry. He was a graduate of Hope and took his Ph.D. degree at the University of Michigan. He was often honored as one of the best Chemistry teachers in the country. He held an honorary degree from Hamline University and received a Doctor of Science degree from the college in 1964. In 1956 he won a prize of $1000 from the Scientific Apparatus Makers. But not all the grants came to the Chemistry Department. The Psychology Department won a grant for research in the problem of youth delinquency, which they did under the direction of the Sheriff of Kent County. $45,000 was received from the Merrill Foundation for study of unemployment in Michigan. In 1960 the National Science Foundation began to give yearly grants for teachers of Chemistry and Mathematics. $30,000 was received from the United States Office of Education for a study by Dr. Robert De Haan of the Psychology Department. A grant of $18,000 was received by Dean John W. Hollenbach from the Ford Foundation for a study of college curriculums.

Town and Gown

Never in the history of Hope were the relations between the college and community better than in the Lubbers era. Some of the credit for this must belong to the President, who was always ready to promote good relations and always willing to listen to any individual or group who had an interest in improving these relations. He himself promoted the cause by speaking persuasively to individuals and groups concerning the possibilities of the liberal arts college in the present age, and the need of larger support. The alumni were organized into a National

Alumni Association with chapters East and West. The publication of an alumni magazine of high quality by a competent
editor made a significant contribution to the cause. And as new
buildings were erected and the old buildings revamped, the college took on a new look.

Individual faculty members began to develop projects that
were of great value to the citizens of Holland. For example,
Dr. Ellert persuaded the Board of Education to let him try an
experiment in the teaching of foreign language in the elementary grades. Efforts were made in behalf of the Achievement
House, which was a joint venture of the college, the Community
Chest, and the city of Holland. The college furnished the teachers, and the Community Chest bore a large part of the costs.
It was incorporated, with officers representing all three parties.
The Achievement House was dedicated to the training of retarded
children between the ages of five and fourteen. It all began
when a parent made a survey of public sentiment and sold the
idea to the college and the Community Chest. The school became a reality in February 1958, and was designed to train re-

*On her official state visit to America in 1952, Queen Juliana of the
Netherlands visited Hope College and is here shown being escorted by
President Lubbers.*

tarded children socially, emotionally, physically, and academically. The college began to assist the community in providing lectures of high quality and assumed leadership in providing Community Concerts.

Athletics had long been a link between the college and community. The college now had a well-rounded athletics and Physical Education staff and participated in all sports. Over the period the coaches were Schouten, Hinga, Vanderbush, Visser, De Vette, and Brewer. Athletics took on new meaning, with Hope College winning its share of victories. Homecoming processions were eagerly awaited and very large crowds came out to see the Homecoming events. The work of William Schrier in oratory and debate upheld the splendid traditions established by Dr. John B. Nykerk. One of the successful winners in the Michigan Intercollegiate Speech League, Guy Vander Jagt, is now a United States Congressman.

A New Faculty

By the end of the Lubbers era, most of the faculty brought to Hope College by President Dimnent were retired or deceased. In 1966 only Dr. Clarence De Graaf was left. Thomas Welmers came to the campus as Professor of Greek in 1920. When Wichers resigned as Registrar in 1925, Welmers took over those duties, and held the office until his death in January of ' 1947. He left a widow and two brilliant sons who later earned the Ph.D. degree. Known as "Tossic" by the students, he taught them much more than Greek. He was a good preacher and organist. Professor Egbert E. Winter became head of the Department of Education in 1919, and served the college for thirty years until his sudden death in February of 1949. Through the years, he made a strong impression upon his students. Albert E. Lampen was Professor of Mathematics from 1919–1956. He was kind and the soul of goodness, but he also was an able mathematician and a skilled teacher. Milton L. Hinga came in the fall of 1931 as Instructor in History and athletic coach. After twenty-five years of coaching in high school and college, his former students presented him with a new automobile. In 1944 he became Dean of Men, and Dean of Students a few years later. He died May 31, 1960, and out of respect for his memory the college dedicated

The Anchor of Hope.

to him the large ship's anchor now found on the west side of
the campus. The Hinga children were both alumni of Hope.
Miss Laura A. Boyd came in 1921 as Professor of German,
and retired in 1955. The Reverend Paul E. Hinkamp came

in 1918 as Professor of Bible and became Professor of Philosophy in 1922. For some time he served as College Pastor, and was Registrar from 1945 until he retired in 1958. Other faculty members retiring were Nella Meyer and Mrs. Marguerite Meyer Prins, Professors of French, and Oscar Thompson, Professor of Biology since 1926. Edward Wolters retired in 1966 and John L. Schouten in 1962. Schouten had been with the college since 1920 and received from the college an honorary A.B. degree in 1945. Miss Metta Ross retired in 1960 after many years of teaching History. She organized Palette and Masque, a drama organization. Upon her retirement she was voted a life membership in the national organization.

For two years after World War II, students sent tons of clothing to students and faculty of Sarospatek College in Hungary. As a token of appreciation, Dr. M. Eugene Osterhaven was named an honorary member of the faculty of the Hungarian College and President Lubbers an honorary trustee. Dr. Joseph Zsiros was brought to Hope College as Professor of Greek. The Reverend A. Dykstra was appointed Director of Development for Hope College and the Reverend Allen B. Cook became Dean of the Chapel and Director of Kollen Hall. The Reverend Dykstra passed away in 1966, and the Reverend William Hillegonds, pastor of Hope Church, succeeded Allen B. Cook as Chaplain. Mr. Danforth gave the college $25,000 for a chapel, but with his consent the purpose of the gift was changed, and it is now used to augment the chapel program. Mrs. Isla Pruim Van Eenenaam succeeded Miss Emma Reeverts as Dean of Women.

Fund Raising

No President has ever been free from the agonizing labor of raising funds for the operation of the college, and perhaps none ever will be. This was particularly true in the Lubbers administration because of the rapid expansion of the college. Until the Dimnent era there were no tuition charges, but in the years 1945–1968 tuition charges were gradually increased until they reached $600 a semester. In 1966, students were paying approximately 80 percent of the entire cost of operating the college. Recently the question has been asked how high tuition can go for the average member of the Reformed Church, for the percentage of non-Reformed Church students has been steadily increasing, as have the tuition rates. Although the endowment has been raised to a little more than $2 million, it is still far below most of the colleges in the GLCA.

It was President Lubbers' idea that the three Reformed Church colleges plan collectively. The plans were called the Eendragt Campaign and the College Roll Call. Both were successful in a measure and brought some money into the treasury. But it was not enough, and so the college employed the firm of Marts and Lundy to outline a program that might really be successful. This company outlined and recommended a campaign for $3 million. The Holland-Zeeland quota was $300,000. This part of the campaign opened in the Civic Center in Holland with the Reverend Norman Vincent Peale and his friend Mr. Kresge as the chief speakers. In Holland, the campaign was under the leadership of Willis Diekema, son of a long-time Trustee of the college, and in Zeeland under the guidance of Jack De Witt, an alumnus of Hope. The slogan was "Looking Ahead with Hope" and the campaign was loyally supported by the various alumni chapters. The New York chapter of the National Alumni Association was host to the largest banquet of its kind to be held in the Waldorf-Astoria. In Los Angeles, more than three hundred alumni and their guests met together and pledged $20,000. These are but examples of the response to the college's appeal, and in due time capital funds in the amount of $3 million were raised.

The centennial fund had its origin in 1947 when Dr. Otto VanderVelde presented a report of a committee at the annual alumni dinner. It proposed that each alumnus should pledge an annual gift to the college. Since 1947, all alumni gifts have been reported in this fund regardless of the source of the gift. From 1947 to 1963, 2150 persons subscribed the total sum of $1,550,998, including the gift of Mr. G. J. Van Zoeren. It did not include a gift of $200,000 by Dr. John Heneveld of Muskegon and now of Florida, which is still in the development stage as part of the college endowment.

Efforts were also put forth to increase giving by alumni and the churches for operating funds. In 1947, 942 individuals gave the total sum of $40,800, while in 1963 the Reformed Church and the alumni were giving more than $250,000 each year for the support of the college. Both the alumni and the churches have raised their sights as to the needs of Hope College.

Such was the work and labor of President Lubbers. In eighteen years he had created a college that was receiving recognition in state and national circles. In eighteen years, he had created a college of distinction.

Convinced that younger leadership was needed, he resigned the presidency as of January 31, 1963. The college gave him many honors at the annual alumni dinner at the end of the second semester. He was without a peer in college administration, and did a great deal to give the other church colleges new hope. On February 15, 1963, he became President of the Iowa Association of Private Colleges and Universities. In the period 1960 to 1963, he was elected Vice President of the National Council of Churches, and in 1962 was elected President of the North Central Association of Colleges and Secondary Schools. In 1964, he was appointed by the Governor of Iowa to serve on the Iowa Higher Education Facilities Commission. He returned to Hope College to give the commencement address in 1963 and to receive the status of President Emeritus. During the centennial celebration in 1966, he returned to give a historical account of the early years of the college. His portrait, done by John Coppens of Bloomfield Hills, Michigan, hangs in the presidents' room in Graves Hall. Vice President Hollenbach was charged with the administration of the college for the second semester, 1963.

15: THE CENTENNIAL YEAR

CALVIN ANTHONY VANDERWERF, son of the Reverend and Mrs. Anthony VanderWerf, was born in Friesland, Wisconsin, January 2, 1917. He completed his secondary education in Holland High School in 1933, and received his A.B. degree from Hope College in 1937, graduating as the valedictorian of his class and serving as editor of the *Anchor* and president of the student body. He received a graduate assistantship in Chemistry from Ohio State University, where he earned the Ph.D. degree in 1941. He then accepted a position as Instructor of Chemistry at the University of Kansas. Named Assistant Professor in 1943 and Associate Professor in 1945, he was advanced to a full Professorship in 1949, becoming Chairman of the Department of Chemistry in 1961.

In 1954, Dr. VanderWerf became a member of the Advisory Committee of the Faculty Senate of the University of Kansas. He was a member of the Kansas University Athletic Board from 1957 to 1963, and chairman of that board from 1960 until he resigned to come to Hope College in 1963.

In addition to his teaching and administrative work at Kansas University, he carried on an active research program in medicinals, organophosphorus compounds, and the nitrogen compounds of petroleum. With his students he has published more than a hundred articles in national chemical journals. He is also the author or co-author of three General Chemistry textbooks, an Organic Chemistry laboratory manual, and a definitive monograph on acid-base theory. As consulting editor for Organic

Chemistry and Biochemistry for the Reinhold Publishing Corporation, he pioneered in 1961 in publishing the first special-topic paperbacks in Chemistry, an idea that has since swept the publishing field. In addition to his teaching, writing, and research, Dr. VanderWerf served on the Industrial Development Commission of the State of Kansas.

Dr. VanderWerf served as Secretary and Chairman of the Division of Chemical Education of the American Chemical Society. Later, as a Visiting Scientist for the National Science Foundation and a Lecturer at many National Science Foundation Summer Science Institutes, he appeared before very many audiences of scientists and Science teachers, both in this country and abroad. In 1961, he was awarded an unrestricted grant of $50,000 by the Petroleum Research Fund for use in imaginative basic research. Dr. VanderWerf has received honorary doctorates from three institutions.

Mrs. VanderWerf is the former Rachel Good, daughter of Professor and Mrs. Harry G. Good of Columbus, Ohio. Professor Good was a member of the faculty of the Department of Education at Ohio State University. Dr. and Mrs. VanderWerf, who were married in 1942, have six children, Gretchen, Klasina, Julie, Lisa, Pieter, and Marte.

When Dr. VanderWerf began his work at Hope in the fall of 1963, he quickly dispelled the fears of some constituents of the college that as a highly professional and dedicated scientist he might completely change the traditional arts emphasis. His passion for inspired learning and exciting teaching and his determination to establish a climate that would foster such teaching and learning were soon evident. In his first two major addresses, the convocation address to the students on September 12, 1963, and the inaugural address in November, President VanderWerf made it clear that college studies are demanding disciplines that challenge the utmost capabilities of all students. He said, in the convocation address:

> As you enjoy the rich educational experience that is Hope College, I trust that you will develop a deep and abiding love of learning; commitment to truth in all its forms, the joy of seeking truth, the peace of finding truth, and the courage of living

Calvin A. Vander Werf, president, 1963-

truth, love of what is good and excellent, love of law, love of life and of people, and a passion for justice in our times.

But, above all, I would like to invite you in the midst of all the bewildering array that is spread before you to a spiritual experiment, to the development or the deepening of a real, a vital, an abiding personal faith which will become for you through all your life your most important single possession; a faith that answers the questions, "Why am I here?", "Where am I going?", "What is my purpose in life?"

The inauguration ceremonies were held on November 16. They were attended by delegates from 137 colleges and universities and 22 learned societies. The President's inaugural address set the tone that was to prevail at Hope College for the coming years when he said:

Society entrusts to our fellowship and tutelage its most precious and priceless possession, its youth, the stuff of which the future is fashioned.... I dedicate all the talents and energy I possess to the task of providing leadership in fostering the climate which will encourage the faculty and students to grow together as a community of free and consecrated scholars in the high tradition of Hope College.

Mr. Ekdal Buys, Chairman of the Board of Trustees and a classmate of President VanderWerf, delivered the charge, to which the new President responded, accepting the responsibility to provide a quality education for all who were to come to Hope College. Following the ceremonies, an inaugural luncheon was held in Phelps Hall, with Vice President John W. Hollenbach as master of ceremonies. Dr. Hollenbach introduced Dr. Matthew Peelen, Vice Chairman of the Board of Trustees, the Reverend Harvey B. Hoffman, who spoke for the Reformed Church in America, Dean William Vander Lugt, who spoke for the faculty, Mr. Lamont Dirkse, who spoke for the National Alumni Association, David R. Mouw, who spoke for the students, and Mayor Nelson Bosman, who spoke for the citizens of Holland.

The first and most important task confronting the new administration was the building of an enlarged faculty. The growing fame and reputation of the college as a superior educational institution was attracting an increasing number of students. The National Council for Accreditation of Teacher Education

Dykstra Hall, completed September, 1967.

granted the college full accreditation in 1964. Applications from deserving high school graduates tripled from 1963 to 1966, and this pressure could not be ignored.

It soon became apparent that, both in order to give thoughtful consideration to every one of the many applicants and in order to identify and attract Freshmen for whom competition had become keen, an expanded admissions program was necessary. As a result, the admissions staff was increased from two to four, and a spacious home was purchased as headquarters for the office.

The knowledge explosion also figured in the decision to increase the faculty. With the burgeoning of discovery, many two- and three-man departments found they were below critical size and could no longer offer a major of integrity in their particular discipline. In order to cover the field for both majors and non-majors in traditional disciplines, the faculty had to be enlarged, especially in the humanities and social sciences.

The new decision to admit more students and hire more faculty was a serious one, for it had to be made at a time when most of this nation's colleges were also seeking additional staff.

Difficulties in building a faculty were compounded in the early years of Dr. VanderWerf's administration by the loss, through death and retirement, of a number of outstanding teachers who had devoted their entire professional lives to service at Hope.

Dr. J. H. Kleinheksel, Professor of Chemistry for thirty-seven years, died unexpectedly in December 1965. At a memorial service held in Dimnent Chapel, January 5, 1966, Dr. Vander-Werf said, "We who have sat at his feet in Freshman Chemistry or in an advanced course in Analytical Chemistry will tell you that we have never known a finer, a more masterful teacher."

Four professors, all appointed by Dr. Dimnent, retired June 1, 1964. These four, affectionately known on the campus as "The Four Horsemen," were: Dr. Gerrit Van Zyl, Chairman of the Department of Chemistry since 1923; Professor Clarence Kleis, Chairman of the Department of Physics since 1920; Professor Garrett Vanderborgh, Chairman of the Department of Education since 1922; and Professor Albert Timmer, Professor of Latin and Admissions Director since 1923. Together, these four served Hope College for 166 years. (As a footnote to this remarkable record of outstanding service, the writer is pleased to add that the Michigan State Senate, at the suggestion of Senator Clyde Geerlings, passed a resolution honoring these four great teachers. A framed statement, now hanging in the new Hope College Alumni House, attests to this recognition.)

Two women, Mrs. Esther Snow of the German Department, and Miss Nella Meyer of the French Department, retired in 1965. Mrs. Snow had first taught at Hope College in 1937, and Miss Meyer had been on the faculty since 1942.

Professor Edward Wolters, who taught Latin for thirty-six years at the college, retired June 8, 1966, along with Dr. Tunis Baker, who had been a member of the Education Department since 1957.

The year 1967 brought the retirement of two more professors of long experience. Mrs. Helen Schoon, of the Education Department, and Dr. Dwight B. Yntema, Chairman of the Department of Economics, had both joined Hope's faculty in 1946.

Yet, in spite of the retirement of these outstanding and beloved teachers and the crucial national shortage of college professors, at the end of the centennial year the faculty totalled 117 and the student-faculty ratio had been decreased substantially.

Based on the annual ratings of the American Association of University Professors, faculty salary increases represented a shift upward from Class E to Class C.

Along with bigger salaries came new fringe benefits. A funded retirement program was instituted in cooperation with the Teachers Insurance and Annuity Association. Optional coverage was provided in the College Retirement Equities Fund. An expanded health and hospital insurance program was provided for all employees, faculty children were granted free tuition at the college, and a generous sabbatical leave program was established.

Innovations in the academic areas included the naming of Dean William Vander Lugt to be Distinguished Professor-at-Large, and the presence of two visiting professors on the campus. Dr. James Muilenburg, Professor Emeritus of Old Testament at Union Theological Seminary, New York City, and Dead Sea Scrolls scholar, spent the spring semester, 1966, as Theologian-in-Residence; Dr. William Welmers, Professor of African Languages at the University of California in Los Angeles, was Visiting Professor of Linguistics during the spring semester, 1967.

Under Chaplain William Hillegonds a campus church was organized and began to hold regular Sunday morning services in Dimnent Chapel. Trustees for the church were selected from the student body. Chaplain Hillegonds and visiting clergy cooperated in the preaching, but a student trustee presided regularly.

During this same period construction of new physical facilities continued. Among the several new buildings dedicated in the fall of 1963 were Gilmore Hall, a dormitory for women, a large complex of residence halls for fraternities, and the Physics-Mathematics Hall. The financing of the Physics-Mathematics Hall represented a new departure at the college. For the first time in its history, the college floated a loan for a classroom building. The $600,000 loan was reduced to less than half in three years.

A greenhouse for the Biology and Botany departments was dedicated on May 30, 1965. It was a memorial to Dr. William George Hoebeke of the Class of 1911, a gift from Mrs. Hoebeke.

An attractive home on 12th Street was turned over to the alumni, and maintained under the direction of Mrs. Marian Stryker, Alumni Secretary. The first floor was used as a lounge and for alumni offices. Guest rooms for overnight visitors were furnished on the second.

Like colleges and universities everywhere, Hope, too, was confronted with the skyrocketing cost of education. The 1963 enrollment of 1571 rose to 1818 by September 1966. That fall the cost for tuition, room and board was $1800, and the President and Trustees worried that some students from Reformed Church homes would be forced, from financial necessity, to enroll elsewhere. With a small, inadequate endowment of $2 million, the college asked churches and alumni to increase their gifts to the operating budget of the college.

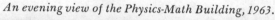

An evening view of the Physics-Math Building, 1963.

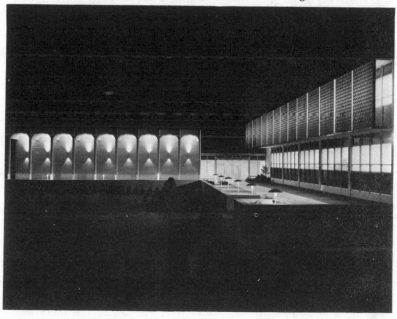

The William G. Hoebeke Greenhouse, 1965. Dr. Paul Van Faasen,
Assistant Professor of Botany.

The fine response to this request can best be shown in figures.
Hope College alumni, through their alumni fund, donated
$37,460 in 1962, $104,050 in 1963, $127,623 in 1964, $158,292 in
1965, and $196,869 in 1966. In 1965, an additional $100,000 was
received in matching gifts.

The Chapel Choir giving a concert in Europe, 1967.

This splendid record of alumni giving brought the college the American Alumni Council's first-place award for coeducational colleges for improvement in alumni giving, and the second-place grand award for colleges and universities of all types. The second-place grand award carried with it a $3000 prize from the U. S. Steel Foundation.

A thoughtful and well-documented appeal for support was made to individual churches and to the Reformed Church headquarters. Increased giving from this source also helped balance the operating budget. In 1962, Hope College received $123,277 in operational funds from the church; in 1963 this figure was $131,272; in 1964, $138,669; in 1965, $155,511; and in 1966, $222,761.

International Programs

In 1964, Professor Paul Fried was named Director of International Programs. Eight years earlier, in 1956, Dr. Fried had founded the Hope College Vienna Summer School with fourteen

students. Under his enthusiastic tutelage in the ensuing decade
the Vienna Summer School grew steadily in distinction and for
the past several summers it has been necessary to limit enrollment to sixty students. Each group has spent a summer of study
and travel in Europe. Both western and eastern European tours
are now part of the Vienna program.

In 1965, the first Hope College Alumni Seminar in Vienna
was held, with twenty-two alumni participating. The theme
was "Vienna: East/West Intersection."

Because of Dr. Fried's experience and because of the college's
outstanding record with the Vienna program, Hope was chosen
to be the coordinating center for the Great Lakes Colleges Association Iron Curtain program. Dr. and Mrs. VanderWerf had
visited Yugoslavia in the summer of 1964 at the request of the
U. S. State Department, and Dr. VanderWerf had helped make
initial arrangements for an American-Yugoslav student inter-
change. Hope served as host school for eight Yugoslav students
in the summer of 1966. This program, under the sponsorship of

*The Reverend Gordon Van Wyk, Professor of History at Meiji Gakuin
University, Tokyo, with the first group of Japanese participants in the
summer "Intensive American Studies" program, 1965.*

the Great Lakes Colleges Association and the U. S. State Department, had sent twelve students to the University of Ljubljana for the first in a series of East-West dialogues the previous year. With the arrival in this country of the Yugoslav students, Hope became the first college in the United States to welcome to its campus a sizeable group of undergraduate students from an Iron Curtain country.

But Europe was not the only continent included in the college's international outreach. The year 1965 saw the establishment at Hope of a summer program for Japanese students. In 1964/65, a faculty seminar on Japanese culture had been located at the college by the Great Lakes Colleges Association with Dr. Masanoa Kano, a Japanese historian from Waseda University, as the leader. In June, thirty-seven Japanese undergraduate students from Tokyo, of Meiji Gakuin University, under the leadership of the Reverend Gordon Van Wyk, '41, arrived to spend six weeks on the campus. In 1966 and 1967, a second and third group arrived.

The second year the studies of the Japanese students were integrated with those of the eight Yugoslav students, and with students from the Netherlands and Germany as well. An American seminar for foreign university students had been inaugurated. Appropriately, it was dubbed a "Vienna Summer School in Reverse."

Other international studies in which Hope faculty and students participated included the Junior Year at American University in Beirut, Lebanon, organized by the GLCA. Dr. John Hollenbach served as GLCA coordinator in Lebanon in 1965/66. Sixteen Hope students have also been enrolled in the GLCA's Latin-American Center in Bogota, Colombia. Professor Werner Heine spent the summer of 1965 in Tanzania working under the sponsorship of a GLCA research grant, and Professor Hubert Weller also studied in Spain and Peru with GLCA funds.

New Instructional Programs

Membership in the Great Lakes Colleges Association has brought participation in major national programs in addition to the international ones just mentioned. Beginning in 1963,

Dr. Robert De Haan, chairman of the college's Department of Education, served as director of a GLCA three-year experiment on new methods of instruction. This research program was made possible through a $250,000 grant from the U. S. Department of Health, Education and Welfare.

In 1966, President VanderWerf was asked to serve as Science Coordinator for the GLCA. In this capacity he heads a committee to design cooperative projects that will be a model and inspiration for liberal arts colleges everywhere in the nation, as they work to provide an intellectual climate that is exceptionally favorable for the education of scientists and of scientifically literate laymen.

In January 1967, Hope was selected by the Alfred P. Sloan Foundation as one of twenty liberal arts colleges to share in a $7.5 million experiment in science curricula and teaching. The college received $375,000 to be used for the development of a broadly innovative and integrated curriculum for all the sciences.

The Kettering Foundation Internship program, another of the GLCA programs in which Hope has participated, annually brought a young scientist to the campus to explore the profession of college teaching. Three young Ph.D. scientists, one biologist and two chemists, have each been interns at Hope. In 1967 the program continued under the aegis of the National Science Foundation, and Hope College now has three teaching interns, in Chemistry, Biology, and Psychology.

Scholarships and Awards

It is not surprising, with a lively, growing faculty and an increasingly well-qualified student body, that Hope students were beginning to win a substantial number of awards and scholarships. In three years Hope students won thirteen Woodrow Wilson Fellowships, many Danforth, Ford Foundation, National Science Foundation and other fellowships. Two students, David Mouw, '64, and Cheryl Richardson, '66, won Fulbright Scholarships to study abroad, and Lynne VandeBunte, '64, received a Marshall Scholarship, one of twenty-four awarded nationwide, for study in Philosophy at Cambridge University.

In 1965, Suellen Prins received the *Chemical and Engineering News* Outstanding Merit Award given annually to the nation's twelve top all-around Senior Chemistry majors; Roger Abel received honorable mention.

Three times the Hope College Music Department produced a winner in the national Congress of Strings competition.

In oratory, Jacob Ngwa, '66, Hope student from Cameroon, won first place in the 1964 Interstate Oratorical Association Final Contest. Richard Rietveld won first place in the State Oratorical Contest in 1967.

Each year approximately 40 percent of the graduating class continued their education in the graduate schools of leading universities, many supported by graduate fellowships, assistantships, and scholarships.

Grants and Special Gifts

In 1964, Hope College was given a $60,000 grant to conduct a National Science Foundation Summer Institute for high school teachers of second-year and advanced-placement Chemistry under the direction of Dr. Eugene Jekel. The grant for this successful program was renewed annually, and in 1967 funds ($52,000) were also received from the National Science Foundation for a similar institute in Mathematics. Other National Science Foundation grants were $12,000 for special apparatus in Physics, $35,000 matching grant for a computer, and $25,000 for undergraduate research.

At a critical period in 1964, when veteran teachers were retiring, the science program received crucial support through a grant of $43,000 from the Research Corporation. This proved to be just the added boost the college needed to move ahead vigorously in strengthening its traditionally preeminent role in the education of scientists and of scientifically literate laymen.

Individual professors also received grants from the Research Corporation, as well as from the Office of Saline Water, the Petroleum Research Fund, and the National Science Foundation.

Seymour and Stuart Padnos, local businessmen, established the Louis and Helen Padnos Community Education Fund at Hope College to further education at all levels in the city.

Dormitory funds were given by two Grand Rapids churches: Eighth Reformed Church bought a residence on East 12th Street and presented it to the college for an honors house for girls;

Central Reformed Church sent $25,000 toward a new dormitory, with the promise to commend to future consistories similar gifts toward a total goal of $500,000.

Ground was broken for the new dormitory on March 13, 1967. The construction contract specified completion of the dormitory by September 1, 1967, in time for fall occupancy. The Hall is designed on the "cluster" plan and has space for 284 students.

A matching grant of $50,000 was received from the U. S. Office of Education. It provided half the total cost of a nuclear magnetic resonance spectrometer, as well as money for much-needed equipment for the Departments of Education, Mathematics, Music, Speech, and Sociology. The actual purchase of the NMR was made possible by a donation from the Holland-Suco Division of the Chemetron Corporation, which gave $10,000 toward the instrument. Of the $17,500 needed to match the government's grant for the instrument, the remaining $7500 was provided in smaller grants from other firms.

The Alcor Society becomes the Mortar Board, 1961.

Hopes for a new science facility to house the Departments of Chemistry, Biology, and Geology came close to realization with the news that the college had received a grant of $1 million from the U. S. Higher Education Facilities Act, and a loan of $2,026,-000 from the U. S. Department of Health, Education, and Welfare. The Trustees proposed raising the remaining funds necessary for the $4 million building through the sale of revenue bonds. This step was taken when it was learned that the present Science Hall, although soundly constructed, could no longer meet present-day safety and fire codes for facilities for science instruction. Remodeling the old building to bring it up to safety standards was first considered, but later dropped when the price turned out to be much higher than the original cost of the building. With minimum expense, however, Science Hall can be remodeled into an excellent office and classroom building for non-laboratory departments.

Application for the government grant and loan was made possible because the college had once again begun to show signs of growth after the five-year period, 1960–64, when enrollment was stagnant at approximately 1560 students. With the 1965 enrollment at 1707, and the 1966 enrollment at 1818, Hope forcefully demonstrated its eligibility for assistance in its building program.

Another source of capital funds was opened to the college by the Capital Funds Campaign of the Reformed Church in America. Scheduled to run from January 1 to June 1, 1967, $4.9 million of the $6 million goal had been pledged by July 1967. Hope College is to receive $2 million from this national campaign. The money will be used for the construction of a student center and a major addition to the Music Building. On June 22, 1967, word was received that Hope College was awarded, by the federal government, under Title I, a $410,995 grant to be used toward the construction of the academic portion of the Student Cultural-Social Center.

Buildings were not alone in placing demands on the capital funds available. The college was also faced with funding a retirement program for present faculty members. With an inadequately funded retirement plan and many instructors under the program approaching retirement age, capital funds for this program are crucial. An actuaries specialist has projected that $780,635 in investments is still needed to fund completely the total retirement program now in force.

One further gift — of another sort — must be mentioned before we leave this section on Grants and Special Gifts.

On January 10, 1965, Mr. H. A. Hoogendoorn, Counselor of the Netherlands Embassy for Press and Cultural Affairs, presented an original oil painting, "The March to the Feast of Whitsuntide," by Kees Sabee, to Hope College from the Netherlands government. The painting hangs in the lobby of Van Zoeren Library where it was unveiled by Dr. G. John Van Zoeren, the library's donor.

The Centennial Year

On April 10, 1965, Prince Bernhard of the Netherlands gave a convocation address at Dimnent Chapel, formally opening the Hope College Centennial Year. In response, President Vander-Werf announced the establishment of Hope's Center for International Education, to be directed by Dr. Paul Fried, and of the Prince Bernhard Scholarship Fund, designed both to bring young scholars and teachers from the Netherlands to Hope College, and to offer Hope students and faculty an opportunity to study in the Netherlands. Jan Huber was the first Netherlands scholar to enroll at Hope. He arrived in September 1965. Paul Schaap, a Senior majoring in Chemistry, was the first exchange fellow to go to the Netherlands. He left Hope for a semester at the University of Groningen in February 1967.

In the fall of 1965, the Education Department began a Professional Semester program which permitted prospective teachers to teach on a full-day basis.

Henry Steffens was promoted to Vice President and Treasurer, Dr. Morette L. Rider was named Dean for Academic Affairs, Clarence J. Handlogten was appointed Director of Business Affairs, and a full-scale development program, with Larry Ter Molen as director, was inaugurated.

With 1400 residential students compressed into two city blocks having few and inadequate recreational facilities, the Trustees and administration recognized that the need for a student center was imperative. Early in the centennial year, the students them-

Mr. H. A. Hoogendoorn presenting Kees Sabee's painting to President Calvin A. Vander Werf, 1966.

selves opened a drive for a student union, which they named the Student Cultural-Social Center. A rally at the President's home kicked off a series of projects — the sale of SCSC buttons, car washes, various benefits — which raised $3000. Older friends also contributed, and the fund for a student center soon surpassed $150,000.

During the centennial year, the annual Fine Arts Festival followed a Dutch theme, bringing to Hope five Dutch personalities: Dr. Ivo Schöffer, Professor of Dutch History at the University of Leiden; Edo de Waard, twenty-one-year-old Assistant Director of the Amsterdam Concertgebouw Orchestra; Max Tak, radio commentator, author, and musician; Miss Tina Ferringa, diplomat in the Netherlands Foreign Service; and Miss Dola de Jong, novelist.

Dr. Norman Norton, Chairman of the Biology Department, was a participant at the International Conference on Palynology, held at Utrecht, the Netherlands.

A series of centennial lectures, open to the public, were given by faculty members representing various disciplines. Distinguished alumni were also invited to give convocation addresses.

In the summer the President was a lecturer at an International Seminar on the Teaching of Science held in Buenos Aires, spon-

Prince Bernhard of the Netherlands welcomed to Hope College, 1965.

sored by the Organization of American States. In 1965, he was appointed to the Research Corporation Board of Trustees; a year later he was named Fellow by the New York Academy of Sciences. In 1967, he was the recipient of the American Chemical Society's award as "Visiting Scientist of the Year."

Three important print collections were hung in the Van Zoeren mezzanine gallery; one by Toon Wegner, Dutch printmaker; an exhibition of biblical prints by Sadao Watanabe; and original works by Leonard Baskin.

Centennial Homecoming Celebration

A gala centennial Homecoming celebration in October 1966, was a long-to-be-remembered event of the first few years of the VanderWerf administration. The keynote address was delivered by Governor George Romney on October 12 in the Holland Civic Center, on the centennial theme, "Education for Respon-

The traditional annual Pull between freshmen and sophomores through the Black River.

The De Witt Cultural Center. Construction on this $2.2 million student and community center will begin in 1969. Money-raising projects conducted by students, a Federal grant, a capital-funds campaign in the Reformed Church in America, and gifts from friends of Hope were important contributions. The facility is named in honor of Jack ('32) and Richard (Prep. '31) De Witt, whose gift was the largest ever made to Hope College.

sible Leadership." Earlier that evening the Governor had been honored at a reception given by President and Mrs. VanderWerf in their home.

The Governor's talk was preceded on October 11 by a lively debate between socialist Norman Thomas and *Newsweek* editor Kenneth Crawford on U. S. policy in Vietnam. Seminars relating to the general Homecoming theme were held on Friday, October 14. Dr. Mortimer Adler, Great Books scholar, spoke on philosophy; Lester Trimble, music critic for the New York *Herald-Tribune,* spoke on music; Colonel John Powers, voice of Mercury Control, spoke on science; Dr. Yale Brozen, University of Chicago, spoke on economics. That same day, Mrs. VanderWerf addressed the Women's League for Hope College at their annual meeting in Durfee Hall. Arthur Allyn, owner of the Chicago White Sox, spoke at the H-Club luncheon the following noon.

On Saturday evening, October 15, the traditional alumni

dinner was turned into a recognition banquet. A $15 million master plan for the physical development of the campus was unveiled, complete with the architect's renditions of five new buildings, two additions to present buildings, and an improved campus layout. New major gifts were announced. These included two memorial funds, the George B. and Anna B. Dalman Scholarship Fund, and the Becker Foundation for Research in Economics to endow a Chair in the Department of Economics.

The Loutit Foundation of Grand Haven gave $25,000 for the student center fund.

Mrs. Matthew J. Wilson of Scottsdale, Arizona, was presented with a sterling silver centennial medallion, the only one cast, in appreciation of her gift of stock certificates to fund the new faculty benefit program. On display at the banquet was the valuable Matthew J. Wilson proof coin collection, another of Mrs. Wilson's gifts to the college.

An honorary LL.D. degree was given Ekdal J. Buys, retiring Chairman of the Board of Trustees. Hugh De Pree, incoming Chairman, was introduced and spoke on the master plan.

The Homecoming celebration concluded Sunday, October 16, with a morning service in the Dimnent Memorial Chapel, led by Dr. Ernest T. Campbell, minister of the First Presbyterian Church of Ann Arbor. In the afternoon, a recital by Dr. Anthony Kooiker dedicated one of the centennial gifts, a new Steinway concert grand piano.

A valuable and interesting pictorial alumni magazine was edited by Mrs. Marian Stryker, secretary of the Alumni Association, and published in October 1966.

EPILOGUE: A LOOK AHEAD

By ACTION OF the Hope College Board of Trustees at its meeting, May 1964, the President was authorized to appoint a Profile Committee, to be made up of a representative cross section of the Board, alumni, faculty, and administration. The commission of this committee, as given it by the President in his appointment letter, was to present a "sharp, incisive, bold, imaginative blueprint for the future. This blueprint should delineate aims and goals, purposes and objectives; it should chart the future — for student body, faculty, campus, curriculum, facilities and finances."

Nineteen men and women devoted to Hope College made up the Profile Committee, under the leadership of Dr. John Hollenbach. This group met frequently during the winter of 1964/65, discussing the direction the college could, and should, take as its second century opened. The completed profile report was presented to the Trustees the following June (1965).

Charting a course of a different type is the new master plan for the campus, prepared by Edward Stade and Associates, Architects. This master plan calls for a minimum of five new academic buildings plus residence halls.

These two plans for the future outline wonderful new dreams for the college, geared to meet the challenges and opportunities of a world in revolution. Totally committed to the conviction that one's responsibility is never discharged simply by the announcement of virtuous ends, President VanderWerf clearly has a large task before him. Parts of the forward-looking pro-

271

gram are under way. The Reverend John A. Dykstra Hall for
Women has been completed and is now occupied. The Student
Cultural Center will soon be a reality. Other programs will
follow as the work of one hundred years moves into the future.
All this will be the fulfillment of Dr. Van Raalte's hopes and
the hopes of those who follow in his train. Under the guidance
of Almighty God, Hope College has toiled and persevered to
translate dreams and visions into a reality that lives and grows
in the lives of its students.

APPENDICES

THE ARTICLES OF INCORPORATION CONSTITUTE THE CHARTER (1865)

We, the undersigned, associate together to become a Corporation, for the purpose of founding and establishing a college under the laws of the State of Michigan, entitled "An Act to provide for the incorporation of Institutions of Learning," approved February 9, 1855, and the Acts amendatory thereto.

Name

The name of the Institution is Hope College. The Trustees and their successors are to be a Body corporate, and their corporate name is "The Council of Hope College."

Location

The location of the college and of the corporation is at Holland, in Ottawa County, in the State of Michigan.

Character and object

The character and object of the school and of the Corporation are to provide the usual literary and scientific course of study, in connection with sound evangelical religious instruction, according to the standards of the Reformed Church, as based on the Holy Scripture.

Although the College is Denominational in character, yet students shall be admitted to all its advantages, without respect to their ecclesiastical connections, subject only to the general rules and regulations of the Institution.

Departments

The Departments of Instruction which it shall be the special endeavor of the Council to maintain, are the following:

1. Grammar School Department, preparatory for business or for higher courses of study.

2. The Academic Department, qualifying for the degree of Bachelor of Arts.

275

3. In addition to these, the Council may institute such other departments as are in harmony with these Articles of Incorporation.

Funds

The amount of funds or capital stock donated or given to the Trustees or Council of the said college, is as follows:

The General Synod of the Reformed Church in America, a body corporate under the Laws of the State of New York, and authorized to hold property for educational purposes in the State of Michigan, has, in good faith and in due form, donated or given to the said Trustees or Council, for the purpose of endowing such college, the sum of thirty thousand dollars, of which sum six thousand dollars has already been paid to the Associates or Trustees, for the use of this college. In addition to this, The General Synod has set apart for the use and purpose of this college and incorporation the real estate and premises in the County of Ottawa and State of Michigan, known as the Holland Academy. And, moreover, the said General Synod, as a Body Corporate, holds in express trust for this corporation and college, independent of the aforesaid thirty thousand dollars, already donated and heretofore set forth, in subscriptions, promissory notes, and cash, twenty thousand dollars, and which sum is from time to time becoming increased by donations.

Original Incorporators

The following are the names and places of residence of the Trustees and length of time of their continuance in office:

Albertus C. Van Raalte, Holland, Michigan until September 1, 1895 or during his ecclesiastical connection with the Particular Synod of Chicago but not exceeding thirty years.

Philip Phelps, Jr. of Holland, Ottawa County, Michigan ex-officio member as President of Hope College, while President but not to exceed thirty years.

John L. See, New Brunswick, New Jersey ex-officio member as Corresponding Secretary of the Board of Education, R.C.A. while such Secretary but not to exceed thirty years.

John Mason Ferris, Flatbush, Long Island, New York until September 1, 1866.

Solomon Cummings, Centreville, Michigan until September 1, 1867.

Samuel J. Rogers, Geneva, New York until September 1, 1868.

Schuyler Colfax, South Bend, Indiana until September 1, 1869.

John S. Joralmon, Fairview, Illinois until September 1, 1866.

John N. Rogers, Davenport, Iowa until September 1, 1867.

Cyrus G. Van Der Veere, Davenport, Iowa until September 1, 1868.

Edward P. Livingston, Bushnell, Illinois until September 1, 1869.

Seine Bolks, Zeeland, Michigan until September 1, 1866.

Hessel O. Yntema, Vriesland, Michigan until September 1, 1867.

Peter J. Oggel, Holland, Michigan until September 1, 1868.

Arie C. Kuyper, Pella, Iowa until September 1, 1869.
N. D. Williamston, Chicago, Illinois until September 1, 1866.
Jacob VanZanten, Low Prairie, Illinois until September 1, 1867.
John Vandermeulen, Milwaukee, Wisconsin until September 1, 1868.
Roelof Pieters, Alto, Wisconsin until September 1, 1869.

Under the foregoing articles we, the undersigned, do hereby associate for the purpose of forming a corporation under the name and for the object aforesaid. (Signed personally by the preceding names, except Rev. John Vandermeulen and John N. Rogers.)

COMMENCEMENT ODE — 1866

By Dr. Phelps

When first we met within these walls,
    Our hands had helped to rear,
The dawn of college life began
    In beauty to appear.
Excelsior our watchword was —
    We've kept it e'er in sight,
And higher yet, with zeal we look,
    On this Commencement night.

In Freshman days, how bright the hope,
    Which did each soul possess!
And ev'ry coming Freshman Class
    Delights itself in *Spes.*
Oh, ne'er cut loose the anchor, boys!
    The anchor sure, of hope!
But in its strength, outride each storm
    And with the billows cope!

Yet toil alone can bring success,
    The trusting heart to cheer;
And *Diligentia* must mark
    The Soph-o-more's career.
That work is light, which with it bears
    The spirit's cheerful choice;
And so, may loving Diligence,
    Your Soph'more way rejoice!

As through our college days we glide,
　　How earnest grows the tie,
Which joins our sentiments in one,
　　And brings us eye to eye!
　　Concordia! ye Junior boys!
　　　Firm concord bringeth might!
And let your class's maxim be
　　A union for the right!

When came the last of college years,
　　That erst had seemed so far,
Then this, the purpose of our hearts,
　　Per-se-ve-ran-ti-a!
Oh, Seniors! Perseverance 'tis—
　　Endurance to the end,
Which makes us men, and bids our steps
　　To full success ascend.

And now, for all our future time,
　　As thro' life's maze we go,
Be this our motto, brothers all!
　　Spera tu in Deo!
Yes! Hope In God, when it is dark,
　　And hope, when it is light!
For hope shall never cease to be,
　　Till lost in perfect sight.

Allusions — *Excelsior* is the motto-word with which the highest class
of the Grammar School pursues and completes its preparatory course.
Spes, Diligentia, Concordia, Perseverantia, are respectively the motto-
words of the Freshman, Sophomore, Junior and Senior classes.

LETTER FROM DR. PHELPS TO THE COUNCIL

ALBANY, NEW YORK
195 HAMILTON STREET
JUNE 17, 1885

TO THE COUNCIL OF HOPE COLLEGE
DEAR BRETHREN:-

A great deal of time was devoted by me to the preparation of the original diplomas, and very unusual care was taken so that the engraver promised to send them from New York even a number of days before the first commencement. But to the great disappointment of all of us, they did not arrive until the class had dispersed to their homes. There was no immediate haste then and soon afterwards there arose a desire on the part of all concerned to change the original device, which could not be done until the constitution of the college had been amended. Meanwhile, however, I had secured the signatures of members of the Council on the diplomas of the first, second and third classes. The new diplomas were first distributed to the class of 1873, and by that time there had arisen serious embarrassments as to the autographs of the members of the Council for the several years 1866–1872. It was not till last summer that I succeeded devising a plan as follows: for the classes of 1866, 1867 and 1869, I retained the early parchments carrying the signatures of original Council and filled them out obtaining also the names of the Professors and Teachers for the several years for the classes of 69, 70, 71 and 72. I filled out blank diplomas, most of which had been a long time in my possession and procured signatures of Professors and Teachers for the several years as before, and also of as many members of the council as practicable, while for the deceased members I obtained fac simile of their autographs, from previous diplomas, so skillfully executed that even an expert could not have told the difference. Some of the diplomas had to be sent to different parties by express for their signatures, as for instance, Drs. Ferris and Crispell in the east. Next I wrote a letter to each alumnus explaining the facts as above and stating which signatures were original and which were fac simile. Thus the first three classes had original autographs by members both of the Council and Faculty, and the others had them of the Faculty in every instance, and in most cases of the Council also, with one or two exceptions. . . .

— DR. PHILIP PHELPS, JR.

280

The poem delivered by the Reverend John M. Vandermeulen
at the fiftieth anniversary of the college in 1916.

Oh, Dutchmen, we have met today to clasp each other's hand;
We have made a noble clearing where our settlement now stands.
Now let us view the consummation of our present hopes and fears,
Let's see what lies before us in the coming fifty years.

Our Alma Mater standeth not as in days gone by,
She has heaved this new gymnasium roof against the flowing sky,
She has called her new professors in to stimulate their peers,
And it's no Van Winkle sleep she'll have these coming fifty years.

She has made a noble effort in the space 'twixt now and there,
For Kollen's financiering was no castle in the air,
And our lads have won the championship and hold it by the ears,
And they'll make a blazing record now these coming fifty years.

Professors, some are still at work who ground us through the mill
And Vennema to furnish power to run us with a will.
May pockets open to him and all hail to him who steers
The largest progeny to him these coming fifty years.

They will watch the microbe hunted down and slaughtered in his lair
They will chuck the automobile and go sailing through the air;
They'll catch and photograph a spook in spite of Yankee sneers.
They'll colonize the North Pole these coming fifty years.

They will smash a score of precedents that now appear so bold;
They'll climb into the governor's chair, great pulpits they will hold—
They cannot all be presidents, but in their several spheres
They'll cut their eye teeth handsomely, these coming fifty years.

Here's a health to each alumnus whose cheerful greetings fail,
We bless him if in congress and will bless him if in jail:
And a tender thought for those, through rising mists of tears,
Whom death will snatch too early these coming fifty years.

Let us bravely face the future now for church and native land
To do whatever honest work God places in our hands;
For country, friends and college, let's give three rousing cheers
And serve our Christ through Hope these coming fifty years.

HONORARY DEGREES CONFERRED
BY HOPE COLLEGE

Name	Hope Grad	Degree	Year
Baert, George, M.D.		A.M.	1901
Baeta, Rev. Christian G.		LL.D.	1959
Baker, Rev. Peter Garrett	1920	D.D.	1951
Banninga, Rev. John	1898	D.D.	1917
Barnouw, Hon. Adrian J.		Litt.D.	1941
Bast, Henry, Rev.	1939	D.D.	1956
Beardslee, Rev. John W.	1898	D.D.	1913
Bedell, Edward	1873	Mus.D.	1894
Beltman, Rev. Henry	1916	D.D.	1949
Beyer, Rev. A. F.		D.D.	1902
Birkhoff, George, Jr.		A.M.	1896
Blekkink, Rev. E. J.	1883	D.D.	1909
Blekkink, Rev. Victor J.	1909	D.D.	1936
Boer, Rev. Nicholas		D.D.	1932
Boers, H.	1878	A.M.	1881
Boeve, Rev. Lucas	1903	D.D.	1925
Bok, Edward W.		LL.D.	1910
Boot, Rev. Harry P.	1900	D.D.	1932
Bovenkerk, Rev. Henry G.	1927	D.D.	1957
Broek, Christian A.	1905	A.M.	1916
Brouwer, Wm. L.		LL.D.	1928
Brower, Rev. Bert	1923	D.D.	1964
Brown, Rev. Willard Dayton		D.D.	1921
Bruce, Rev. W. P.		D.D.	1912
Brucker, Wilber M.		LL.D.	1958
Brummelkamp, Rev. A.		D.D.	1911
Bruggers, Rev. John Henry	1915	D.D.	1954
Brush, Rev. Alfred H.		D.D.	1897
Brush, Hon. Donald Livingston	1912	LL.D.	1954
Burrell, Rev. David J., D.D.		LL.D.	1902
Buys, Ekdal J.	1937	LL.D.	1966
Cadman, Mrs. Grace Hazenburg	1909	A.M.	1919
Campbell, Rev. Allen D.		D.D.	1903

Name	Hope Grad	Degree	Year
Case, Rev. Clifford P.		D.D.	1916
Chamberlain, Rev. Jacob		LL.D.	1900
Chamberlain, Rev. Wm. I.		D.D.	1907
Chellanpa, Bishop David		D.D.	1957
Churchman, Rev. Arthur B.		D.D.	1926
Colenbrander, Rev. Henry	1913	D.D.	1951
Coles, J. Ackerman		LL.D.	1903
Cooper, Wm. H.	1903	A.M.	1907
Dame, Rev. Clarence P.	1913	D.D.	1938
Danhof, James J.		A.M.	1884
De Jonge, Rev. Gerhard	1882	D.D.	1921
De Kleine, Wm.	1902	D.Sc.	1937
Den Herder, Marius	1901	LL.D.	1947
Den Uyl, Simon D.	1919	LL.D.	1956
De Pree, Rev. Henry Peter	1902	D.D.	1931
De Pree, Rev. James	1867	D.D.	1926
De Pree, Rev. P.		D.D.	1894
Dethmers, Hon. John Roy	1925	LL.D.	1954
De Valois Siebers, Bernadine	1930	Sc.D.	1956
De Velder, Rev. Walter	1929	D.D.	1964
De Witt, Jonkheer H. M. Van Haersma		LL.D.	1935
De Young, Rev. Abraham	1900	D.D.	1937
De Young, Chris Anthony	1920	Litt.D.	1952
Diekema, Hon. G. J.	1881	LL.D.	1913
Dimnent, E. D.	1896	L.H.D.	1919
Dirksen, Hon. Everett M.		LL.D.	1949
Ditzen, Lowell R.		L.H.D.	1961
Dosker, Rev. Henry E.	1876	L.H.D.	1926
Dosker, Herman N.		A.M.	1882
Douwstra, Rev. George A.		A.M.	1907
Douwstra, Rev. Richard		A.M.	1907
Dressler, Louis R.		Mus.D.	1897
Dubbink, Rev. G. H.	1892	D.D.	1904
Dykstra, Clarence A.		LL.D.	1937
Dykstra, Rev. Dirk	1906	D.D.	1936
Dykstra, Mrs. John A.	1912	LL.D.	1957
Dykstra, Rev. John A.	1909	D.D.	1924
Dykstra, John Dean	1940	D.D.	1962
Elson, Edward L. R.		LL.D.	1961
Englund, Rev. Harold		D.D.	1960
Fell, Egbert E.		LL.D.	1935
Flipse, Rev. M. Eugene	1916	D.D.	1940
Gardener, Cornelius		A.M.	1896
Gardner, Rev. J. S.		D.D.	1911
Gebhard, Rev. John G.	1878	D.D.	1906
Geyer, Rev. Julius		D.D.	1895
Gillespie, Rev. John H.		D.D.	1898
Gispen, Rev. W. H.		D.D.	1898
Graves, Nathan F.		LL.D.	1894
Green, Hon. Fred Warren		LL.D.	1927

Name	Hope Grad	Degree	Year
Hager, Rev. Harry	1920	D.D.	1937
Hager, Titus W.		LL.D.	1962
Hambro, Hon. Carl Joachim		LL.D.	1944
Harrison, Paul W.		D.Sc.	1923
Heemstra, Rev. Jacob	1910	D.D.	1939
Hekhuis, Rev. Gerrit J.	1885	D.D.	1929
Hill, Rev. Wm. Bancroft		Litt.D.	1924
Hoekje, John C.	1906	M.Ed.	1939
Hoekje, Rev. Willis G.	1904	D.D.	1934
Hoffman, Rev. Harvey B.	1932	D.D.	1939
Hoffman, Rev. James E.	1917	D.D.	1948
Hoffman, Rev. Milton J.	1909	D.D.	1918
Holkeboer, Tena	1920	LL.D.	1949
Hondelink, Rev. Gerrit	1900	D.D.	1942
Hospers, Rev. Henry	1889	D.D.	1916
Huizenga, John	1867	A.B.	1867
Huizenga, Thomas G.		A.M.	1901
Humphrey, James W.		A.M.	1895
Joralman, Rev. J. S.		D.D.	1909
Juliana, H. R. H. Princess		LL.D.	1941
Kempers, Rev. John R.	1921	D.D.	1950
Koeppe, Rev. Edwin W.	1914	D.D.	1946
Kollen, Mrs. Martha Diekema		Litt.D.	1948
Kolyn, Rev. Matthew	1877	D.D.	1908
Kremers, Rev. Harry	1890	D.D.	1927
Kremers, Henry		A.M.	1884
Kruithof, Rev. Bastian		D.D.	1951
Kuizenga, Rev. John E.	1899	D.D.	1916
Kuyper, Rev. Abram		D.D.	1908
Kuyper, Rev. Lester J.	1928	D.D.	1928
Landwehr, August H.		D.Sc.	1928
Lepeltak, Rev. Peter		D.D.	1904
Lockwood, Rev. Henry		D.D.	1916
Lubbers, Irwin J.	1917	Litt.D.	1945
Luben, Rev. Barnard Maurice	1926	D.D.	1952
Luidens, Rev. Anthony	1912	D.D.	1942
Lumsden, Alex		L.H.D.	1967
MacKay, Rev. Donald Sage		D.D.	1906
Malik, Charles, Hon.		D.Sc.	1953
Mandeville, Rev. Giles H.		LL.D.	1895
Marcus, Beth	1942	LL.D.	1960
Mason, Rev. A. De Witt		D.D.	1909
McCracken, Harold		Litt.D.	1957
McLean, Charles Myron		LL.D.	1929
Meulendyke, Rev. Josias	1873	D.D.	1933
Meury, Rev. E. J.		D.D.	1916
Middlebush, Frederick A.		LL.D.	1937
Miles, Hon. Fred T.		LL.D.	1938
Miller, Rev. Edward R.		D.D.	1914
Moerdyke, Rev. Peter	1866	D.D.	1905

Name	Hope Grad	Degree	Year
Moerdyke, Rev. Wm.	1866	D.D.	1922
Muilenburg, Dr. James	1920	L.H.D.	1956
Mulder, Arnold	1907	Litt.D.	1923
Mulder, Rev. John R.	1917	D.D.	1931
Murray, Roger F. II		LL.D.	1960
Muste, Rev. Cornelius B.	1914	D.D.	1932
Neevel, Rev. Alvin J.	1926	D.D.	1957
Nettinga, Rev. S. C.			1919
Nykerk, John B.	1885	Litt.D.	1920
Oggel, H. P.		A.M.	1869
Olert, Rev. Frederick H.	1926	D.D.	1963
Oudersluys, Rev. Richard		D.D.	1945
Paul, Mrs. Josephine Bay		LL.D.	1961
Peale, Norman Vincent		LL.D.	1962
Peale, Ruth Stafford		Litt.D.	1962
Peeke, Rev. H. V. S.	1887	D.D.	1913
Pelgrim, Rev. Carleton	1905	D.D.	1905
Pennings, Rev. Gerrit J.	1905	D.D.	1934
Phelps, Rev. Philip	1882	LL.D.	1894
Pieters, Rev. Adrian J.	1887	D.D.	1906
Pieters, Rev. Albertus	1887	D.D.	1924
Poling, Rev. Daniel A.		D.D.	1925
Poppen, Rev. Henry	1914	D.D.	1941
Poppen, James Leonard	1926	D.Sc.	1953
Potter, Francis Marmaduke		L.H.D.	1927
Potts, William J., M.D.	1918	D.Sc.	1964
Prins, Rev. Jacob	1924	D.D.	1944
Pyle, Rev. H. W.	1921	D.D.	1942
Raap, Albert		A.M.	1910
Romney, Lenore (Mrs. George)		L.H.D.	1967
Ridder, Rev. Herman J.	1949	D.D.	1965
Riggs, Arad		LL.D.	1953
Roosevelt, Hon. Theodore		LL.D.	1901
Rottschaefer, Rev. Bernard	1906	D.D.	1933
Runk, Charles L.		LL.D.	1928
Sanford, Francis B.		LL.D.	1935
Schnucker, Rev. G.		D.D.	1923
Shaw, John		A.M.	1879
Sizoo, Rev. Joseph R.	1907	D.D.	1925
Slutter, Rev. Henry	1899	D.D.	1935
Spaan, Rev. Cornelius	1899	D.D.	1935
Steffens, Rev. N. M.		D.D.	1884
Stegeman, Henry Van Eyck	1912	D.D.	1928
Straaks, Rev. H.		A.M.	1899
Strick, Edward J.	1903	D.Sc.	1924
Sutherland, Rev. R. R.		A.M.	1878
Takenaka, Jiro		Litt.D.	1950
Ter Keurst, Rev. Henry D.	1914	D.D.	1940
Thompson, Rev. Elias W.		D.D.	1916
Torchiana, Hon. H. A. Van Coenen		LL.D.	1933

Name	Hope Grad	Degree	Year
Tsai, C. T.		D.D.	1946
Tsuru, Rev. Senji		D.D.	1949
Turner, Fennell Parrish		Litt.D.	1931
Van Dyke, Rev. Henry	1917	D.D.	1959
Van Ess, Rev. John	1899	LL.D.	1934
Van Kersen, Rev. Wm. J.	1894	D.D.	1925
Van Kleffers, Hon. Eelko Nicolaas		LL.D.	1949
Van Peursem, Rev. Gerrit D.	1907	D.D.	1947
Van Peursem, Rev. John	1902	D.D.	1935
Van Putten, Wm.	1869	A.B.	1869
Van Raalte, D. B. K.	1867	A.B.	1867
Van Roijen, Hon. J. J.		LL.D.	1928
Van Strien, Rev. David	1909	D.D.	1947
Van Swinderen, Hon. R. De M.		LL.D.	1908
VanZanten, Rev. John W.		D.D.	1926
Van Zoeren, Gerrit John	1912	Sc.D.	1960
Van Zwaluwenburg, Cornelius		D.Sc.	1925
Vandenberg, Arthur H.		LL.D.	1926
Vanderlaan, John		D.Sc.	1933
Vander Lugt, Gerrit T.		Litt.D.	1960
Vander Meulen, Cornelius, LL.B.	1900	L.H.D.	1966
Vandermeulen, Rev. Jacob	1854	D.D.	1897
Vandermeulen, Rev. Jacob	1897	D.D.	1921
Vandermeulen, Rev. John M.	1891	D.D.	1909
Vandermeulen, Rev. John	1855	D.D.	1892
VanderVeen, Arend	1860	A.M.	1866
VanderWerf, Calvin	1937	D.Sc.	1963
Vanderwerp, Hon. John		LL.D.	1930
VanderVelde, Otto	1915	D.Sc.	1955
VanderVries, John N.		LL.D.	1922
Van Zyl, Gerrit	1918	D.Sc.	1965
Veenboer, M., M.D.		A.M.	1878
Veldman, Rev. Henry J.	1892	D.D.	1920
Vennema, Rev. Ame	1879	D.D.	1904
Vennema, Hon. John	1889	LL.D.	1930
Vermeulen, James M.	1926	LL.D.	1951
Visscher, John Paul	1917	LL.D.	1950
Vroom, Rev. W. H.		D.D.	1898
Vruwink, Rev. Henry A.	1910	D.D.	1942
Walvoord, Rev. Wm.	1908	D.D.	1958
Warnshuis, Rev. A. L.	1897	D.D.	1916
Warnshuis, Fred G.		D.Sc.	1922
Warnshuis, Rev. John H.	1910	D.D.	1932
Wayer, James	1901	D.D.	1955
Welmers, Everett T.	1932	D.Sc.	1966
Welmers, Rev. Thomas E.	1903	D.D.	1945
Welmers, William E.	1936	D.Litt.	1967
Wichers, Edward	1913	D.Sc.	1941
Wichers, Wynand	1909	LL.D.	1931
Wierenga, Rev. Cornelius R.	1917	D.D.	1931

Name	Hope Grad	Degree	Year
Winter, Rev. E.	1858	D.D.	1890
Wormser, A.		A.M.	1881
Wyckoff Rev. J. H.		D.D.	1892
Yang, You Chan		LL.D.	1955
Yntema, Leonard Francis	1915	D.Sc.	1927
Yntema, Theodore Otte	1921	D.Sc.	1960
Yonkman, Frederick	1925	D.Sc.	1955
Zimmerman, Rev. Frederick		D.D.	1938
Zimmerman, John		A.M.	1900
Zwemer, Rev. James F.	1870	D.D.	1905
Zwemer, Rev. Samuel M.	1887	D.D.	1952

Presidents of:
Council of Hope College, 1865-1927
Board of Trustees, 1927-1966

Rev. A. C. Van Raalte, D.D.	1865-1876
Elder Lodewecus D. Viele	1877-1878
Rev. Roelof Pieters	1878-1880
Rev. John H. Karsten	1880-1883
Rev. Nicholas M. Steffens	1883-1884
Rev. Peter Lepeltak	1884-1889
Rev. John Vandermeulen	1889-1890
Rev. Alonzo Paige Peeke	1890-1891
Rev. William Moerdyke	1891-1893
Rev. Derk Broek	1893-1894
Rev. Cornelius Brett, D.D.	1894-1895
Rev. Peter Moerdyke, D.D.	1895-1896
Rev. Peter De Bruyn	1896-1897
Rev. William Moerdyke	1897-1900
Rev. Gerhard De Jonge	1900-1902
Rev. James F. Zwemer	1902-1907
Rev. William Moerdyke, D.D.	1907-1913
Rev. Albert Vandenberg	1913-1919
Rev. Henry J. Veldman, D.D.	1919-1920
Rev. Gerhard De Jonge	1920-1930
*Mr. Wynand Wichers	1930
Rev. Nicholas Boer, D.D.	1930-1939
†Rev. John A. Dykstra, D.D.	1940-1961
Mr. Ekdal Buys	1961-1966
Mr. Hugh De Pree	1966-

†"Chairman" adopted instead of "President"–1959
*Resigned Oct. 9, 1930, upon appointment as President of the college.

Hope Men
Who Have Died in the Defense of Their Country

Korean War
John Essebagger, Class of 1950
Awarded Congressional Medal of Honor posthumously

World War II

John W. Anderson '37
Chester Arnold '45
John T. Ayers '45
Eugene R. Baker '44
E. Raymond Boot '38
Edward W. Buteyn '38
Peter Cupery '58
Hollister G. De Motts '39
Edward O. De Pree '42
Jack A. De Zeeuw '45
John P. Eisenberger '42
LeRoy M. Ellerbrook '41
Lewis J. Geerlings '28
Charles Holcomb '43
John Kleis '44
Rowland Koskamp '37
Lester Lampen '43
Kenneth M. Leighton '45
Clarence J. Lokker '40
Gerard M. Looman '44
Marvin H. Merrick '37

John E. Palmer '42
Leonard G. Pape '45
Robert A. Passell ASTP*
Clark V. Poling '33**
Everett Potts '32
Wallace Riemersma '43
Willis A. Smallegan '43
Thomas Slager '42
George Steininger '16
Arthur Taylor '43
Edwin T. Tellman '31
Louis A. Van Dyke '44
Gerald Van Dyke '41
William C. Van Fassen
Harold Van Lente '44
Roger J. Van Oss '38
Milton J. Verburg '44
Benjamin Ver Meer '31
Leonard J. Vos '46
Ralph L. Wallace '42
Joseph W. Whitworth '42

*Army Specialized Training Program

**Awarded the Distinguished Service Cross posthumously

World War I
William A. Jansma '20   George J. Roosenraad '20
                    Walter Wissink '17

Civil War
William Goetchius Ledeboer Prep 1862

BIBLIOGRAPHY

I. UNPRINTED MATERIALS

Excelsiora, a semimonthly magazine by students of the preparatory school, 1870-1893. All in longhand script, not paginated. Hope College Archives.

Minutes of the Academic Faculty of Hope College, from 1871. Hope College Archives.

Minutes of the Board of Regents and the School Board of Holland Academy, 1858-1874. Hope College Archives.

Minutes of the Executive Committee of the Council of Hope College, 1874-1885. Hope College Archives.

Minutes of the Council and Board of Trustees of Hope College, 1885-1929. In Hope College Archives; 1930 to present in Hope College Administrative Office.

Treasurer's Ledger for the Visscher period, 1901-1915. Hope College Archives.

The C. Vander Veen Papers, 1856-1896. In Calvin College Library, Heritage Hall.

The A. C. Van Raalte Papers, 1836-1876. In Calvin College Library, Heritage Hall.

Xerox copies of more than seventy unpublished letters from Van Raalte to President Phelps of Hope College. In the author's possession,

II. PRINTED MATERIALS

Books:

Acts and Proceedings of the General Synod of the Reformed Church in America. Annual volumes from 1767. Board of Publication of the Reformed Protestant Church, New York. Western Theological Seminary Library.

Corwin, E. T. *Manual of the Reformed Church in America.* Fourth Edition. Board of Publication, New York, 1902.

Dosker, H. E. *Levensschets van Rev. A. C. Van Raalte, D.D.* Nijkerk, The Netherlands, 1893.

Hyma, Albert. *A. C. Van Raalte and His Dutch Settlements in Michigan.* Grand Rapids, 1947.

Lucas, Henry. *Dutch Immigrant Memoirs and Related Writings.* 2 vols. Assen, The Netherlands, 1955. Netherlands Information Office, Holland, Michigan.

289

Lucas, Henry. *Netherlanders in America*. University of Michigan, 1955.
Mulder, Arnold. *Americans from Holland*. The Peoples of America Series, ed. Louis Adamic. Philadelphia, 1947.
Phelps, P. T. *A Brief Biography of Rev. Philip Phelps, D.D. LL.D.* 1941, publisher unknown. Hope College Archives.
Reformed Church in America, Minutes of the Particular Synod of Chicago. From 1858. Western Theological Seminary Library.
Pieters, Aleida. *A Dutch Settlement in Michigan*. Grand Rapids, 1923.
Risseuw, P. J. *Landverhuizers*. Trilogy in one volume. Baarn, The Netherlands, 1959.
Schroeder, J. A. *Secession and Emigration*. Amsterdam, 1947.
Stegenga, Preston. *Anchor of Hope*. Grand Rapids, 1954.
Van Eyck, William. *Landmarks of the Reformed Fathers*. Grand Rapids, n.d.
Van Schelven, G. "Historische Schetsen uit het Koloniale Leven," series of articles in *De Grondwet*, Oct. 1913——June 1915.

Hope College Printed Publications:

Hope College Annual. A student publication. One issue only, 1905. Hope College Archives.
Hope College *Milestone*. A student publication. Annual since 1916. Hope College Archives.
Hope College *Anchor*. Student newspaper since 1887. Hope College Archives.
Hope College *Remembrancer*. Report of the first inauguration and the first commencement. 1866.

Printed Pamphlets:

Ebenezer 1847-1947. A souvenir of the centennial celebration in Holland, ed. Henry Lucas. Hope College Archives.
Hyma, Albert. *When the Dutch Came to Michigan*. December 6, 1947. Hope College Archives.

Newspapers:

De Grondwet. Dutch language weekly, Holland, Michigan, 1860-1939. Copies from December 1871 in Netherlands Museum, Holland, Michigan. Earlier issues presumably lost in 1871 Holland fire.
De Hope. Dutch language religious weekly, 1865-1933. Western Seminary Library.
Holland *City News*. English weekly, established 1872. Holland Public Library.
Holland *Evening Sentinel*. Established 1896. Holland Public Library.
Ottawa County *Times*. English weekly, 1892-1907. Holland Public Library.
Christian Intelligencer. A religious weekly of the Reformed Church in America published in New York 1830-1933 (called the *Christian Intelligencer and Mission Field* after 1922). Previously (1827-29) the *Magazine of the Reformed Church*. Became the *Intelligencer-Leader* in 1934 and the *Church Herald* in 1944. Official organ of the Reformed Church in America. Western Theological Seminary Library.

INDEX

Abel, Roger, 261
Abrams, Frank, 237
Achievement House, 242
Adler, Mortimer, 269
Adrian College, 237
Africa, 60
Albany, N.Y., 19, 20, 23, 24, 45, 123, 128, 215
Albany Academy, 53
Albany Emigrant Aid Society, 20, 25
Albemarle Canal, 98
Albion College, 120, 170, 190, 218, 239
Alcor, Senior Women's Society, 213
Alcott (Diekema), Mary E., 90
Alcott (Whitenack), Sarah Gertrude, 89
"All-College Sing," 214
Allegan, 11, 21, 23, 29, 118
Allegan County Bible Society, 178
Allyn, Arthur, 269
Alma College, 151, 237
Alpha Chi, 177
Alumni Association, see National Alumni Association
Alumni House, 253
Alumni Seminar in Vienna, 258
Amelia County, 98
Amelia Courthouse, 98
Amelia Institute, 89
American Alumni Council, 257
American Association of Universities, 211
American Association of University Professors, 254
American Association of University Women, 240
American Bible Society, 130, 178, 179
American Chemical Society, 240, 249, 267

American Council on Education, 240
Anchor, 119, 132, 159, 165, 166, 170, 248
Anderson, John J., 175
Ann Arbor, Mich., 176, 269
Annville, Ky., 179
Antes Fort, 106
Antigone, 164
Antioch College, 239
Arabia, 180-182
Arendshorst, Bernard, 197
Army Specialized Training Program, 222, 223
Arnhem, The Netherlands, 16, 19
Articles of Association, 67, 72, 75, 83, 275-277
Association of American Colleges, 240
Association of American Universities, 212
Atlanta, Ga., 58

"B Natural Chorus," 190
Badeau, John S., 218
Baker, Tunis, 253
Barnouw, Adriaan J., 218
Baskin, Leonard, 267
Basrah, Arabia, 182
Basquettes, 169
Beach House, 193
Beardslee, John W., Sr., 123
Beardslee, John W., Jr., 162, 175
Beck, Professor T. Romeyn, 61, 74, 83, 85, 90, 101, 118, 124
Becker Foundation for Research in Economics, 269
Bedell, Edward A., 128
Bedminster, N.J., 139
Beidler, Rev. F., 39
Bell, Helen, 189

302 A Century of Hope

Suydam, James, 42, 80, 85, 86, 95
Synod of 1836, 16
Synod of 1871, 99
Synod of the Reformed Church in
America, see General Synod

Tak, Max, 266
Talmage, Rev. John Van Nest,
60, 61
Taylor, Rev. Andrew B., 22, 30
Taylor, Anna B., 35, 40
Taylor, Henry Courtney, 40
Taylor, Hugh Woodruff, 35
Taylor, Margaret W., 35, 40
Taylor, Walter T., 35, 36, 37, 39, 40,
50, 66, 98
Taylor, Rev. William J., 113, 123
Teachers Insurance and Annuity
Association, 254
Tennyson, Alfred, 210
Ter Molen, Larry, 264
Te Winkle, Rev. John W., 69
Thebaud, Victor, 224
Third Reformed Church, Holland,
Mich., 96, 189
Thomas, Norman, 268
Thompson, Abraham, 47
Thompson, Oscar, 245
Timmer, Albert H., 229, 253
Tokyo, Japan, 259
Torchiana, Henry A. Van Coenen,
216
Tri Alpha Men's Union, 222
Trimble, Lester, 269
Trowbridge, Hon. C. C., 21
Turner, Harvey E., 237
Twichell, J., 123

Uiterwyk, Rev. Henry, 92
Ulfilas Society, 119, 122, 167
Ulrum, The Netherlands, 15
Ulster County, N.Y., 41
Union College, 22, 53, 79, 87
Union School (Holland, Mich.),
75, 89
Union Theological Seminary, 254
University Idea, 82-84
University of Beirut, Lebanon, 228
University of Cairo, 228
University of California at Los
Angeles, 254
University of Chicago, 198, 269

University of Groningen, The
Netherlands, 264
University of Illinois, 160, 218, 233
University of Kansas, 248
University of Leiden, The Nether-
lands, 16, 31, 266
University of Ljubljana,
Yugoslavia, 259
University of Michigan, 120, 158,
170, 189, 198, 201, 204, 208, 210,
218, 241
University of North Dakota, 211
University of Pittsburgh, 160
University of Wisconsin, 210
U.S. Army, 185, 226
U.S. Department of Health, Educa-
tion and Welfare, 260, 263
U.S. Higher Education Facilities
Act, 263
U.S. Office of Education, 262
U.S. State Department, 258, 259
Utrecht, The Netherlands, 266

Vance, Rev. James I., 178
VandeBunte, Lynne, 260
Van de Luyster, Jannes, 228
Vandenberg, Arthur, 202
Vanderborgh, Garrett, 192, 253
Vanderbush, Alvin W., 243
Vander Haar Farm, 23, 28
Vander Jagt, Rep. Guy, 243
Vanderlaan, John, 160
Vander Lugt, William, 229, 251, 254
Vander Meulen, Rev. Cornelius,
24, 27, 37, 48
Vander Meulen, Cornelius, 162
Vandermeulen, Rev. Jacob, 40
Vandermeulen, Rev. John M., 92,
119, 123, 152, 164, 175
VanderVeen, Arend, 69
Vander Veen, Rev. Christian, 16,
36, 37, 40, 91, 92, 122
Vander Veen, Cornelius, 40
Vander Veen, R. E., 197
VanderVelde, Otto, 229, 246
VanderVries, John, 184
VanderWerf, Rev. Anthony, 248
VanderWerf, President Calvin
Anthony, 248, 249, 253, 255, 258,
260, 264-268, 271
VanderWerf, Gretchen, 249